BLUEBEARD AND AFTER

RAYNER HEPPENSTALL

Bluebeard and After

THREE DECADES OF MURDER IN FRANCE

PETER OWEN · LONDON

ISBN 0 7206 0192 4

PETER OWEN LIMITED
12 Kendrick Mews Kendrick Place London SW7

First British Commonwealth edition 1972
© 1972 Rayner Heppenstall

Printed in Great Britain by
Bristol Typesetting Co. Ltd
Barton Manor St Philips Bristol

| CONTENTS

CONTENTS

ILLUSTRATIONS

| PREFACE

As I FIRST defined it to myself, the subject of this book was to be murder in France between the two world wars. That is still the heart of my subject, but I have extended it a little as to both time and place. The trials of Landru himself and of Raoul Villain both took place within our period, and so it seemed natural enough to go back to a point very shortly before the Great War, when the first of their crimes was committed. At the other end of the scale, it is true that the extraordinary sequence of murders for which Dr Petiot is famous did not begin until after the Germans had occupied Paris, but there is a very strong presumption indeed that he was responsible for two disappearances and one sudden death at Villeneuve-sur-Yonne in the 'twenties. He was certainly very much in the Landru tradition. It has not needed me to point out to what extent his trial, just after the Second World War, paralleled Landru's just after the First.

I have also dealt, though not at great length, with four acts of culpable homicide committed by French nationals in and around London and thus within the jurisdiction of our courts, though one was not in fact tried here. There are national criminal traditions, and three of these cases belong to ours in this sense, that they are frequently mentioned by British writers on criminal history, but never by French ones. It is remarkable how self-contained national traditions are, in this as in other fields. Political assassinations in one country are noted in others, and I dare say that most English readers of my generation know who Jean Jaurès was and that he was murdered, if not by whom. A few American cases of common murder are known about in the United Kingdom and no doubt vice versa. The Victorians knew about Marie Lafarge and Troppmann. Otherwise, the only French murderer the British public seems ever to have heard of is Landru, while the French knew about Jack the Ripper, *l'Eventreur*, but no other homicidal anti-hero of ours until, more recently, Heath and then the Moors murderers.

9

This is one of the reasons why I have taken to writing about French crime. I have been asked why I do it by both British and French acquaintances, by the former commonly with the implied suggestion that criminality in my own country ought to be good enough for me, by the latter with something of the same but also with signs of latent fear that, on the one hand, I may not quite understand and, on the other, that I may be creating the impression that the French are a peculiarly criminal nation. As a matter of statistical fact, they are, on average, rather more than twice as murderous as ourselves, not only in bright rooms and dark lanes but in their cars on the roads, but I try to avoid saying that. My usual answer is that I write about French crime because, as I do it in English, I face little competition.

I have, now and then, referred to murderous courses that were being pursued contemporaneously in the United Kingdom, the United States and Germany. My purpose is to remind older British and American readers, including the many whose first language was German, of what they may have been reading or hearing about at home while French indignation was being stirred by the cases in this book. I hope thus that I may situate these cases in what for some of my readers will be an order of meaningful time. It is true that I also hope to persuade the reader that simple ignorance of, or disregard for, the history of crime in my own country and more widely abroad is not the sole explanation of the fact that I have concentrated on murder in France. Had I taken sooner to crime and had I known more languages, I might have aimed at becoming a universal criminal historian.

That is all I should have wished to be. New psychiatries and sociologies, measures of penal reform and demands for yet more of it, modifications of legal procedure, even developments in scientific criminology, interest me only as historical facts. There are circumstances favouring crime, but none known to me which cause it and so no general cure. There is a common human propensity to murder, and we can only marvel at the variety of its manifestations, though indeed we might wish for more variety, for there is also something monotonous about it. We may find national differences, but closer examination often shows these to be temporary, local and confined to a single class.

During *la Belle Époque*, there were upper-class French crimes one could not have imagined in any part of the United Kingdom or the United States, though one might have imagined them in

Rome or Vienna. In our period, Mme Fahmy seems to belong to
la Belle Époque, which lingered on through the 'twenties in high
life. In any case, Mme Fahmy, though French, killed her husband
in London, and the touch of Oriental inscrutability not in her but
in her victim is not to be found in any of our all-French cases, while
the English provinces at least offer Chung Yi-miao and Dr Buck
Ruxton. Between the wars, the only murders in France I find in-
conceivable elsewhere, except perhaps in Berlin, were those between
foreign nationals in Paris for political reasons. Even the Corsicans
in Marseilles and Montmartre had their counterparts in Chicago,
Genoa and even Soho. There is also the curious list of British
nationals murdered in France. That we failed to return the com-
pliment was no doubt due to our poor touristic facilities and the
comparative solidity of the pound sterling. There was also the
Occupation, but other countries had that.

It is always nice to end a preface with expressions of personal
gratitude. For this one, I seem able to manage little more than
renewed thanks to tireless Jean Tsushima and to G.H. Brook, book-
providers, to whose names I must add those of J.H.H. Gaute and
Colin Wilson, while, on Ibiza, B.S. Johnson kindly undertook field-
research into the last years of Raoul Villain, somewhat blocked by
the authorities. My debt to the books, to some more than others, I
indicate in a short bibliography. Getting off to a good start with
Morain, I could not have continued without Montarron.

1 | THE MURDER OF JEAN JAURÈS

THE OLDEST of our *dramatis personae* were to be victims, three of them leading statesmen. But even a murderer may take time to ripen, and two of ours were born before the Franco-Prussian War, Landru himself in 1869 and Mme Bessarabo the year before that. She was born in Lyons to the silk trade. Henri-Désiré Landru was born in the 19th *arrondissement* of Paris, that north-easterly district known after the Buttes-Chaumont park which it contains (but it also contains the La Villette cattle-market and slaughter-house). His father worked in an iron foundry.

Landru was educated by the Christian brothers in the Rue de Bretonvilliers on the Île St Louis and sang in the choir at St Louis-en-l'Île near by. His voice did not break until he was fifteen, and for a short while thereafter he continued to serve Mass, vested, if not properly ordained, as a sub-deacon. He took an elementary course in engineering, performed his military service in the infantry at St Quentin and attained the rank of quartermaster-sergeant. In 1893, he made an honest woman of a second cousin by whom he had a daughter. The following year, he returned to civilian life. That year, the future Mme Bessarabo went to Mexico, where she met her first husband, a traveller in silk, M. Paul Jacques, twenty years older than herself. By him, she had a daughter, Paule.

In 1900, Max Kassel, a villain but a victim, and Georges Sarret both reached the age of twenty-one. *Né* Sarrejani in Trieste under Austrian rule, Sarret, who from the age of four had received a good French education, lived in Marseilles, where for the moment he practised journalism. Born at Riga but taken in childhood to Paris and there first apprenticed to a furrier, Max Kassel, a powerfully built, red-haired Jew, was already a figure in *le milieu*, the world of Montmartre poncedom, and even had a girl from the Moulin Rouge working for him in Soho. Red Max's subsequent career in *la traite des blanches* (the white-slave traffic, international *proxénétisme*) was to be, as we might say, exemplary, but, while he is of

13

special interest to us in London, he provides us with no example of murder in France. A Frenchman four years older than he, a butcher, Louis Voisin, may also be said to belong rather to our own criminal tradition, as may Jean-Pierre Vaquier, in age between the two, engineer and inventor, whose whereabouts would remain shrouded in obscurity until he appeared, mending the wireless, in a hotel lounge at Biarritz.

Adolescent in 1900 were Raoul Villain, son of the clerk to the civil court in Rheims; Guillaume Seznec, whose father had a saw-mill at Morlaix, in Brittany; and Shalom Schwartzbard, the son of poor Jewish parents in the Ukraine, apprenticed to a watchmaker. Children, of ages ranging down from ten to two, were Pierre Bou-grat, son of a university teacher in Lyons; Marie-Marguerite Alibert, who was to figure prominently in British juridical history under another name, in Paris; Paul Gorguloff, a big lad whose parents were kulaks in the Caucasus; Mieczyslas Charrier, weak-chested, one of the numerous illegitimate children of scurvy-ridden, alcoholic Left Bank anarchist gasbag Goldberg and a woman from Marseilles who, after afflicting her son with his father's Polish Christian name, took the child home with her; Marcel Petiot, a postman's son in Auxerre; Emile Courgibet, youngest of six, in Paris; and Christine Papin, in Le Mans.

That year, Landru, already turned thirty, was for the first of no fewer than seven times convicted of fraud. The past six years had gone very badly for him. A prospective employer had absconded with a deposit. A scheme for a bicycle factory had come to nothing. The pattern of the next thirteen years of his life was to be one that most of us would have found monotonous in the extreme. A woman of, as we say, uncertain age or, as the French say, *d'un certain âge* would complain that, with a false promise of marriage, he had deprived her of her savings and furniture. He would then spend anything from thirteen months to three years in prison, return to his wife and beget a child, deprive another widow or elderly spinster of her furniture and savings, return to prison and so on.

During those years, Mme Jacques returned from Mexico and by 1904 is to be found in the Rue de Sèvres, mistress of a literary *salon*, herself printing poems and stories under the name of Héra Myrtel. That year, with another socialist, Aristide Briand, Auguste-Marie-Joseph-Jean Jaurès founded *L'Humanité*. Born the following year were the younger of the Papin sisters, Léa, at Le Mans, and, on the island of Réunion, Alain de Bernardy de Sigoyer, an engineer's son

of unsound aristocratic pretensions. Not on French soil at all but at
Frankfurt-am-Main, Eugen Weidmann was born on February 5th,
1908. That year, two young Italians, Bartolommeo Vanzetti, aged
twenty, and Nicola Sacco, aged seventeen, sailed to the New World.
In French criminal history, those were the years of Jeanne Weber,
the tireless child-strangler, of the *chauffeurs de la Drôme* and of
Mme Steinheil, presently to be replaced in popular favour by the
Bonnot gang.

In 1910, never a much-travelled man, Landru spent his penulti-
mate period out of prison operating as far afield as Lille. There, a
widow, Mme Izoré, who had answered a matrimonial advertisement
inserted in a local paper by him in the name of Morel, parted with
her savings and furniture, complained when he absconded and saw
him sent to prison for three years. Landru's parents had gone to
live in the country, at Agen. His mother died in 1912. M. Landru
père went to stay with his daughter-in-law in Paris. Henri-Désiré
was still in prison. Grieved no doubt in part by the evil courses of a
son now in his forties, towards the end of August old Landru put
an end to his days in the Bois de Boulogne. Coming once more out
of prison the following year, young Landru found himself the
richer by the ten thousand francs his father had left him. This was
two-thirds as much as the savings of Mme Izoré, so briefly in his
possession.

BORN, IN 1859, at Castres in the south-west, Jean Jaurès had first
been elected a deputy for the department at the age of twenty-six
and had also lectured brilliantly in philosophy at the university of
Toulouse. By 1913, at the age of fifty-four, he had been the undoubted leader of the Socialist Party for nine years past. His socialism was a French product and anti-Marxist. Though devoted to
notions of human brotherhood and international working-class
solidarity, Jaurès was a patriot, and he was interested in military
problems. His best-known book was *L'Armée Nouvelle*, 'a nation in
arms' being its central idea. It was this very idea which had made
him oppose the extension of military service to three years.

As war began to seem inevitable, this extension of military service
assumed the highest importance. The population of Germany was
greater than that of France, and far more Germans were under
arms. To the political Right, those who opposed or had opposed
the three years' extension seemed traitors and dangerous. The

attacks on Jaurès were vicious. *L'Action Française* was already whipping up spy fever. In February 1913, Léon Daudet claimed that Kub Maggi advertisements throughout the countryside had been planted to indicate strategic points to the invader, and in March the paper stated that in Paris there was an army of ten thousand German and German Jewish spies ready for acts of sabotage, more particularly the sudden cutting off of food supplies. In April, a *Paris-Midi* journalist wrote :

> In two hours, 258 Prussian battalions will have crossed our frontier. . . . Never mind, General Jaurès will look after it all. It is he who, at the head of his private army, will negotiate the surrender of Paris. That day, *L'Humanité* will appear in two languages, as it has already tried to do. That will be the end of Paris.

In May, Charles Maurras described Jaurès as an intermediary between German corruption and the already corrupt of French anti-militarism and as the Kaiser's spokesman and added :

> A serious investigation would reveal, throughout his articles and speeches, the taint of German gold. We must not let this traitor out of our sight.

A Forain cartoon in *Le Figaro* bore the caption :

> M. Jaurès dreamt in German all night.

That kind of thing was perhaps to be expected. These were political journalists after all, however much we may respect Forain also as an artist. But Charles Péguy is considered a great writer. He *had* been a socialist himself and a friend of Jaurès. It is supposed that he had turned spiteful in the first place when he was not asked to write for *L'Humanité*. In the *Cahier* he published that April, Péguy wrote :

> I must beg the reader's pardon for mentioning here the name of M. Jaurès. It is a name which has become so low and filthy that, when one sets it down to be sent to the printers, one feels that one may be exposing oneself to some legal penalty. . . . Jaurès, the representative in France of German imperialism, has sunk beneath contempt. . . . This born traitor betrayed socialism in the first place. He betrayed the cause of Dreyfus in the name of

reasons of State and for profit. He is doing his best to betray France to the profit of German policy. He has indeed met with some resistance here, and he would do well to take warning. In time of war, there is only one policy, and it is that of the Convention. It means Jaurès in a tumbril and the roll of drums to cover his big voice. . . . Jaurès is a pan-Germanist. He is a German agent. He is working for greater Germany. It is always a handful of wretched intellectuals who in the end ensure that a people shall be massacred.

It appears from the reminiscences of another very considerable writer, Romain Rolland, that to him, at about this time, Péguy further said :

At the outbreak of war, the first thing we shall do is shoot Jaurès. We shan't leave such traitors behind to stab us in the back.

But of course Raoul Villain would not know that.

This younger son of the clerk to the civil court in Rheims had reached his late twenties without quite settling to anything. He had formerly taken a diploma at the agricultural college in Rennes and worked for a while as a farm steward, but in 1913 he was in Paris, intermittently employed as a *surveillant* at the Collège Stanislas and following courses in Egyptian archaeology at the École du Louvre He had travelled previously, being taken by his father to Switzerland and Italy to convalesce after a bad attack of typhoid when he was twenty. In 1913, he visited England, where a Miss Francis of Langton in Kent befriended him, and Greece. He joined a League of Young Friends of Alsace-Lorraine, which had close ties with Action Française, and was also attached to the militant Catholic *Sillon* group. Péguy was his favourite reading. His first murderous fantasies were directed against the Kaiser, but he decided that William II was not merely difficult to get at but also the most highly cultivated man amongst European royalty. The thought that his mission was perhaps rather to kill Jaurès first occurred to him in December at a performance of Corneille's play *Le Cid* at the Comédie Française. His lodgings at the time were in the Rue d'Assas, where he paid a monthly rent of 35 francs. None of his landladies had ever found anything to complain of in his behaviour.

Nor, in any important way, had his teachers, of whom the most important in his development had no doubt been the Jesuits in Rheims, whom he had left, after six years, without taking his *baccalauréat.* He was neither an utter fool nor particularly bright, perhaps lacked powers of concentration. He had friends, but somewhat kept himself to himself. His military service at Bar-le-Duc had been spoilt for him by the fact that the other young soldiers read *L'Humanité* and made fun of his addiction to Joan of Arc. He was never in serious financial difficulties. There was always money from home, if not a great deal. It was not a broken home, but rather an odd one. The paternal grandmother had never stirred out of her room, where she lived in a state of undress, having visions and talking to the Virgin. At the age of two, his mother had dropped little Raoul out of a window and was thereafter confined in an asylum. On the other hand, elder brother Marcel, though equally patriotic, had grown up sensible enough and had followed his father into the lower reaches of the magistracy.

We may be quite certain that Jaurès had never heard of Raoul Villain and never would hear of him. The two were never to meet face to face, and it could only be for a moment and without interest if, the evening before the one on which they were to come closest to each other, the young man's face crossed Jaurès' retina. One thing the two had in common was that both were fair in colouring and blue-eyed, Jaurès bearded of course, the young man clean-shaven, wider-browed and in general with better features than his senior, the mouth shapely if rather unpleasantly set, the eyes apparently not without humour.

ON THE morning of March 5th, 1914, in his room at 107 Rue de Sèvres, M. Paul Jacques, first husband of the future Mme Bessarabo, was found dead, with a revolver at his feet. A verdict of suicide was returned, though rumour had it that M. Jacques had expected to be murdered by his wife, who had some weeks earlier tried to poison him by putting corrosive sublimate in his soup. A fortnight later, the wife of the Minister of Finance, Joseph Caillaux, a politician almost as unpopular on the Right as Jaurès, shot the editor of *Le Figaro* in his office. Though Caillaux resigned his ministerial post that same evening, the fact that his wife lay in prison facing murder charges did not prevent his parliamentary constituents from re-electing him on April 26th. Jean Jaurès also was re-elected with an increased majority, and the total of socialist deputies rose to over a hundred.

Despite this success or because of it, their leader received a shoal of threatening letters, and the public attacks continued. It was, as Jaurès said, those keenest on order and civilisation who most prodigally threatened him with imprisonment, firing squads and the guillotine. Within six months, he said, France would no doubt be at war, and it wouldn't surprise him if he were the first casualty. He could forgive whoever killed him. The guilty would be those who put the weapon in the murderer's hands. It was in fact from a teacher at the Collège Stanislas that Raoul Villain first borrowed, at about this time, a 6.35 millimetre Browning automatic pistol, a light weapon to practise with. He returned it to its owner in June. On June 28th, he just scraped through examinations at the École du Louvre.

That day, in Sarajevo, the Archduke Franz Ferdinand, heir to the Austro-Hungarian double crown, and his consort were shot dead in the street by a Bosnian, Gavrilo Prinzip, with a weapon supplied by Serbian officers. It was not at that moment clear that this shocking incident must inevitably lead by a roundabout way to the outbreak of war, even on a small scale in the Balkans. The French were planning their summer holidays. Even Raoul Villain thought of going to Langton again. He wrote to Miss Francis in early July. But then he heard that his grandmother was ill (the mad recluse who had visions and talked to the Virgin). He stayed for the moment in Paris.

The President of the Republic, Raymond Poincaré, went to Russia. Those, like Jaurès, who still hoped that war might be averted, were particularly afraid of the Russian commitment. It seemed to them that the Russians wanted a war and would drag France into it. At a meeting of the parliamentary Socialist Party, attended as a delegate by the German socialist Liebknecht, Jaurès propounded the idea of the workers of their two countries in the last resort stopping war by a concerted general strike. This brought vicious reaction. *La Sociale*, for example, wanted Jaurès stuck on the wall with the mobilisation orders, and *Paris-Midi* recommended that four men and a corporal should then fill his brain with lead at point-blank range. It was a dangerous notion, of course, and Jaurès had to insist that the kind of strike he had in mind could only be concerted and bilateral, or would not take place.

July 19th was a Sunday. With a priest from school, Father Jean Calvet, Raoul Villain attended a parish fair at Sèvres. Father Calvet was later to recall that Villain spent the whole afternoon on the shooting range, blazing away like a maniac. From his other col-

league, he again borrowed the 6.35 automatic. And next day he
went home to Rheims. That day in Paris, the trial of Mme Caillaux
opened. In Rheims, Villain is on record as saying that there would
be a war and that he would be glad. That was on Wednesday, July
22nd. Next day, the Austrian ultimatum to Serbia was delivered.
On Friday, the German ambassadors in Paris, St Petersburg and
London delivered notes stating that in the view of their government
the Austrian demands were just and would have to be met. That
day, old Mme Villain died. A graveyard attendant recalled hearing
Villain hold forth to a group including his brother, on the way out
of the cemetery after their grandmother's funeral, that there were
politicians who ought to be killed at once. This was taken by the
others to mean Jaurès and Caillaux, but Villain pointed out that
Caillaux hadn't been making pacifist speeches lately.

On Sunday the 26th, Jaurès travelled to Lyons to support a
socialist candidate in a by-election. He visited the art gallery and
enthused about the beauties of nature in a park. On his way back
to Paris, the train was derailed, and he spent the night in Dijon. In
Paris on Monday evening, there was a procession of 10,000 anti-
war demonstrators in the *grands boulevards*. In the Boulevard
Bonne-Nouvelle, they smashed the windows of *Le Matin*, and there
was a charge by mounted police, with serious casualties. President
Poincaré was on his way home by sea from Russia, which had
started mobilising. On the 28th, Jaurès went to Brussels for a conference of socialists from fourteen countries. His first question on
arrival was whether the Caillaux verdict had come through on the
telegraph. It had. Mme Caillaux had been acquitted. Jaurès thought
this was wrong. There had, after all, been violence, he said.

In the evening, he addressed a crowd of 8,000 at the Cirque
Royale. They acclaimed him and his country. '*Vive la France!*' was
the heartfelt shout of the Belgians. About Jaurès' patriotic feelings
and loyalty to the Viviani government at that moment, there is no
conceivable doubt.

In acclaiming France, comrades, it is peace you acclaim, for you
know that France wants peace. When I go back to Paris, I shall
say with what emotion I, who am denounced there as a man of
no country, heard the France of the great Revolution saluted
here. For us French socialists, our duty is quite straightforward.
We have no need to impose a policy of peace on our government.
Our government is pursuing such a policy. I who have never
been afraid to bring on my head the hatred of our super-patriots

by my obstinate wish for Franco-German friendship, it is my
duty to say that at this moment the French government is working for peace and its continuance. All we have to do is insist that
it speaks firmly to Russia. If Russia will not listen, then we must
say : the only treaty we recognise is that which binds us to the
human species. Beneath that dynasty of absolute masters, the
earth is mined. Revolution unloosed will say to them : 'Get you
away, and beg forgiveness from God and man !' But this I must
also say. If our homeland is nevertheless put in danger, we shall
be the first at the frontier to defend the France whose blood
flows in our veins, the France whose proud genius represents the
best we have in us.

At dawn, in Belgrade, shells were bursting, the first among millions
in the Great War. That afternoon, Raymond Poincaré reached
Paris.

Raoul Villain left his home at Rheims in a rage, accusing his
brother and then more hotly his father of lukewarmth in their
patriotism. It had been a father-son quarrel on an archetypal scale.
The son caught a late-afternoon train at six o'clock and arrived in
Paris at eight. *L'Action Française* was saying : 'We do not wish to
incite anyone to political murder. But should M. Jaurès be seized
with a fit of trembling. . . .' Jaurès was still in Brussels. Villain
booked in at a hotel near the Gare de l'Est and took a bus west to
Passy, where for over an hour he hung around the streets near
Jaurès' house in what is now the Villa, but was then the Impasse,
de la Tour, arousing the suspicions of the watchman on a nearby
building site. The 6.35 automatic was in his pocket. Next morning,
he went to a gunsmith in the Rue de Rennes and bought a heavier
weapon, a Smith & Wesson .32 revolver. He called at the lodging of
his school colleague, meaning again to return the borrowed automatic, but his friend was out. Villain went back to his old room in
the Rue d'Assas.

Jaurès spent his last two hours in Brussels at the art gallery,
looking at the Flemish Primitives. Reaching Paris in the late afternoon, he called at the Elysée Palace and was reassured about
Poincaré's intentions, with which he declared himself fully satisfied.
He went to his office at *L'Humanite* in the Rue Montmartre, wrote
his editorial for next day, dined at his usual restaurant, the Coq
d'Or, a few doors away, and returned to his office. That was
Thursday, July 30th. That day, the order for general mobilisation
went out in Russia. Towards midnight, Jaurès and three of his col-

leagues left the newspaper building and called in for a last drink at the Café du Croissant. Villain was lurking. He asked a passing workman whether that was M. Jaurès and, told that it was, said he'd expected Jaurès to be older. Inside, Jaurès said to his friends : 'This war is going to rouse all the bestial passions that are asleep in humanity's heart. We can expect to be murdered at any street corner.' Raoul Villain was looking in at the window. Presently, he went away. He slept that night in the Rue d'Assas.

Friday, July 31st. Jean Jaurès spent most of the day at the Chamber of Deputies, then went to his office in the Rue Montmartre. Not much is known of what Villain did that day or whom he saw. It is known that he picked the name-tabs and makers' labels off his clothes and that he visited Notre Dame, where he lighted a candle, to what saint is not known (it cannot have been Joan of Arc, who, though beatified, was not yet canonised). In the evening, he treated himself to an unaccustomed blow-out at an Italian restaurant, with a half-flask of Chianti (by his standards, serious drinking). Then he set off towards the Rue Montmartre. He carried a raincoat over one arm to conceal the Smith & Wesson, too big to lie inconspicuously in his pocket. It was loaded. The Browning automatic lay in his left-hand jacket pocket, unloaded, though in his right-hand waistcoat pocket were five cartridges of the smaller calibre.

At nine o'clock, Jaurès and his colleagues went out to eat. They went not to the Coq d'Or but to the Croissant, which was quieter. It was a warm evening, and the windows were open, behind each al-coved wall seat a light curtain on a brass rail. Two tables were put together, cornerwise to a third, for the party from *L'Humanité*. In all, there were fifteen of them, including two women. Jaurès sat with his back to a window on the Rue du Croissant side. He ate quickly. By half-past nine, he was starting on the pudding, a strawberry tart. A colleague was passing around a snapshot of his little girl. Jaurès duly admired. The curtain behind him was drawn back from outside the window. There were two shots. One broke a mirror across the restaurant. Jaurès fell against the friend on his left, a .32 bullet in his skull, brain matter oozing. A policeman on his beat had just reached the corner. He saw Villain back away from the window and turn in unhurried flight towards the Rue Réaumur. It took Jaurès five or six minutes to die. It was a quarter to ten. Villain, under arrest, was on his way to the police station in the Rue du Mail.

FOUND OUT again, Landru should have appeared in a lower court on July 20th, the day on which the trial of Mme Caillaux opened. As he was unable to be found, he was sentenced *in absentia* to four years' imprisonment, after which he would have been *relégable*, that is to say, deported and forced to live out the term of his natural life either on the fringe of the penal settlements in French Guiana or in New Caledonia. It may be supposed to have been at about this time that he grew the beard which was to form so characteristic a feature of his unusual physical appearance. It seems odd that a man who looked like that should have gone unchallenged all through the war years in Paris, the typical beards of the time being those grown in the trenches by soldiers, who were therefore known as *poilus*, and the sartorial style and manner of this bald, bowler-hatted, neat little man being quite unlike those of any soldier on leave.

He continued to answer, or to insert, matrimonial advertisements in the papers. One of the first of those with whom these brought him into relations was a Mme Cuchet, a widow with a nineteen-year-old son, who had a milliner's shop at St Denis and some thousands of francs of savings. She was not alone in the world. She had a sister and a brother-in-law, who warned her against the man she knew as Raymond Diard, having discovered what his real name was and that he was not a bachelor, as he pretended, but had a wife and four children. For a while, this discovery was effective, but love conquered, and in December 1914 the widow and her son went to stay with Landru at a villa rented for her in the outer suburbs, not yet at Gambais but Vernouillet.

The date after which the Cuchets were never seen again was January 4th, 1915. On May 1st of that year, Landru inserted a matrimonial advertisement in *Le Journal*. Among those who answered it were three widows, Mmes Laborde-Line, Guillin and Héon, aged respectively forty-seven, fifty-one and fifty-five. All three thus made the acquaintance of a bald, black-bearded, thoughtful and polite man they knew by various names, including that of Cuchet. All three were to disappear in the course of the year, the first two in summer at (or from) Vernouillet, Mme Héon not until December at or from the more suitable, because more isolated, villa at Gambais, rented in the name of Dupont. Their names, or code-names applicable to them (Mme Laborde-Line, born in Buenos

Aires, was shown as 'Brazil'), were duly entered in a little notebook.

That year, the Widow Jacques known on the literary fringes as Héra Myrtel took her daughter to Mexico to clear up her late husband's silk interests there. While mother and daughter were staying at a rich man's *hacienda*, he was shot dead. Mme Jacques told a story of masked men, which the police believed. In Mexico, she met a M. Weissmann, who went by the name of Bessarabo, a Rumanian timber-merchant who also had oil interests. Him she married, presently to return with him and her daughter to Paris and take up her former life as literary hostess, with, apparently, a succession of young lovers which her fearsome appearance, in bombazine, a black velvet band about her unlovely neck, makes it hard to credit.

Files on Raoul Villain were sent in March to the equivalent of our Director of Public Prosecutions. He found them unsatisfactory and flung them back at the examining magistrate, who saw further unhelpful witnesses. There was no solid evidence of complicity, but Villain's movements on the last two days of Jaurès' life remained mysterious. Villain expressed no regret, but on the contrary said that he had acted from a sense of duty and was satisfied with what he had done. An indictment was drawn up in October, and he was committed for trial before the court of assize in Paris on December 20th. At the Cour d'Appel, it was argued that revelations made in court might disturb the unity of the nation, while not to make them would impede his defence. The case was postponed *sine die*. For two years more, Raoul Villain was to remain undisturbed at the Santé prison. He would protest intermittently. In British criminal history, 1915 had been the year of the Brides in the Bath, George Joseph Smith having been arrested in February, tried in June and executed in August.

FOR A year, there are no further recorded disappearances at or from Gambais. The next was that of Mme Collomb, again a widow but younger than Mme Guillin or Mme Héon, a mere forty-four. If she was indeed murdered, then it would be either at the very end of 1916 or in the first days of 1917. On February 13th of this latter year, 'Mata Hari' was arrested. On March 29th, a girl of nineteen, Andrée Babelay, was taken to Gambais, where she remained, alive, for about a fortnight. Not only was she much younger than any other of Landru's presumed victims, but also she had no money or prospects, so that the motive for killing her must have been different. As it has never been suggested that Landru was a sadist or 'sex killer' in the usual sense, it seems likely enough that she found out something about the previous disappearances which made her a potential dangerous witness.

Landru had picked up Andrée Babelay in tears on a railway platform in the Underground. It was on a bus that, in May, he picked up Fernande Segret, aged twenty-five, whose discretion was to be quite remarkable, so that she never stood in serious danger. She was a slight, fair young woman, not exactly pretty but pleasing, who worked in a furrier's shop but sang nicely and hoped to make a career as an *artiste lyrique*. In the same month, among those Landru met as a result of his matrimonial advertisements was a Mme Jaume, aged thirty-eight, separated from her husband, whom she proposed to divorce. The name under which he was passing at that time was Lucien Guillet.

An ingenious but, for the moment, unsuccessful murderer active at the time was Henri Girard, a middle-aged dandy who had indeed one past success to his credit, having given a friend typhoid by putting a culture of germs in drinking water and then, upon the friend's slow recovery, finishing him off with an injection. That had been two years before the war. On May 10th, 11th and 14th, 1917, Girard fed another friend with poison toadstools and doctored

25

drinks, unrewardingly. In August, Mme Buisson, a widow, forty-four, who had answered a matrimonial advertisement, went to Gambais with Landru, whom she knew as Frémyet, and disappeared.

I am uncertain whether 'Mata Hari' comes properly within my purview or not. The documents in the case are still difficult of access, but I am somewhat persuaded by the Sam Waagenaar volume, published in 1964, that this big, jolly Dutch tart and exhibitionist was no more a spy, dear reader, than you or I, though less careful what company she kept, and that her execution by a firing squad, on October 15th, 1917, was a true example of judicial murder in the only sense which, to my mind, that much-abused expression can properly bear, that is to say, wilful murder committed by an individual using the judicial process as one might use arsenic or a hammer. The murderer, in this view of the matter, was a Captain Ladoux, who got her arrested out of jealousy and spite, well knowing what must follow in the climate of spy mania prevalent in that darkest year of the war.

In early November occurred one of our four murders committed by a French individual (in this case, on another French individual) in or near London. On the morning of Friday 2nd, a roadsweeper in Regent Square, Bloomsbury, found the headless trunk and handless arms of Emilienne Gérard, thirty-two, wrapped in a sheet and a meat sack, while her legs lay near by in a brown-paper parcel. A laundry mark on the sheet led to the establishment of her identity and to her address, a mile or so westward, towards Regent's Park. A photograph over her mantelpiece showed Louis Voisin, aged forty-two, a big, florid butcher in Charlotte Street, half a mile south, in a neighbourhood then, as indeed twenty years later, a kind of northerly extension of Soho. An I.O.U. for £50 signed by him was also found in Mlle Gérard's flat. In his basement were found her head and hands, the head viciously battered but without fracture of the skull, signs also about the neck of strangulation. There was dried blood everywhere, including the interior of a pony-trap in a stable at the back. Louis Voisin was sitting in his kitchen with another Frenchwoman Berthe Roche.

Asked about Emilienne Gérard, he said that he had last seen her on Wednesday and that she had asked him to look after her cat, as she was going to France for a few days. The body had been dismembered with an expertness which suggested the hand of a butcher. The clue to Voisin's guilt which has, however, delighted

generations of British amateur criminologists was that, on a piece
of brown paper with the remains, had been written 'Blodie Belgiam'.
The intention had, presumably, been to conceal the identity rather
of the victim than of the killer, but other possibilities may occur to
the reader's mind. Voisin was asked to write out 'bloody Belgium'
and with dogged persistence five times spelled it the same way. The
orthographical error being pointed out to him, he changed his tale,
saying that on Thursday he had called at Emilienne's flat, found
her head and hands on the table and panicked. In favour of Berthe
Roche's complicity, to say the least, was the fact that the skull,
though savagely struck a dozen or so times, had not fractured,
which suggested a feminine lack of physical strength. There was
also neighbourly testimony to the fact that she had not, as she said,
just called in to see Voisin but had stayed in his basement flat on
Wednesday and Thursday nights.

A tidier man than his exiled compatriot, Henri-Désiré Landru
seems to have effected, on November 26th or 27th, the disappearance at Gambais of Mme Jaume. His affair with Fernande Segret
continued, to their evident mutual satisfaction. He already knew
Mme Pascal, aged thirty-three and divorced, a milliner without
assets.

In January 1918, Louis Voisin appeared at the Old Bailey and was
sentenced to death by hanging. In France, the office of the Director
of Public Prosecutions for Paris and the Seine called for psychiatrists' reports on Raoul Villain, who was still confined at the Santé
prison. He was found fit to plead and to stand trial, which was
perhaps not what *le Parquet* had hoped. However, for the moment,
nothing was done. Mme Pascal's turn to disappear at or from Gambais came in early April. As with Andrée Babelay, Landru was left
none the richer, except by a few articles of clothing.

At the time, Henri Girard, having failed to kill his friends with
successive banquets of mushrooms, was taking out insurance policies
on the life of a Mme Monin and at the same time cultivating
bacillus typhosus in his laboratory. The Phoenix policy was dated
April 9th. On the 24th, in the northerly suburb of La Villette, a
gang garrotted and robbed Mme Dreyfus, a slaughterhouse-owner.
On the 30th, at Girard's new apartment near the Gare de l'Est,
Mme Monin drank a quinquina loaded with bacilli and afterwards
collapsed on the station platform of the Underground. In Russia,

there had been a change of government, and on July 16th, the deposed monarch, Nicholas II, was murdered in a cellar at Tobolsk.

In August, Raoul Villain was transferred from the Santé out to Fresnes, where the air was better. There, towards the end of the month, he was joined by Henri Girard. In September, Landru made the acquaintance of a Mme Falques who, in October, visited Gambais but survived. On November 11th, at 11 a.m., a solemn hush fell on the Western and other fronts. Three days later, an undersized youth of sixteen, Emile Buisson, was convicted of petty larceny and given a fortnight's suspended sentence at Paray-le-Monial in Burgundy. His period of greatest fame lay thirty years ahead, though some of his doings at earlier dates may seem worth noting as we come to them. In Paris, a week after the Armistice, an Emile four years older, Emile Courgibet, who in due course was to be closely associated with 'Mimile' Buisson, faced trial for his life, having stabbed to the heart a fickle mistress for whose sake he had failed to return to his regiment at the end of a period of sick leave. He was sentenced to eight years' hard labour in the Guiana penal settlements, to be followed by ten years' *interdiction de séjour*, thus to seventeen years of deportation in all.

He sailed for Cayenne the following year in the *La Martinière*, a German vessel renamed. In January of that year, Mme Marchadier, thirty-seven, whose boarding-house in Paris Landru had been proposing to buy, went with him to Gambais and was seen no more. But that month also the mayor of Gambais received puzzling letters from a Mlle Lacoste and a Mme Pelat, both concerned with the disappearance of sisters, respectively a Mme Buisson and a Mme Collomb. They had visited Gambais in the company of a bearded gentleman whom one correspondent remembered as M. Frémyet and the other as M. Cuchet. He evidently resembled the M. Dupont who indeed rented a villa in the commune, from which he was absent, however, when enquiries were made. The mayor suggested to each of the questing sisters that she should get in touch with the other and passed both letters to the police at Mantes, who sent them to the headquarters, in the Rue Greffulhe, Paris, of No. 1 *brigade mobile* of the Sûreté Générale, already concerned with the disappearance of a Mme Cuchet and her son, last known to have gone with a M. Diard not to Gambais but to Vernouillet. That month also, the La Villette gang resumed its activities on an unrewarding scale with safe-blowing in a bank vault.

On March 4th, Raoul Villain was brought from Fresnes to the

Conciergerie, adjacent to the Law Courts on the Île de la Cité. His trial opened on the 24th, four years and eight months after the murder with which he was charged. It was an odd trial. The indictment or act of accusation, equivalent to the opening speech for the prosecution in British courts but read by the clerk to the court, was the one drawn up in 1915 by an earlier Director of Public Prosecutions and omitted, as might have been only tactful at the time, any reference either to such evidence of complicity as there was or to Villain's political affiliations. In early 1919, no general demobilisation had yet taken place, and the average age of the jury was exceptionally high, the youngest being fifty-three. All but one of the twelve jurymen could be described as *bourgeois*. The number of witnesses had greatly increased, while of those originally cited some were dead, and some had been unaccountably dropped. These included the policeman who had so promptly arrested Villain and the priest who on a Sunday afternoon had watched him practising like a madman on the shooting range at a parish fair in Sèvres. The presiding judge's questions were indulgent, the concluding speech for the prosecution mild and ambiguous. The protracted irrelevance of the *partie civile* was barely credible.

Criminal and civil proceedings are kept quite separate in British courts. Half-way through a French murder trial, it is common for speeches to be made and, on occasion, for witnesses to be called by barristers acting on behalf of the victim's next-of-kin, the *partie civile*. The abuse that this practice most frequently leads to is that a black-gowned member of the Order of Advocates, who in theory cannot directly prosecute, will in effect be leading for the prosecution and sometimes doing it with a vindictiveness which leaves his red-gowned colleagues in the magistracy standing. In the Villain case, that was not the trouble. It is known that Jaurès' widow had not been anxious to constitute herself civil complainant at all. She herself was not a socialist, and the Party had taken the matter out of her hands. For three days on end, the trial quite ceased to be concerned with Villain's guilt and became a succession of tributes to the dead man, paid in turn by no fewer than seventeen eloquent gentlemen more or less of the Left. They included three former prime ministers, generals and a former Minister of War, a Nobel Peace Prize winner, d'Estournelles de Constant, and, to become the best-known of them all outside France, Léon Blum, who compared Jaurès with Chateaubriand, Victor Hugo, Mirabeau, Bossuet, Michelet and Rousseau. Leading counsel for the *partie civile*,

Maître Paul-Boncour, was himself to become a leading statesman and sounded that way set.

Defending counsel, Maîtres Zevaès and Henri Géraud, were both bearded. We shall meet them both, but especially the latter, again. At the age of forty-seven, his beard was already long. During the next twenty years, he would grow to look more and more like an Old Testament prophet. I quote one fragment of his concluding speech :

> FOR THE DEFENCE, ME GÉRAUD : He knew nothing of the easy-going comradeship of editorial offices, the cosy humbug of parliamentary life. Those displays of moral indignation, the angry cries, the shaken fists, meant nothing, my poor Villain, except to you, in your impossible chastity, your patriotic dream. Out of the public eye, those gentlemen were all the best of friends over their port.

And then of course he asked the jury for an acquittal.

In a French criminal trial, the last word is always with the defence. There exists, nevertheless, a 'right to reply' (but then also a right to reply to the reply), which is not infrequently exercised by the red-robed prosecutor. Irregularly, it was in this case exercised by a *partie civile* lawyer, and the pleas ended with an angry exchange between Mes Géraud and Paul-Boncour, the latter pointing out that, when all was said about reconciliation, a man had been killed and another had killed him, the former insisting that he had tried to look beyond the grave.

> PRESIDENT OF THE COURT, M. BOUCARD : Discussion is now closed. Raoul-Marie-Alexandre Villain, have you anything further to say in your defence?
>
> VILLAIN : Mr President, I ask the victim's pardon and forgiveness for my father and my brother. The grief of a widow and an orphan girl will leave my life devoid of happiness.

That is the kind of thing which a person accused of a grave crime is expected to say in conclusion, and we may assume that Villain had been drilled in it. Even so, we find it welling up from unconsciousness that his father and brother were to blame, when he was meant to be asking forgiveness for himself in order to spare them.

There were two questions put to the jury. First, was Villain guilty of having committed wilful murder upon the person of Jean Jaurès?

Second, was the said murder committed with malice aforethought, premeditation or lying in wait? The jury retired. The prisoner was removed. Those twelve old men were out for no more than half an hour.

> PRESIDENT : Mr Foreman of the Jury, be so good as to acquaint the court with the result of your deliberations.
>
> FOREMAN : On my honour and on my conscience, before God and before men, the jury's answer to both questions is no, by a majority of more than seven to five.

That is the formula. Villain was brought back and informed that he would be immediately released unless he were required to face some other charge in another court.

It was a bad verdict in itself, and its consequences were to be bad. To begin with, in the debate on the civil issue, which followed the prisoner's discharge on criminal counts, not only did Mme Jaurès receive no damages, but costs were awarded against her. The award must strike us as iniquitous, but it was not due to personal iniquity on the part of the judges in that particular court. It was, as Le Clère makes plain in his excellent little book on the case, inherent in the Penal Code from Napoleonic times, no amendment being introduced till 1940. There was an element of logic in it. Since Raoul Villain was proved not to have wilfully caused her late husband's death, Mme Jaurès, in seeking damages from him, could be thought to be indulging in what a British judge might call vexatious litigation. As it was only Socialist Party pressure which had led her to constitute herself plaintiff in the first place and as it was they who had turned the *partie civile* into a three days' political demonstration, with which she can have felt little sympathy and which must have put the jury's backs up more than somewhat, one would like to think that they dipped into Party funds to relieve her of the expense. But, as we shall see, the acquittal itself was to create a dangerous precedent.

As WE know, Fernande Segret, now twenty-seven, though she also worked in a furrier's shop, fancied her chances as an *artiste lyrique*. Nor can her middle-aged boy-friend for the past two years, the man she knew as Lucien Guillet, engineer, small, dark-bearded, bald, but so polite, attentive, poetical and amusing, with whom she commonly lived in the Rue Rochechouart but with whom she had also stayed six or seven times at a funny little, ill-furnished villa between the churchyard and the forest at Gambais, have been altogether unmusical. In the first week of April 1919, they went together to a performance of Massenet's *Manon* at the Opéra Comique and were much taken with one song in it, '*Adieu, notre petite table, un même verre était le nôtre, chacun de nous. . . .*' They had just bought a new table, and on Saturday, April 5th, they went to a big shop in the Rue de Rivoli and chose a new, white dinner service. Then they took an afternoon train to Houdan, and Papa Louis drove them to Gambais as so often before.

It does not appear that Fernande was either a particularly observant young woman or one to worry unduly. If, at the shop in the Rue de Rivoli, she had noticed a middle-aged woman staring at her companion or seen him meet the woman's eyes briefly and look for a moment uneasy, we may suppose that she said nothing and that she soon forgot about the matter. He would recognise the woman and think quickly what he must say if she addressed him but she did not and was presently lost to view. He cannot have known that, earlier in the day, a man from the Sûreté had called to see her at the house where she worked as a domestic servant and that his last instructions to her had been that, if she saw the man she knew as Frémyet, she was to call a policeman and have him arrested. She did not do this, but presently she rang up the Rue Greffulhe and spoke to young Inspector Belin. She was Mlle Lacoste, sister of the Mme Buisson last seen at Gambais in the late summer of 1917.

Fernande Segret and the man she knew as Lucien Guillet stayed at Gambais all week and returned to Paris on Friday evening. They did not know that, as soon as he saw them back, the caretaker at the house in the Rue Rochechouart went to a nearby bar and told Inspector Belin, who had been calling at the house since Monday with a warrant issued not in Paris but at Mantes and in the name not of Guillet but of Frémyet, the address having been established from a visiting card left with a deposit at the crockery shop. Because of regulations about making arrests on private premises during the hours of darkness, Inspector Belin spent part of that night in the caretaker's lodge and part on the landing, but they didn't know. Saturday, the 12th, was Landru's fiftieth birthday, but seems likely enough that Mlle Segret didn't even know that, any more than she knew her Lucien's real name.

Movements concerning the two, unknown to them, began at day

break. First of all, Inspector Belin stationed a uniformed policeman outside the house. Then he sent the caretaker to the Rue Greffulhe to fetch another inspector with a car, himself meanwhile going along the road for a cup of coffee. It was after nine o'clock when knocking started at the flat door. Eventually, Lucien, in his pyjamas, opened it a couple of inches, and the detectives pushed in. From the next room, Fernande heard them say that they were investigating the disappearance of two women, Mmes Collomb and Buisson, that foul play was suspected and that Frémyet, Guillet, Diard or whatever his name was would have to get dressed at once and go with them. Fernande Segret fainted. When she came to, she found 'Lucien' holding a glass of water to her lips and stroking her hair. As he left with one of the detectives and the uniformed policeman, he sang to her, wryly, '*Adieu, notre petite table. . . .*' Inspector Belin remained and asked her whether she minded if he had a look round. At that moment, even he did not know what Landru's real name was, but he discovered it later that morning and, on the way to deliver his prisoner at Mantes, called with him at Gambais, where for the moment no more was discovered than the bodies of three little dogs, which had been strangled with wire.

French newspapers being quite uninhibited about commenting on matters *sub judice*, it was not many days before Fernande Segret knew all about her lover's early convictions for fraud, the fact that he had a wife and four children at Clichy, his earlier villa at Vernouillet, the presence of various ladies at Gambais before she met him and, alas, the presence of others there since, one as recently as January. Their names somewhat explained the initials on her blue dressing-gown and various other articles of feminine apparel which had long been or more lately appeared in the flat. From papers which Inspector Belin had taken away, it seemed that, during the past four years, the man she supposed she would always think of as Lucien had received 283 replies to matrimonial advertisements and that he'd followed up 179 of these, including those from some of the ladies who had disappeared. From two little notebooks she'd often seen him with, the police had discovered even more significant information.

For a fortnight, he was in prison at Mantes. Then they brought him to the Santé, where, as it turned out, he was to remain for over two years, after which he would be transferred to Versailles, where at present, it seemed, politicians of many countries were haggling about a peace treaty. He was famous. In the streets soldiers, elsewhere more successful *artistes lyriques*, sang songs about him. In prison he received countless proposals of marriage. At the elections, voters spoiled their ballot papers by writing his name across them. He was known as Bluebeard.

THE TREATY of Versailles was signed on June 28th, to become effective six months later. It may be worth glancing here at the military records of a number of those whose names we must hear again. Georges Sarret, for instance, *né* Sarrejani, of Marseilles, had performed non-combatant duties. It may be remembered that, before the war, he had practised journalism. Now, demobilised at the age of forty, he took up the study of law and might presently be seen in an office of his own at which he advised businessmen on the legal side of their undertakings and projects. Pierre Bougrat, who had started his medical studies at Lyons before the war, was to complete them with distinction in 1920 and put up his plate in Marseilles, where a doctor father-in-law ceded him half of his practice. As *aide-major* or assistant medical officer, Bougrat had served with exceptional merit. He had been wounded six times in France and Salonika and had received both Croix de Guerre and Legion of Honour, being five times mentioned in dispatches. One of several head wounds had deprived him of sight for a period of five months, but, quite recovered, he was, at twenty-nine, a well-made, good-looking young man, dark hair brushed smoothly back, moustache closely clipped over a mouth sensuously full.

Also to be a doctor, Marcel Petiot, on the other hand, had given the Army nothing but trouble. In 1919, he was not yet finished with it, but, the following year, would still be in hospital in Orleans under psychiatric care. He was younger, a mere twenty-two, a native of Auxerre, son of a postman who had died when he was eight. Psychiatric grounds had first been pleaded in his defence when, in 1918, he had been charged with stealing drugs from a casualty clearing station and selling them to his own profit. At sixteen, he had come before the juvenile court in Auxerre for robbing letter-boxes. He, too, had been wounded, in the foot by a hand-grenade. He was dark to the point of swarthiness. A year older and brought up in Marseilles, Mieczyslas Charrier had served as a hospital orderly. I have no note of the wartime activities of Guillaume Seznec, let alone those of Jean-Pierre Vaquier or Max Kassel, these two already in their forties.

Of those born in the Ukraine, Shalom Schwartzbard had been in Paris when the war broke out, had volunteered for the French army, served with the Foreign Legion, been wounded in 1916, decorated and invalided out. He had then returned to the Ukraine, where he still was at the time of the worst pogroms, when fifteen members of his Jewish family were slain. Pavel Gorguloff may have taken an active part in the torture and shootings. He had served in the Russian army until the Treaty of Brest-Litovsk, had been wounded in the head, had started medical studies at Rostov, there contracted a first marriage, fought again in the civil war on the side neither of Whites nor of Reds but of the Greens, who were little more than bandits, fled to Poland and contracted a second marriage (and would presently be found in Czechoslovakia for nine years). Among others of alien nationality who would eventually find their way to Paris, Eugen Weidmann, in 1919, was only eleven. He was back in Frankfurt-am-Main, having spent the war years in Cologne with grandparents, while his father served in the German army and his mother worked in an insurance office.

Among our ladies, it may be noted that in 1919 Marie-Marguerite Alibert married a M. Laurent, by whom she had a child and whom she presently divorced on grounds of desertion. He made her a large allowance. For reasons unknown to me, she adopted the name of Maggie Mellor, was to be seen at the races and sometimes appeared at embassy parties. In Le Mans, the sisters Christine and Léa Papin had both left the Good Shepherd hard-case convent and started their life together in domestic service. They still had a mother who expected her share of their wages. They could never be induced to take service in different houses.

3 | A WORLD AT PEACE

READERS OF M. Simenon's Maigret novels become almost obsessively familiar with a building in the Quai des Orfèvres. This part of the south embankment of the Île de la Cité extends from the Pont Neuf, near the westerly tip of the island, to the Pont St Michel, beyond which it is continued to the east by the Quai du Marché Neuf and the southern edge of the open square before the cathedral of Notre Dame. Behind the Quai des Orfèvres lie, first, the Place Dauphine and then the Law Courts (the spire of Sainte Chapelle rising from a yard in that constellation of buildings). Behind the Quai du Marché Neuf lie the headquarters of the Prefecture of Police, whose west front faces the main entrance to the Law Courts across the Boulevard du Palais. It is the P.P. for the department of the Seine, which means, or until recently meant, Paris and its suburbs. The Quai des Orfèvres building, No. 36, housed the *police judiciaire* or P.J. of the P.P., confined in its operations to that area, which indeed alone properly lay within the jurisdiction of those Law Courts.

In Paris also, however, in the Rue des Saussaies, two miles to the north-west and forming part of the Ministry of the Interior or, as we should say, Home Office buildings, were the headquarters of the Sûreté Nationale, whose writ ran throughout France and which also had its *police judiciaire*, including that Garde Mobile to whose 1st flying squad, separately housed in the Rue Greffulhe, Inspector Jean Belin belonged. Confusion sometimes arises because '*la Sûreté*' has often been popularly used to mean the P.J. in the Quai des Orfèvres. This would matter less now than it did, the French police now being more effectively integrated than they were. During the years with which we are concerned, there was often damaging rivalry between the two *polices judiciaires* in and around Paris. Jean Belin had indeed arrested Landru in Paris, but it was with a warrant made out in Mantes-la-Jolie. A man from the Quai des Orfèvres, armed with a P.P. warrant, signed by a Seine magistrate, might have chased him westward all through Neuilly but could not have crossed the bridge and continued to Nanterre.

One understands that Maigret was largely based on Chief Superintendent Massu. His predecessor was René Faralicq, appointed on October 15th, 1919, at the age of forty-one, a big man of exceptional strength, who wrote poetry and studied the works of Dante with scholarly attention. He was head of what we may indeed call the crime squad but which, until the end of the Second World War, was not the Brigade Criminelle but the Brigade Spéciale, the other main section of the P.J. of the P.P. being the vice squad or Brigade Mondaine, to which a drug squad or Brigade des Stupéfiants was adjoined in ever-increasing strength. Under him, Chief Superintendent Faralicq had fifty men, mainly *inspecteurs* and *brigadiers*, these latter equivalent, in the United Kingdom, to detective-sergeants and detective-constables. His office at the Quai des Orfèvres was on the third floor (on the fourth is now the police museum, which anyone may visit). As though in the opening pages of a Maigret novel, he describes the view from his windows, on the one side over the Place Dauphine, with children roller-skating, on the other of the Seine, with the Pont des Arts, the Pont Neuf and sunsets.

At the French murder rate for the time, during the first ten months of Faralicq's occupation of his new post there must have been over a hundred acts of culpable homicide in the Paris region alone. In his reminiscences, he was to deal with investigations into a mere nine of these. The victims were a uniformed policeman who had challenged a gang of tyre robbers, an old maid who kept a boot shop, an eccentric old woman who lived in a wagon, a yet older woman who, gagged, had choked on her false teeth, a floor manager at the Grand Hôtel, a travelling woman, a dressmaker, a lady's maid and a rich, elderly businessman, found in a trunk as far away as Nancy. For each a murderer was eventually found, though the cases against two of the men were non-suited. Of those undoubtedly guilty, one was an anarchist, though his ill-treatment and robbery of the old lady with false teeth seems to have been attributable only to the most general political motives. Only to the uniformed policeman, the proprietress of the boot shop and the hotel floor manager, among the victims, does Faralicq give a name, and only to the murderer, Burger, of this last, painstakingly dismembered, his trunk pitched over the parapet of the Pont Mirabeau into the Seine, which then carried it as far as Bougival. The rest are referred to only by initials, as Mother C, Mmes L, O and P, Mlle C's maid and Monsieur C. In a way, this is natural enough. The Chief Superintendent was not much concerned either with the psychology of the criminals or with the public hearing of the cases against them except in so far as the one may have helped or hindered their arrest and as the other resulted in a conviction or failed to do so, but only in the success of the operations conducted by his own section, while even in this connection he deprives one of his men of glory by naming him only as Brigadier W. The police side of his matter is one which the criminal historian should never ignore, and Faralicq is in general good about dates. In other respects, however, it does not facilitate the historian's task to deprive him of names. I have not felt that mattered in all but one of the cases above. It would have been dreadful not to know from other sources that Monsieur B was M. Bessarabo, that Mme B was Héra Myrtel and that Mlle J was her daughter by a first husband, Paule Jacques. For, while the rest (apart perhaps from the case of the hotel floor manager, Jobin, whose flighty wife was involved) might be regarded as a mere succession of *faits divers*, this was to be something of a *cause célèbre*.

Among other sources, we are lucky to have, and in English, the reminiscences also of the prefect of police in Faralicq's day, a twinkling little man with a closely trimmed beard, awarded the C.B.E. for services of some kind during the Great War or on the occasion of a royal visit. From him, as (once we know who Mme B was) from Faralicq, we may gather that the presence of Bessarabo's body in a trunk at Nancy resulted from a shot fired by his wife on July 30th (not the first that month, but ten days before she had missed) and the subsequent, frenzied activities of herself and his stepdaughter, who took after her mother and, for no very good reason, hated him. Mme Bessarabo, who used drugs, had frequently threatened her second husband. One night two years ago, he had awakened with her hands on his throat. He knew very well that she had killed her first husband, and had expressed the fear that his turn would come. He would have left her, but she was apparently in a position to blackmail him over some irregularity in his business dealings.

In England and Wales during those months, a sixty-year-old labourer, Albert Burrows, killed his young mistress and her two children (one of them also his) and pitched their bodies down the air-shaft of a disused mine in Derbyshire. A green bicycle, found in a Leicestershire canal, connected Ronald Light with the murder, seven months before, of Bella Wright. The body of a Mrs Greenwood was exhumed, and her husband, a solicitor in Kidwelly, Carmarthenshire, was charged with poisoning her. Also in Wales, a boy called Harold Jones, of Abertillery, committed the first of his two murders on younger girls. An army deserter, Percy Toplis, shot a taxi-driver in Wiltshire and a policeman and another man in the Scottish Highlands and was himself shot down by police in Cumberland. Two unemployed labourers, Field and Gray, brained and robbed a Scottish typist near Eastbourne. The Communist Party of Great Britain was founded. A young ex-soldier, John Reginald Halliday Christie, married a girl called Ethel Simpson Waddington, in Sheffield.

At a small town in New England, on April 15th, 1920, a pay-clerk and his security guard were gunned down, finished off and robbed in broad daylight by men in a car which then made off rapidly. It was one of a series of such acts of banditry. One is tempted to say that it was destined to become the crime of the decade, but in fact the crime itself was soon forgotten. What is remembered is that at about this time two Italian anarchists, Sacco and Vanzetti, were arrested and charged with a crime of some kind, perhaps a wholly imaginary one. They were in fact arrested on May 5th, largely on the basis of a reliable ballistics *expertise*. That month in Chicago, an ageing Italian super-ponce, Colosimo, known to gangster-fans as 'big Jim', was gunned down on premises of his own, of which there were many.

In hungry Germany, on August 13th, a young woman who may have been the Grand Duchess Anastasia of Russia fell victim to the first and possibly the greatest of the decade's curious succession of German mass-murderers, Grossmann, who then sold the fleshier parts of her body for meat and made black pudding of the blood. Returning to Paris from the Ukraine, Shalom Schwartzbard set up as a watchmaker in Ménilmontant. In prison for fraud at Grenoble and there discovered to be tubercular Mieczyslas or Mécislas Charrier made the acquaintance of two habitual criminals, Thomas and Bertrand. It may be assumed that the three discussed future prospects and that Goldberg's bastard acquainted his less intellectual companions with the anarchist justification of crime as *reprise individuelle* and propaganda by deed. In Paris, on October 18th, a lower court than the one he had earlier faced convicted Raoul Villain on a currency charge.

The leader of the La Villette gang was René Jean, who seemed respectable. He had been the Dreyfuses' head clerk, and with money acquired by the murder of Mme Dreyfus two years before he had bought himself a partnership in a scalding-house. After two attempts to kill and rob the principal collector for the slaughterhouses, he contented himself, on October 21st, with hammering to death, in the great central hall of the cattle-market, the young cashier of a smaller firm, whose name we may discover from Morain (Faralicq spares the whole gang and gives their victims no more than initials) to have been Mme Desserre. Two Arabs, heard boasting that they had been offered a part in the job, gave him and others away. Near Boulogne-sur-Mer, at the end of November, disappeared William Gourlay, a young London tourist agent, one of a long series of British visitors to vanish or to be found unaccountably dead in France between the wars.

The year itself ended with a Socialist Party congress at Tours, at which the moderates, led by Léon Blum, were outvoted by others whose leaders had recently been to Moscow for orders. A French Communist Party still had ten months to wait for its formal constitution, but *L'Humanité*, founded by Jean Jaurès to propagate a socialism with French roots, fell at once into the hands of the Marxists. 'At the Tours congress,' said one of Blum's friends, 'Jaurès was murdered for the second time.' Not that it would save his name thenceforward from being taken in vain on the Marxist behalf.

IN THE examining magistrates' wing at the Palais de Justice on the Île de la Cité, M. Bonin must have been the object of some envy, since not only Landru had been allocated to him but, more recently, Mme Bessarabo as well. The unusual length of time he had already spent in preparing the Landru *dossier* was justified by the fact that the *prévenu* (he would not be *accusé* until the case against him was complete and a true bill had been found by the *chambre des mises en accusation* of the Cour d'Appel) admitted nothing and more obviously by the further fact that everything had to be done to trace no fewer than 179 women. Mme Bessarabo, on the other hand, had confessed that it was her hand which had fired the fatal shot, though under extreme provocation and almost by accident, and incriminated her daughter only as what we should call an accessory after the fact (helping with the trunk and so on). True, on January 18th, 1921, a month before her trial, she suddenly retracted her confession and reverted to an earlier story about armed gangs, but by then it was too late to halt proceedings, and her counsel was perhaps able to assure the *Parquet* or Public Prosecutions department that in court his client would plead as intended, which does not mean that he may not also have encouraged the retractation. Though best known for his beautiful voice and moving eloquence, that short but handsome Corsican was also a crafty strategist and may have planned to confuse the jury.

He was Vincent de Moro-Giafferi, last of the great *ténors du barreau* (operatic tenors of the Bar, an expression for which it may be we never needed an equivalent, even in the nineteenth century reserving that style of eloquence for the House of Commons). He was also in due course to lead and plead for Landru, the case against whom must provide its own confusion, if only by reason of the number of counts in the indictment, though most of the women had been traced by now (all would be) except the ten listed in that awkward little notebook. In the Bessarabo case, what Moro could not hope to control was the behaviour of his client's daughter, Paule Jacques, who was already on record as saying to a prosecution witness, 'I would like to show you how we use revolvers in Mexico.' She had also hinted darkly that there was in the matter a secret concerning her mother which she had no right to reveal without her mother's consent.

There was in fact talk of armed gangs at the trial which opened on February 15th. Doubt was even cast on whether the body found in the trunk at Nancy had been M. Bessarabo's at all. The *coup de théâtre* occurred, however, after the formal pleas, as the jury were about to retire. Asked whether she had anything to add in her defence, Paule Jacques told all. This resulted in her acquittal, twenty years' hard for her mother.

Faits divers of the spring and early summer included the award, at Lyons, of a year's imprisonment for breaking and entering to Emile Buisson, the suicide in prison of Henri Girard and an attempt on the life of the prince regent of Yugoslavia, due to accede to his father's throne, as Alexander I, in two months' time. Henri Girard was the toadstool and microbe poisoner. Awaiting trial with the practical certainty of a capital sentence, he somehow obtained a test-tubeful of *bacillus typhosus*, of which he died in his forty-sixth year. 'Mimile' Buisson, it may be remembered, was small and had been put on a kind of probation three days after the Armistice, when he was sixteen. He came from a bad home, not a 'broken' one

but one made wretched by a drunken father, such as seems to have
been as common a childhood affliction in France during our period
as in Victorian or Edwardian London. The Papin sisters had one.
He had also forced sexual intimacy upon the elder, Christine, who
had in her turn initiated the feeble-minded younger, Léa, into
Lesbian practices, whence the fact that the two were inseparable.

In New England, the trial of Sacco and Vanzetti, begun on May
31st, ended on July 14th with the conviction of both for murder in
the first degree. There were at first no perceptible repercussions
abroad, except in Italy. The most spectacular French crime of that
month and indeed of that year was committed on the Paris-
Marseilles night express, known as Train 5, on July 24th-25th. Just
after midnight, a row of first-class compartments was invaded by
three masked men, who collected a fair amount of money and jewellery, then pulled the communication cord and, as the train slowed
up, jumped off it at a point between Beaune and Mâcon in Burgundy. The one passenger who offered any resistance, a young Army
lieutenant, had been shot and left dying. The bandits were traced
back to Paris, and on July 30th, just after midday, two of them
shot it out with the police at a bar in the Batignolles. The two
bandits were killed and a policeman fatally wounded. The names
of the two dead bandits were Thomas and Bertrand. The third,
taken into custody early that morning, had immediately confessed
and given his older companions away. He was the Mécislas Charrier
whom they had met in prison at Grenoble, a tall, thin young man
with thick, dark hair brushed back, professing those anarchist
principles which are indeed peculiarly suited to anyone proposing
to take up a life of crime or vagabondage. At the Santé prison, he
wrote both prose and verse. He was not the first or last young
criminal to do that either.

As it was committed in the provinces, the crime on Train 5 had
fallen within the jurisdiction of the Sûreté Nationale, not that of
the prefecture in Paris. In this case, however, the two forces co-
operated rationally, and it was in fact inspectors from the Quai des
Orfèvres who carried out the arrests and one of whom was killed.
Their *patron*, Faralicq, was at the time on holiday in Savoy, reading Dante perhaps.

In the Soviet Union, anarchists were daily liquidated. This had
not prevented the master minds of the Comintern from seeing revolutionary possibilities in a world outcry against the Sacco-Vanzetti
verdict (sentence had not yet been passed). By mid-September, the

plan had been formulated and orders sent out. On the 20th, the Central Committee for Action of the newly formed French Communist Party passed a resolution in these terms :

Only direct and unambiguously revolutionary action can save the Italian liberators, Sacco and Vanzetti, from the death penalty to which they have been sentenced.

L'Humanité opened a subscribers' fund and declared :

There is an American embassy in Paris. We owe it a visit !

Towards the end of September, 8,000 comrades and sympathisers attended a rally in the Salle Wagram. On their way out, a hand-grenade was lobbed into the midst of the *service d'ordre* of police, producing casualties but none fatal. On October 19th, another, jokily or with intended guile wrapped in a copy of *L'Action Fran-çaise*, arrived by post at the Embassy and injured the attendant who opened the parcel. On the 24th, the vast crowd of demonstrators outside had to be held back by 10,000 police and 18,000 troops. A smaller demonstration in London was washed out by rain. Then, in Europe, the revolutionary heat was turned off, though it continued in Latin America. The Landru trial opened on November 7th, at Versailles.

This was because the eleven murders alleged had all taken place in what until recently (most of it is now Yvelines) was the department of Seine-et-Oise. Landru had been brought to Versailles from the Santé on June 14th. The prison of St Pierre, adjoining the courthouse, was small and at the time full, and he had been lodged at once in what was the condemned cell. A further delay had been sought by reason of his poor health, but this had resulted in no more than the issue of a free pair of new spectacles. Landru had asked for a pack of cards to play patience and tell fortunes with. These had been refused, on the ground that they were issued only to prisoners under sentence of death. Landru had answered that he was, after all, in the death cell. In the end, he made himself a pack out of the numerous picture postcards he received from admirers. His wife, meanwhile, had initiated divorce proceedings, unmollified by the gold watch and chain he had sent her, once the property of Mme Cuchet.

EVERYONE MUST have a first murderer, and for my generation it could only be Landru, 'the French Bluebeard', whose immensely photogenic (the word was not in use then, of course) face stared magnetically out at us, when we were ten, from the pages of the *Daily Mail*. His beard looked black, but I supposed it to be a kind of navy-blue. That he was a Frenchman must somewhat have predisposed me to the studies I have latterly pursued, half a century later. The only other Frenchmen I was aware of were Marshal Foch and the handsome light-heavyweight boxer Georges Carpentier, on whom I won sixpence when he beat Joe Beckett.

Among the photographs I have looked at recently, the one which most nearly corresponds to what I remember shows him, in a dinner jacket (but with a white tie), side by side with Fernande Segret, taken, presumably, in May 1917, on the day of their formal betrothal. The photographs of him in court, most of which I saw for the first time only recently, give a different impression. The beard is certainly not black, let alone blue. From conflicting accounts of it, I suppose it to have been a reddish grey. It had also been allowed to grow ragged. Perhaps at one time he had dyed it, for even when it was dark such observers as the young Inspector Belin would seem to remember a reddish glint. In several of the photographs of Landru in the dock (peering down through a pair of metal-rimmed spectacles or with the fingers of one hand eloquently spread, while the other holds the spectacles, or, simply, in profile, expostulating) he reminds me uncannily of a dear, and by then much older, friend, Sir Richard Rees, in his last years. Rees was a tall man, but so thin is Landru's nose, so angular are his frozen gestures, that from photographs alone one might have supposed him tall.

The first day's hearing was taken up with formalities, with the reading of the indictment or act of accusation and with a legal argument between Maître Moro-Giafferi and the *représentant du ministère public,* the *avocat-général,* red-gowned M. Godefroy, leading for the prosecution. On the second day, the presiding judge, M. Gilbert, took the defendant through the earlier part of his *curriculum vitae,* with which we are already familiar. Mme Izoré of Lille was heard. So was Inspector Belin, with evidence of arrest. At one point, Moro gathered up his papers and threatened to leave the court. On succeeding days, Landru was questioned, and witnesses were called, in respect of each of the alleged victims in turn, beginning with Mme Cuchet and her son, whose names appeared first in the list in the famous notebook.

Mme Cuchet, it may be recalled, had taken her son to Vernouillet in December 1914. Neither was seen again after January 4th, 1915, and four months later Landru inserted a matrimonial advertisement in *Le Journal.* Among those who replied were a Mme Laborde-Line and a Mme Guillin, both widows, aged respectively forty-seven and fifty-one. They disappeared in the course of the summer at (or from) Vernouillet. They had known Landru under the names of Diard, Frémyet and Cuchet. In December, he relinquished the first villa at Vernouillet and took the one at Gambais, out of the village, near woods and adjacent to the churchyard. The first widow after that was Mme Héon, fifty-five. Landru denied that he had made proposals of marriage to any of these women. He had merely bought their furniture for resale and negotiated securities for them.

PRESIDENT OF THE COURT, M. GILBERT : It appears, nevertheless, that on leaving her daughter's house, Mme Héon announced her impending marriage to you.

THE DEFENDANT, LANDRU : I know that she very much wanted to remarry. The idea made her feel younger. She was one of those women who count their age not from birth but from their first communion.

PRESIDENT : But you did not protest when she made the announcement.

LANDRU : It is possible. It pleased the lady. I was only interested in her furniture.

With little exchanges like that, Landru had quickly gained the reputation of a wit. It was now the sixth day of the trial. The appearance of the courtroom had changed. There had indeed been exhibits before : on the day of the Cuchets, for example, the gold

watch and chain which Landru had given to his wife, the blue
dressing-gown which Mlle Segret had been wearing. But now, with
the first Gambais disappearance, a stove had taken its place on a
dais in front of the judges and was to be frequently seen there, a
constant reminder of the gravamen of the prosecution case.

PRESIDENT : This stove was installed, was it not, in December
1915.

LANDRU : The house had stood empty for five years. There was
no proper kitchen installation.

PRESIDENT : And at the same time you ordered three hundred-
weight of coal.

LANDRU : Of course. It was December. It was cold.

PRESIDENT : Mme Héon accompanied you to Gambais on
December 8th?

LANDRU : No.

PRESIDENT : And yet in your notebook under that date we
find the prices of railway tickets from Paris to a station nearby.
One return, 3.85 francs. One single, 2.40 francs.

LANDRU : When I went to Gambais, I cycled. I inquired what
the railway fare was, for future reference. I see nothing unusual
about that.

The next case was one of the two which had led by a roundabout way to Landru's eventual arrest.

PRESIDENT : We come now to Mme Collomb, who gave you
her age as twenty-nine but who was in fact forty-four. You have
no comment to make on that fact?

LANDRU : No.

PRESIDENT : You are not always so chivalrous. On December
19th, 1916, Mme Collomb gave up her position as a typist with
the Prudential insurance company. On the 27th, she travelled
with you to Gambais, and again your notebook records that you
bought one single and one return ticket. Why was that?

LANDRU : I don't understand the question. I had to return to
Paris on business. If I'd bought a return ticket for Mme Collomb,
it would have suggested to her that I wish to curtail her visit.

PRESIDENT : And she never returned to Paris?

LANDRU : In due course, Mme Collomb returned to Paris.

PRESIDENT : Where was she on January 3rd, when you were
next seen at Gambais?

LANDRU : It is five years ago. I cannot remember all the details.

PRESIDENT : In your notebook, there is a figure 4 marked on December 27th. In the opinion of the police, that is the hour at which you murdered Mme Collomb.

LANDRU : Every time a figure occurs in my notebook, I am supposed to have murdered somebody.

PRESIDENT : Mme Collomb has never been seen again. Two years later, her mother, Mme Moreau, whom we shall hear, wrote to the mayor of Gambais.

There followed the case of the servant girl, Andrée Babelay, who had no money or even furniture. According to journalists, by a parallel with the Bluebeard story, she must therefore have been killed for giving way to curiosity and learning too much. The suppression of a potentially dangerous witness is, indeed, one of the commonest motives for murder. This case is certainly outside Landru's 'system' and, if it be thought proved, perhaps the least easily forgiven of his crimes. After Andrée Babelay came Mme Buisson, who, like Mme Collomb, was forty-four, a widow but with an illegitimate son and, unluckily for Landru, a sister who, like Mme Collomb's, did not forget her.

PRESIDENT : In June 1917, Mme Buisson ordered a wedding dress. In August, she went to Gambais. A return and a single ticket were taken. Mme Buisson was last seen on September 1st. On that date, the time 10.15 is noted. Also on that date, it appears that your cash in hand increased by a thousand francs.

LANDRU : It was a business transaction.

The *avocat-général* butted in.

FOR THE PROSECUTION, M. GODEFROY : A woman rarely orders a wedding-dress to transact business in. Nor are her clothes, false hair and papers as a rule found afterwards in a trunk at a garage belonging to the man with whom that business was transacted.

Mme Buisson's sister, Mme Lacoste, was heard. She it was who, by telephoning the police after seeing Landru in the street, had been most directly responsible for his arrest.

MME LACOSTE : Landru treated my sister as his wife. If I had ever had doubts as to the relationship between them, they were dispelled when I myself stayed with them at Gambais that August.

PRESIDENT : On that occasion, you quarrelled with your sister?

MME LACOSTE : A quarrel provoked by Landru. Months passed, eighteen perhaps. My sister's son went blind. I wrote to the mayor of Gambais. A short time afterwards, I had a visit from Mme Moreau, who also had written and been advised to see me.

Sir, if my sister had been living, she would have communicated with her blind son. My sister had been murdered. And by you, Landru, by you, by you!

There were also Mme Jaume, Mme Pascal, Mme Marchadier, last seen in November 1917, April 1918, January 1919. The trial had already lasted a fortnight. On November 22nd, people were fighting for places. Fernande Segret herself was to appear in evidence. She, it must be remembered, had not, after the initial roll-call of witnesses, till then been in court, but had had to content herself with what she read in the newspapers and what may have been told her by earlier witnesses with whom she had struck up an acquaintance or by lawyers. Before she was called, the clerk to the court read an affidavit from Mme Falque, in a sanatorium at the time, the only other woman known to have visited Gambais with Landru and survived. Mme Marchadier had visited Gambais shortly after and had, apparently, not survived.

The appearance of Mlle Segret caused so great a commotion that M. Gilbert threatened to have the court cleared. She wore a long sealskin coat and picture-hat. She was formally identified as Fernande Segret, aged twenty-nine, *artiste lyrique*, of 7 Rue Custine, Paris. She turned back the collar of her coat and disclosed a dainty blouse of pale pink satin. Her voice was pleasing, as that of an *artiste lyrique* might well be expected to be, and she gave an impression of great sincerity.

PRESIDENT : You recognise the prisoner?

MLLE SEGRET : Yes.

PRESIDENT : Please tell us how you became acquainted.

MLLE SEGRET : It was in May 1917. He offered me his seat on a bus. We got into conversation. Next day, we met at the Place de l'Étoile and went walking in the Bois de Boulogne. We boated on the lake. He said that he was Lucien Guillet, an engineer from Rocroi in the Ardennes, and that is what he seemed to me to look like. Everything was respectable and correct, and I did not suppose that we should be more than friends. But every day after that he accompanied me to the furrier's shop where I worked. From mere friends we became fiancés. I introduced M. Guillet to my mother and my relations.

That was on New Year's Day, 1918. The betrothal was arranged for Easter. There was a disappointment. My fiancé did not appear. He wrote that he was detained by urgent business on the Aisne. My mother and I went to Rocroi to learn what we could about him. We found that M. Guillet was unknown at Rocroi. This was a terrible blow. A few days later, however, the gentleman whom I now know to be M. Landru returned, and his explanation convinced us. The betrothal took place in May. Only my mother and my grandfather were present, but everything was beautifully arranged. The flowers were quite wonderful, and afterwards we had a box at the Opéra Comique. Everyone was very happy. We . . . I beg your pardon, Mr President, I. . . .

She had begun to sob uncontrollably and looked as though she might faint. Smelling-salts were produced, but she could not yet go on. Landru viewed her with perfect indifference, as though he had never seen her before. The hearing was suspended for ten minutes or so. The witness returned.

PRESIDENT : You are quite recovered?

MLLE SEGRET : Yes, thank you, Mr President.

PRESIDENT : And we may go on?

MLLE SEGRET : Yes. . . . It was decided that we should be married at the end of the year. At the time of the Armistice celebrations, in fact on Armistice Day, M. Guillet said, 'The war has ended too soon for me.' That was because a soldier at the Front with whom I was in correspondence as a 'war godmother' would be returning.

PRESIDENT : You hesitated between the two?

MLLE SEGRET : Yes. My first fiancé was young, but Lucien, M. Landru, made me very happy. Eventually, I broke completely with the young man. When I called on M. Landru in the evening to tell him of my decision, he went down on his knees to me. That evening, I became his mistress. We went to live in the Rue de Rochechouart.

PRESIDENT : What did your mother say?

MLLE SEGRET : I was of age. My mother did say that the man was an impostor and an adventurer, but he spoke to her with great sweetness and good sense and calmed her.

PRESIDENT : It was understood that your union would presently be regularised?

MLLE SEGRET : Yes, but somehow the marriage certificate. . . .

PRESIDENT : Quite so. Now, during this period of almost two years, you visited Gambais on a number of occasions. How many, would you say?

MLLE SEGRET : Seven or eight times.

PRESIDENT : How did the villa strike you?

MLLE SEGRET : Well, of course, the Hermitage was not well-furnished. In one room, there were guns and cartridges, a revolver. M. Landru was an excellent shot, he said.

PRESIDENT : I see. But otherwise . . . ?

MLLE SEGRET : I found the place charming. I loved our walks in the forest and the country lanes.

PRESIDENT : Did you ever quarrel?

MLLE SEGRET : A little, one day, when a letter came addressed not to M. Guillet but in another name.

PRESIDENT : Did you know what your fiancé's resources were? How did you live?

MLLE SEGRET : The garage at Clichy brought in a good deal.

PRESIDENT : Did you ever visit this garage?

MLLE SEGRET : Yes. It disappointed me a little. Only one apprentice was working there. And then one day my fiancé flew into a rage because I started looking at some business papers at our rooms in the Rue de Rochechouart. I was surprised. He read all my correspondence.

PRESIDENT : Did you know that in a little notebook he designated you by the figure 7?

MLLE SEGRET : I was not informed of that. I often noticed the little books. He said they contained personal memoranda.

PRESIDENT : In your testimony before the examining magistrate, you raised a delicate point about your relations with the defendant. You said that, while very passionate, he was quite normal. Is that so?

MLLE SEGRET : Oh, yes. Very normal.

Moro-Giafferi was permitted to intervene.

FOR THE DEFENCE, ME DE MORO-GIAFFERI : Your last visit to Gambais was on April 4th, 1919.

MLLE SEGRET : Yes. We drove down by cart. My young brother went with us.

MORO : And no doubt you cooked an evening meal. What with?

MLLE SEGRET : With . . . that.

MORO : This stove? Exhibit A?

MLLE SEGRET : Yes.

MORO : It was bought, I believe, from a hardware-merchant at Houdan.

MLLE SEGRET : Yes, M. Solier.

MORO : And you – in the course of two years – used it quite frequently?

MILLE SEGRET : Yes.

MORO : Did you ever see a skull or bones in it?

MLLE SEGRET : Oh, Maître, no! I would rake out the ashes and lay a fire. I never saw anything of that kind!

MORO : Not even on April 4th?

MLLE SEGRET : No, indeed not!

MORO : Yet, according to the prosecution, the last 'murder' had by then been committed. According also to the prosecution, bones were discovered among those ashes on April 13th. . . . Thank you, Mr President.

ON WEDNESDAY, November 23rd, Fernande Segret, no longer kept out as a future witness, sat in the courtroom. It was surprisedly observed that she was all smiles and seemed to enjoy the proceedings. That day and for several days thereafter, the evidence was concerned with the disposal of bodies. There were new exhibits in the form of boxes of bone fragments, teeth, hairpins, dress-hooks, pins, small mother-of-pearl buttons, metal buttons. The stove remained on view. Among those heard was Dr Paul, the French Sir Bernard Spilsbury.

PRESIDENT : Landru, if you had cut up the bodies of your victims, if you had buried them piecemeal in the woods at Gambais or Vernouillet, if you had thrown other parts into the river or a pond, it would have been very difficult to bring to light proof of your crimes. However, all was not destroyed. There remain material traces. Among ashes from the kitchen stove we see before us, medical experts found the remnants of human bones.

MORO : Mr President, we have heard when and how this material was collected.

PRESIDENT : That will be noted. I continue. As to the means by which they met their end, we know you possessed firearms.

LANDRU : I had a .22 rifle for use in the garden.

PRESIDENT : And a revolver, according to Mlle Segret. However, perhaps it was poison. There was found on your premises a book called *The Great Poisoners*.

LANDRU : You can't poison people with a book.

PRESIDENT : In the cellar at Gambais, a succeeding tenant found a number of phials, which he broke.

LANDRU : They contained photographic developers.

PRESIDENT : That was not his impression. We must also consider the possibility of strangling. You 'executed' dogs belonging to Mme Marchadier by hanging them. 'The easiest death,' you said.

LANDRU : Yes, for dogs.

PRESIDENT : However, these are only suppositions. The prosecution's case is that, however they met their end, you burned at least some of your victims. We shall hear the evidence of witnesses who will tell us that they smelled horrible odours as of burning flesh and saw suspicious lights both at Gambais and at Vernouillet.

LANDRU : I should like to know at what point a glimmer of light ceases to be normal and becomes suspicious. A great deal of senseless gossip goes on in the country.

PRESIDENT : Another witness will state that he saw you go out during the night in a motor-car, noticed you standing at the edge of a pond and heard the sound of a heavy object being thrown into the water at that moment. Investigations were carried out at various ponds near Gambais. These are muddy and much overgrown. If nothing was found in them, that is because a thorough search would have involved great risk.

LANDRU : The risk to me is unimportant, of course.

PRESIDENT : However, calcined bones were found and identified.

LANDRU : Identified?

PRESIDENT : They were human bones, and they came from at least three bodies.

LANDRU : The place is next to the graveyard, and there are not only gossips but practical jokers in the country. The place was left unguarded.

Experiments had been conducted with the stove.

DR PAUL : A right foot disappears in fifty minutes, half a skull with the brains taken out in thirty-six minutes, the whole skull in an hour and ten minutes. A human head, with the brain, hair, tongue, etc., takes about one hour and forty minutes. . . .

And so it went on, tooth by tooth, button by button.

The concluding speeches began on the 28th, with the *réquisitoire* pronounced by M. Godefroy.

FOR THE PROSECUTION, M. GODEFROY : When the man you see before you was arrested on April 12th, 1919, and when the examining magistrate established that he had written to 283 women proposing marriage and had killed ten of those unfortunate women and the child of one of them, there was general indignation and stupor. One wondered how such crimes were possible in our time, how so many victims could have disappeared without trace, how a murderer such as we had never seen before could have enjoyed immunity for so long, could have accomplished his work of death undisturbed. There were some who suggested that the affair had been made up out of whole cloth to divert attention from the Peace Treaty. Alas, this man's crimes were only too real. Here was a man who could justly be compared with Jack the Ripper, Mrs van der Zuiden, our own Dumollard or Troppmann. In some countries, whose people are given to sarcasm, he was seen as a sympathetic Punchinello making a mock of the police. But he was a tracked beast. He began as a swindler. When his crimes threatened his safety, he became a murderer. When Mme Cuchet, his first victim, discovered that he was a married man with a family, he saw that the day must come when, deceived and robbed, she must lodge a complaint with the police, who were already looking for him. From that moment, her fate was sealed.

He was admired because, without the physical advantages of a seducer, he so readily charmed and conquered women. He could indeed be patient, as with Mme Pascal or Mme Buisson, but in the case of Mme Laborde-Line little more than a month was needed to seduce and kill her. Gentlemen, you see before you a cruel, callous and ferocious man. Beside one of his fiancées he kneels devoutly in church. An hour or two later, he is bending over her dead body in the act of cutting it up. Then, quite calmly, he will go and repose on the bosom of Mlle Fernande Segret.

How was the killing done? How were the bodies disposed of? To that it has not been easy for us to find an answer, though in the course of this long trial you have seen certain of his victims come from their graves to show us their limbs burnt and calcined in that furnace at Gambais. Vain, proud, a liar, well-acquainted with legal formalities, without any regular occupation, busy with projects each more disreputable than the last, six times convicted of fraud before the war, sentenced again in its first year. . . .

M. Godefroy traced our hero's career.

. . . But in the end truth pierces the darkest clouds. Landru's guile is not forever proof against the devotion of a sister. . . .

A display of close logic and then a little rhetoric.

. . . He committed eleven murders in cold blood, methodically, with the same premeditation you have seen him display throughout this trial, infernal, abject. You may ask, which of us has the right to pass judgment on another? Lamennais said : 'I am seized with apprehension when I consider that there are men who judge other men.' We know what Victor Hugo said again and again. There are indeed limits to human understanding. But here today we have certainty. In this case, no miscarriage of justice is possible. My duty is clear. I demand an affirmative verdict on all the charges. No extenuating circumstances. No pity. I demand the supreme penalty, death, for Landru, the murderer of Vernouillet and Gambais. He is responsible absolutely and wholly for his deeds and with no excuse. Death is the sole fitting punishment. When it is needed for public safety, it is good to erect the guillotine. Voltaire and Rousseau proclaimed this need, and the great Montesquieu, in *The Spirit of the Laws*, wrote : 'A citizen merits death when he has taken life. This punishment of death is the remedy for a sick society.' Gentlemen, I conjure you, do not hesitate, strike without weakness. . . .

And so on. M. Godefroy's gist seems pretty clear.

Moro-Giafferi began his concluding speech for the defence that afternoon. He insisted on two legal points, first on the defendant's right not to answer questions put to him, second on the safeguards needed before death is presumed.

FOR THE DEFENCE, ME DE MORO-GIAFFERI : What is meant by disappearance? I turn to Article 115 of the Civil Code. I read : 'It is dangerous to presume, until after a long interval, that someone who is missing has finally disappeared.' Suppose Landru himself were dead. None of the property of those missing women would be allowed to pass to their relatives. The law would not permit their families finally to presume their death for eighteen years. The task of making this clear to them might well fall on my learned friend, the very man who has just been asking you, with all the eloquence at his command, to send Landru to the guillotine. He would have to say : 'I know I stated at Versailles assizes that' – for example – 'Mme Pascal had been murdered. The law now compels me to inform you that she is not dead, she is alive.' French civil law declares that there is insufficient evidence presented here to establish that any one of those ten women is dead. And yet the presumption which is not allowed when small sums of money or a few sticks of furniture are in question is the very presumption you have been asked to make when what is at stake is a man's head.

On the 29th, Moro started in on the expert witnesses.

Instead of corpses, you produce reports and *expertises*, the greatest danger confronting justice. They parade their theories, 'dogmatic madness' as Montaigne called it, the source, alas, of too many grave judicial errors. During the war, at Verdun, a soldier was sentenced and shot for a self-inflicted wound. *Post-mortem* examination showed that he had been wounded by a German bullet. On the word of a doctor, a hero had been shot as a coward. It might have been the word of Dr Paul. In 1909, at St Malo, a small skeleton was found on the beach one day. The doctor called in to examine it said that it was the corpse of a little girl who must have been attacked and cut up with large blows from a knife. Two days later, the great painter Aimé Morot came forward to say that he had thrown a chimpanzee's body into the sea.

In close and convincing or at least persuasive detail, Moro performed, as it were, his own *expertise* upon the evidence of expert witnesses. Reminding the jury that no trace of blood had been found either at Gambais or at Vernouillet, he came to the famous stove.

There wasn't even *time* for Landru to burn so many bodies in it. In 1897, Carrara took more than twenty-four hours to burn the body of the messenger he killed in his mushroom cellars. In recounting the terrible deaths of the Russian imperial family, M. Gillard, the crown prince's tutor, has told us that the pyre was made of resinous wood soaked with over a hundred gallons of petrol and that the bodies took more than three days to burn away. In the case of Pel the clockmaker. . . .

But let us leave him for the moment. In conclusion, the great Corsican advocate suggested an alternative explanation for so many disappearances of women.

Their papers were found. Well, gentlemen, as you know, there is a type of offender in whose possession women's papers are often found. The dealer in women. I do not wish to insult any of the ladies of whom we have heard. Our laws against the white-slave traffic are designed to protect those who set off, as they believe, to an honest trade, only to find out the truth when they reach their destination. There, when it is too late, they are kept by force from returning. One thing is certain. Those women had all broken with their families. All had signified their intention of travelling abroad. Now remember this. In each case, for two months after they disappeared, Landru strove to reassure their friends. It was always two months. That is the length of time it would take to reach Brazil. After that, friends and the law can do nothing. If they left their identity papers behind, it was because they had been told they must change their names. The times shown in the notebook have been said to be times of death. They might equally well have been times of departure.

Is that the key to the mystery? I must admit, I do not know. Landru has not told me what his mysterious business was. I cannot show you the light. But I can dissipate darkness, that darkness created by the prosecution, who are asking you to act irreparably. Suppose that tomorrow one of those women returns. What faith would you then have in yourselves strong enough to face the stony gaze of the ghost which came to you in the night and said : 'I did not kill ! You killed me !' One day, it could be written in the margin of your verdict: 'They pronounced sentence of death. They were mistaken.' Terrible words.

PRESIDENT : Discussion is now at an end. Landru, stand up. Have you anything further to say in your defence?

LANDRU : Mr President, in his speech yesterday, M. Godefroy attributed a great many sins, vices and even crimes to me. He was kind enough, nevertheless, and I thank him for it, to allow me one noble feeling, affection for my family, love of children and home. By that I swear that I never killed anyone.

PRESIDENT : The jury will now retire.

It was half past seven on the evening of November 29th. During the next hour and a half, the behaviour of the crowd in the court-room was atrocious. They of course brought out their sandwiches and wine. Cameramen set up lights over the dock. Towards nine o'clock, an electric bell whirred, and the jury began to file back. People stood on chairs and benches. Others yelled at them to sit down. The presiding judge, M. Gilbert and the *avocat-général*, M. Godefroy, rebuked the crowd for their heartlessness and cowardice. The latter seems to have said at that point, before the jury had announced the verdict, that a man was about to be (did they not realise?) sentenced to death. Moro warned Landru, when he was brought back, to expect the worst, exhorting him to be brave. Landru said that it had been what he expected all along and that Moro must not be upset. After the verdict and sentence, Moro took a petition for mercy round to the jury, who signed it. So did Mme Pascal's sister. Lawyers for the *partie civile* claimed and were awarded one franc damages. Landru went back to his cell.

December passed. January passed. The Court of Cassation, which is the supreme court, rejected Landru's appeal on February 1st. The date of execution was fixed for the 25th. On the 23rd, Vincent de Moro-Giafferi waited on the President of the Republic at the Élysée Palace. He, at the time, was Alexandre Millerand, who, like so many French politicians, had started public life as a barrister. In 1885, he had acted as junior defence counsel in the case of a young man, Albert Pel, a clockmaker, who had untidily incinerated two women previously dispatched with arsenic. The two cases had been compared in court. The Landru study in Montarron's *Grands Procès d'Assises* assures us that Moro-Giafferi and Millerand compared them that evening. In the course of the judicial inquiry which preceded the Pel trial, a pathologist had obtained a body from the medical schools and caused it to be burnt in a stove identical with Pel's. In somewhat less than forty-eight hours, the body had been reduced wholly to ash, but the stove, bought new, was a mess. Landru's stove had stood there in court for all to see, as good as new.

No doubt Moro also reminded the President that, although Pel had first been sentenced to death, at a second trial extenuating circumstances had been found for him, so that in due course he had sailed for the Guiana settlements, where he presumably still was, alive or dead. Pel's guilt had been fully substantiated. The evidence against Landru had been presumptive. President Millerand would see the point, but he remained unmoved and signed no reprieve.

On the morning of the 25th, H.D. Landru therefore received the attentions of the *exécuteur des hautes oeuvres*, Antole Deibler. To the last, he displayed the dignity, tartness and reserve which had characterised his deportment throughout the proceedings and perhaps most of his life. Always a temperate man, he refused the rum and cigarette, as well as the consolations of religion. It was, he said, merely insulting to ask an innocent man at this stage whether he had anything to say.

His family claimed the body, and so there was no *post-mortem* examination. Mlle Segret said that she had never had anything to reproach him with. She had loved him very deeply. She had been very, very happy with him. It may be supposed that she also believed him innocent, but of that we cannot be sure. It may be doubted whether Moro-Giafferi did. Certainly, his suggestion that Landru's dealings with all those women had been in the interests of white slavery cannot be taken seriously. The son also of the first presumed victim had disappeared. Andrée Babelay was young, Mme Pascal under forty, divorced and not virtuous, but the others were hardly to be imagined as brothel-meat, even in South America or the Middle East. We may speculate, if we please, on what might have happened to Fernande Segret, had her elderly lover remained at large. That she had been meant to remain alive seems likely. In point of fact, she was to go to Lebanon and live there many years, perhaps solely on her gifts as a singer.

It is difficult not to feel a sneaking sympathy with Landru, as perhaps with Crippen and with very few other murderers. His victims were typically women of a certain age, lonely hearts with pitiable savings, which came into his possession, making no great total. From photographs one sees that a fair proportion of them were downright ugly. They found him charming, kind, attentive, and in the first place at least their relatives agreed. The last weeks of the lives of ten women were filled by him with a hope, a happiness, an interest, which eight of them cannot reasonably have expected to find again. The last moments of disillusion were no doubt painful, but, despite those monkey eyes, nothing that we known of the man suggests that they were unduly protracted or attended by unnecessary suffering. By the care with which he cleaned up afterwards, but indeed also by his continuing silence, he spared even the bereaved both trouble and disquieting images, and one of them showed her gratitude in a small way. He was a tidy little man.

WHILE LANDRU awaited trial, a mass-murderer on a far larger scale, the first of a remarkable German series, Georg Karl Grossmann, had been arrested in Berlin. While his appeal was being considered, another German, Peter Grupen, who had killed only two girls, was executed. In the United Kingdom, Allaway and Armstrong were arrested, but the kingdom shrank with the formation of an Irish Free State. V., on Faralicq's manor, at Boulogne-sur-Seine, hammered to death and robbed an Englishwoman, Mrs D., not on Greenwall's list. In London, within a fortnight of Landru's execution, Ronald True murdered Olive Young with a rolling pin, and nine days later Henry Jacoby did much the same with a hammer to Lady White.

On April 22nd, the young train robber, Mieczyslas Charrier, came up for trial in Paris. That oak panelling had reverberated to defiant anarchist speeches in the 'nineties and again to those of Raymond Science and other members of the Bonnot gang the year before the war. It now sounded to less affecting stuff of much the same kind from Charrier. In the condemned cell, he continued to write, and some of what he wrote is coldly vivid.

Furious at the English giving way to their absurd demands, the Irish gunmen killed Sir Henry Wilson on June 22nd (two months later, would murder one of their own men, Michael Collins). On the 24th, the excellent Walter Rathenau was (to use the term, to which German, like French, has no equivalent) assassinated in a Berlin street, Germany's sole contribution to political crime in the 'twenties. In Russia, Lenin became literally speechless with horror at the world he had brought into being. In Chicago, gang warfare was hotting up, no longer so much in connection with vice but with that insipid if thirst-quenching beverage, beer. In New England, an Episcopalian parson and one of his lady choristers were found shot under a crab-apple tree, the fragments of their amorous correspondence scattered around them and the chorister's vocal chords vindictively severed. Just outside London, on the night of October 3rd, Frederick Bywaters fatally stabbed Percy Thompson, and the memorials of another illicit love were released to posterity.

By the 28th, Mussolini reigned in Rome. As if to prove that *la Belle Époque* was decidedly over, Marcel Proust died on November 18th, while at the end of that month, the La Villette gang were brought to justice, not with any capital consequences but with some afflux of population to the Guiana settlements, notably depleted that year by the escape of Émile Courgibet, whose next six years as a free man were to prove somewhat discouraging. On December 26th, in Cairo, the Marie-Marguerite Dalibert whom we briefly glimpsed in Paris as Mme Laurent (also known as Maggie Mellor) contracted a civil marriage with Fahmy Bey, whom she had met at his country's French legation in May. Their internationally romantic affair was already turning nasty.

That year also, Eugen Weidmann, aged fourteen, of Frankfurt-am-Main, a bit of a handful already, had been sent for reformatory treatment to a Schloss Dehrn, which in his later reminiscences sounds delightful, far nicer than an English public school. A psychiatrists report on him at the time, made by a Dr Furstenheim, reads :

> Eugen Weidmann is very well grown for his age and in excellent physical health. What I found striking was the greater sensitiveness of the left side of his body to pin-pricking by contrast with the right. The variable sensitiveness of the right side of the body seems to be affected by psychological influences. There are symptoms of psychopathic instability and some lack of parental control.

Weidmann was to remain left-handed. His delinquency had principally consisted in thieving from his schoolfellows' coats in the cloakroom.

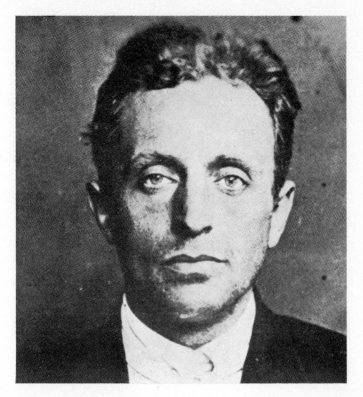

1 Raoul Villain

2 Landru at Versailles, November 1921

FOUNDED AS a monthly in 1899, at the time of the Dreyfus case, *L'Action Française* became a daily in 1908. It had not started out royalist, but had quickly become so under the influence of one of its founding members, Charles Maurras. The young men who sold it on the streets were therefore known as *camelots du Roi*. They belonged to the Ligue d'Action Française, whose general secretary, Marius Plateau, was quickly able to get them out on the streets as intimidating gangs, a political technique he may be said to have originated, at any rate on the Right. At the beginning of 1923, three founding members of the paper were still active in its production, Maurras, Léon Daudet, both men in their middle fifties, and the somewhat younger Jacques Bainville. The paper's editor-in-chief was Daudet. The name of his principal assistant or *secrétaire de rédaction* was Allard. Plateau, a man with a hearty laugh, was a figure of leading importance in their counsels, though not on the purely literary side. Daudet was a member of the Chamber of Deputies. A son of the author of the *Lettres de mon Moulin*, he had been married to, but was divorced from, a grand-daughter of Victor Hugo, by whom he had a son, Philippe. By a second marriage, he was the brother-in-law of his editorial deputy, Allard.

Léon Daudet lived in the Rue St Guillaume, though for editorial purposes his private address was given as Rue de Bellechasse, a few streets away to the west, the home of his mother, the widow of Alphonse Daudet, herself an Allard. Both houses were (and are) on the Left Bank. The church of St Germain l'Auxerrois stood (and stands) across the river, but again, in effect, no more than a few streets away to the east. The offices of the paper, on the other hand, were a mile or so to the north, in the Rue de Rome, near the Gare St Lazare. There, on the morning of Saturday, January 20th, 1923, two telephone calls were received from a woman, who did not give her name but stated that she had information about a communist plot against the paper and against the life of M. Daudet. As he was again not there the second time she rang, she asked if his address was still that in the Rue de Bellechasse and was told that it was. Calling there, she was given his real address in the Rue St Guillaume and walked thus far east, but was told that M. Daudet was not at home. It was suggested to her that she see M. Allard. She was a young woman, not downright bad-looking but with strange eyes and a lop-sided face. Though he did not know she was armed, her manner as reported to Daudet, who was in fact at home and caught a glimpse of her through the lace curtains, was such that he at once reported the matter to the police at the station in the Rue Perronnet, also warning Allard by telephone to be on his guard. Towards the end of the afternoon, she called at the offices of the paper in the Rue de Rome, first sending in a note in which she said that she wished to serve the royalist cause and could effectively do that by spying on the anarchists, to whom she had previously belonged. Allard then received her. With him was Marius Plateau, who laughed and said that her information was too vague and already known to him. Let her bring them something precise for publication. This she promised to do.

ALLARD (*in evidence*) : In fact we formed the impression that, like so many stories of the same kind we had heard before, this one would lead to no more than a request for money.

Louis XVI was executed on January 21st, 1793. As, in 1923, that date fell on a Sunday, the annual commemorative mass was celebrated at St Germain l'Auxerrois next day. On behalf of the paper and of the Ligue, it was attended not by Daudet but by Charles Maurras. It was also attended by the young woman, who would have been just as glad to have Maurras in her sights but found him surrounded by stalwarts and feared to miss. At 1.30 p.m., she reappeared in the Rue de Rome and again sent in a letter, on paper with the heading of a bar near by and addressed this time to M. Plateau. It began :

This is from the person who spoke to you on Saturday with M. Allard. I learned news yesterday, much news. I heard that two plans were afoot. One is to smash up the offices of the *Action Française*, the other to kill both M. Daudet and M. Maurras. I therefore warn them not to go out alone; but it would be better still to remain at home altogether. I cannot explain all in a note. Please give me an interview.

The courageous Plateau did so and was alone with his visitor for over an hour.

By a quarter to three, those in the outer office included the League president, the treasurer and a contributor. From time to time, they heard shouts of laughter from the jovial Marius Plateau. At one point, he came out to ask the treasurer for information. Then the door of his private office closed behind him. A quarter of an hour later, several shots were fired in quick succession. The door opened. Plateau staggered out, collapsed into the arms of the League president and slid to the floor. On the floor of his private office lay the young woman, bleeding from the left shoulder. In another room, Marius Plateau presently died, three bullets having pierced heart, liver and stomach, to say nothing of left lung and right thigh. The young woman had by then opened her eyes and, having been bandaged, told a superintendent of police from the Rue de Lisbonne that, as she had failed to see Daudet, she had indeed come to the office that afternoon intending to kill M. Plateau. She had waited until he went to the door to show her out. It was true that he had turned his back to her once before, but she was then seated and had not been quick enough to take the pistol from her pocket. Her purpose, she said, had been to avenge Jaurès, for whose death Daudet had been responsible. She had no accomplices, but a friend had got her the automatic pistol.

Her name was Germaine Berton, aged twenty, born at Puteaux but largely brought up in Tours, where she had first frequented anarchist circles. Her father, who had come down in the world and worked on the railway, had died three and a half years before, and she had quarrelled with her mother, a schoolteacher. She had come to Paris a year and a half ago, regarded herself as an artist and had, indeed, a certificate in drawing, but also the modest beginnings of a criminal record, having spent three months in prison for disorderly conduct and assaulting a policeman and a fortnight for unauthorised possession of firearms. She was described as doing no work but living on the uncertain gifts of anarchist comrades, to whom she became a passing mistress.

As ANYONE who ever collected stamps knows, 1923 was the year during which German inflation reached its crazy zenith, while Armenia, Azerbaijan, Georgia and the Ukraine again lost their independence, the first three of these briefly enjoying a shadowy combined existence as the Transcaucasian Federation. In Chicago, beer remained at a premium, and three of an Irish racketeer's armed salesmen were dispatched by those of an Italian rival. At a congress in Vienna, Interpol was founded, a worthy but greatly overrated body. The Fahmys were touring Europe, and there were dreadful scenes at the Majestic in Paris, as earlier there had been in a boat on the Nile. At the beginning of July, they came to London and took a suite at the Savoy, on the fourth floor.

July 9th was a day of almost tropical heat in London, and at midnight the makings of a spectacular thunderstorm began to move down the Thames valley, ready to provide a suitable background to international drama at the Savoy. At one o'clock, it broke in rain and splendour. To roll upon roll of thunder, a night porter saw Prince Ali and his wife expostulating at the door to Suite No. 41. As he pursued his way along the corridor, leaving high life to its own devices, he distinguished three sharper sounds and turned back. Later that morning, the former Marie-Marguerite Alibert, intermediately Mme Laurent and Maggie Mellor, though she knew not a word of English, appeared at Bow Street police court, charged with the murder of her husband, and was remanded in custody at Holloway.

In Paris, on July 23rd, an elderly Breton woman of noble birth, Mlle du Bot de Talhouët, shot the rich businessman whose mistress she had been for twenty-six years but who kept her and their son at near-starvation level, a man presumably of Greek extraction, Léonidas Basilionides. In London, the Crown's case against Mme Fahmy was outlined at the Old Bailey on September 10th.

Had she killed Fahmy Bey at the Majestic in Paris, there would have been little likelihood of a capital sentence being passed on Mme Fahmy and none whatever of it being carried out. Its probability in England was real. Provocation only proved motive, and, as Mr Percival Clarke said, in his opening speech for the prosecution (somewhat modifying the popular notion that it is peculiar to English law to assume innocence until guilt is proved):

> Every homicide is presumed to be a murder until the contrary is shown. From the defendant's own lips it is known that she it was who caused the death of her husband, and, in the absence of any circumstances to make it some other offence, you must find her guilty of murder.

Had she been found guilty of murder, she would have been hanged, for clearly she was not mad.

To avoid this horrid eventuality seems to have been everybody's idea, and, as it strikes me, this was achieved by turning the trial, in so far as our rules of procedure and laws of evidence permitted, into a continental trial. Far more background stuff was heard than is usual in our courts, much of it from the accused in French. Though an official interpreter was present, she was also allowed the services of a French woman barrister, Maître Odette Simon. Witnesses were brought from abroad for the sole apparent purpose of being paraded as living proof of the versatility of Prince Ali's sexual tastes. For the defence, Sir Edward Marshall Hall talked about *atmosphere* and used such dramatic effects as crouching like an animal about to spring or dropping a pistol at a crucial and startling moment. A policeman, who clearly knew very little about it, demonstrated the ejection and reloading mechanism of an automatic pistol (he thought that several shots could be fired with one pressure on the trigger). The jury behaved like a French jury, dismissing not only murder but manslaughter, and the public behaved like a French public, cheering the verdict so demonstratively that the judge had to threaten to clear the court.

I don't want to make too much of this point. There was, indeed, evidence, if not proof, that Mme Fahmy did not think the pistol was loaded when she fired at her husband *the first time* (having previously discharged one bullet harmlessly out of the window). As no sentence had been passed it would have been futile for a court of criminal appeal to quash the verdict, even had it been empowered to do so without appeal being made. I feel sure that some defect of form might easily have been found had things gone otherwise. I have seen no expert comment. It is perhaps interesting in itself that no *Notable British Trials* volume was ever devoted to the case, as one would be to another case, the following year, in which a French defendant equally needed an interpreter.

In the next chapter, I shall have to turn back in time to what was perhaps the most notable French criminal affair of 1923 in the private sector. Before we return to political murder in Paris, there are two crimes of that autumn which it is convenient to list here. A dismembered body found in the Seine, near Melun, on October 23rd, turned out to be that of the wife of a butcher in Paris, Louis Dervaux, who had strangled her, sawn her up, wrapped her in oil-cloth, weighted her with a car-brake casing, deposited her in the river near where she was found, reported her disappearance to the police and offered a reward of ten thousand francs for information leading to the discovery of her whereabouts. He was arrested by Jean Belin, Landru's captor. On November 23rd, an English widow from Reading, Dora Hunt, aged fifty-nine, was found battered to death in a hotel bedroom near Cannes. This crime was investigated by Alexandre Guibal, O.B.E., of the Marseilles *police judiciaire*, who failed to solve it (it is thought that a theft of jewels was involved, but these were never recovered). The incidence of British decorations on French policemen's chests has never been high, though we have noted one on a prefect's. Chief Inspector Guibal had received his for services to Intelligence during the war.

POLITICALLY, FRANCE had shifted to the Left (the very notions of political Left and Right being derived from the semi-circular shape of the French Chamber of Deputies and thus applicable only metaphorically elsewhere). This was to be felt in the Law Courts and perhaps even to affect the actual commission of murder. The acquittal of Raoul Villain for the murder of Jean Jaurès had been a bad thing. It is always a bad thing, one of the worst things that can happen within the life of a civilised country, when political opinion affects or seems to affect a legal decision, though few of us, I fancy, are quite free of a tendency to rejoice when a legal decision goes our way politically. The mad Right had exulted in the acquittal of Villain. The Left was now to take its revenge in court. Concluding his address to the jury on behalf of Germaine Berton, her senior counsel, Maître Henry Torrès expressed himself as follows :

FOR THE DEFENCE, ME TORRÈS : You must acquit Germaine Berton, as you acquitted Villain. I say 'you' because, in France, the Jury is One and Indivisible, like the Republic. You acquitted Villain. You know what Jaurès meant to us, and you know the wound that still bleeds in our side. I am asking you to cicatrise it.

By Jaurès' death, a terrible account was opened between the royalists and that great, unanimous crowd which followed his coffin. You must acquit Germaine Berton, gentlemen of the jury, or you will be saying that Plateau was the greater man of the two. A wrong verdict would be to impose sentence on those for whom, now that better times have dawned, Jaurès' religion was conceived. A satisfactory verdict will have to be concordant with the will of him who was not slow to pardon, but who knew that the real instigators of the crime against him would not hesitate to disavow the tool of whom they had made use.

Peace for all, gentlemen of the jury! Justice for all! I do not wish to glorify Germaine Berton, that would be wrong. No more murders, no more bloodshed! But, in order that blood may cease to be shed, in order that the dying hope of Jaurès may be realised, she who struck her blow in sincere homage to his memory must be absolved, as was Villain, and speedily.

An English judge, summing up, might have suggested that two wrongs don't make a right and that the acquittal of a guilty person is as much a miscarriage of justice as the conviction of an innocent one. The defence, however, had long had the last word in French courts. The jury, perhaps all too willingly, adopted Maître Torrès' paradox and found Germaine Berton not guilty on all counts. That is to say, she had either not killed Marius Plateau at all, or she had acted in self-defence. Certainly, there had been no premeditation, let alone lying in wait. That French juries could be so persuaded was noted by a youth from Brescia, a great newspaper reader, Ernesto Bonomini, who had come to France to evade military service and was employed as a waiter. No doubt he had also noticed, in reports of the Berton trial, that uncomplimentary remarks had been made about the young *Fascisti*, with whom the *camelots du Roi* had been compared.

There were many Italians in Paris, some of whom had quite reasonably left home because their earlier political activities had exposed them to danger from the new dictatorial government. To counteract their propaganda, this government had set up a *Fascio* in Paris. Attached to it was a journalist, himself of no great age, Signor Bonservizi, who not only acted as Paris correspondent to *Il Popolo d'Italia* but also brought out a sheet in French, *L'Italie Nouvelle*. This man found that he was being followed and, towards the end of January 1924 (as, near Moscow, Lenin's eyes finally closed), called his local police station to say that a young man was hanging around his apartment in what appeared to be a state of dangerous excitement. The young man was Ernesto Bonomini, who had of course disappeared by the time the police appeared.

He had, however, discovered the restaurant, in the Passage des Princes, at which Signor Bonservizi took his meals. He left his previous job and took one there at lower pay. He had also acquired a revolver. On the evening of February 20th, armed with this, he crept round the *banquette* on which his compatriot was sitting over his coffee and, through a *jardinière* of flowers, shot him behind the right ear with eventual (it took five weeks) fatal effect. For Bonomini's defence also, Maître Henry Torrès was engaged.

AT THE Blue Anchor in Byfleet, Surrey, then no doubt less evidently a London suburb, the new management, the Joneses, were putting up an impecunious Frenchman, curly-haired, curly-bearded, with a big moustache and over one eye a wart, Jean-Pierre Vaquier, aged forty-five. In January, Mabel Jones had met him in Biarritz, where she was taking a holiday for her health. In Biarritz she had been a naughty girl with him, also in Paris on her way home, also, it is to be feared, at the Russell Hotel in London when he followed her to England. Not at the Blue Anchor, where he had appeared and stayed and not yet paid his bill and was in fact rather a nuisance about the place. Jones was one of those publicans who drink the profits, at closing time closing indeed but with friends inside. When he got up on the morning of March 29th, a morning very much after the night before, he mixed himself a dose of the Bromo salts he kept in the bar parlour. They did not effervesce, and they tasted bitter. A few hours later, he had died of strychnine poisoning.

Vaquier was not at once arrested. Indeed, he was still at liberty a fortnight later when his only rival that year for similar attention in British newspapers, Patrick Mahon, a soda-fountain attendant in nearby Richmond, by his own accounts a broth of a bhoy, took a girl called Emily Kaye to Eastbourne and proceeded as though his intention were to make broth of her. Both trials took place in July, Mahon's at Lewes, Vaquier's in the county hall at Guildford. Also that month, in Paris, took place the trial of Mlle du Bot de Talhouët and her son, who were acquitted.

Both Mahon and Vaquier were tried before Mr Justice Avory (it could not have been so in France, where High Court judges do not go on circuit, but each sticks to his departmental court of assize). Mahon was prosecuted, Vaquier defended, by Sir Henry Curtis-Bennett (again, not possible in France, where a prosecutor always prosecutes). In his account of the case, Sir Patrick Hastings tells us :

Jean-Pierre Vaquier was the first and only man whom I have

prosecuted for murder, and I disliked the case intensely. I was Attorney-General when the crime was committed, and as a law officer almost invariably conducts the prosecution in a case of death by poisoning the task fell upon me. I had no sympathy with the strange little man in the dock, but the trial worried me a great deal, partly because I was quite unable to satisfy myself as to the motive for the murder, and partly because the experience of cross-examining a man to his death was one which I never desire to repeat.

Hastings was closely and formidably seconded by Marshall Hall, who, the reader may recall, had defended Mme Fahmy and who was more frequently engaged to defend than to prosecute. We also have an account of the case from the pen of the official interpreter, H. Ashton Wolfe, who had also acted in this capacity at the trial of Mme Fahmy, stepping down when Me Simon appeared. I see nothing wrong with Wolfe's accounts of either case, and I am listing two of his books in my bibliography, but will here warn the reader who consults either of them that, once on territory where he cannot be easily checked by the English reader, H. Ashton Wolfe gave way to the wildest mythomania.

Unlike that of Mme Fahmy, the Vaquier trial was conducted in faultlessly British fashion, it being rather an exhibition of fair play than of any wish to follow continental practice that Sir Patrick relinquished ('being anxious that the prisoner, as a foreigner, should have every possible advantage at his trial') the right which those few dignitaries who at a given moment are 'law officers' enjoy, to speak last, even when the defence has called no witnesses at all or none other than the accused. The effect was odd. I quote Hastings again, not omitting what might be thought some unfairness to his remote French colleagues, as well as his possible misconception about a French word.

The most curious feature of the trial was the attitude of the prisoner himself. His overweening vanity was self-evident, but his knowledge of criminal procedure came entirely from the French courts. He expected to be bullied, not only by the prosecuting counsel, but by the judge himself. He expected to be shouted at and called an assassin. The studied courtesy and impartiality with which he was treated appeared not only to take him by surprise but to raise in his mind an entirely erroneous belief as to the course the trial was taking. As nobody shouted at him he thought they liked him; as nobody called him an assassin he seemed to think that nobody thought he was one. From first to last he appeared to be under the belief that the case was proceeding in an atmosphere of kindness which could only end in a triumphant acquittal.

It was sad also of course, but undoubtedly it was funny, when he discovered his mistake, when the jury came back with their verdict and Mr Justice Avory put on his 'black cap' and pronounced the fatal words.

He screamed that he was innocent, that his trial had been unfair, and he had to be forcibly removed, shouting and raving, from the dock.

Like Mahon, he found his way to Wandsworth and was there, shouting *'Vive la France!'*, hanged on August 24th, Mahon a fortnight later.

AT THE trial of Ernesto Bonomini, on October 23rd, Maître Torrès was allowed to generalise in court about the nature of Fascism.

> FOR THE DEFENCE, ME TORRÈS : What, then, is Fascism? . . . At its inception, I know, the disposition of Fascism was to form a rallying-point about which men of goodwill and of every shade of political opinion could muster. It did indeed so muster veterans whom war had driven from their homes, parted from their families and their customary ways, those veterans not yet successfully re-adapted from a state of war to one of peace, who brought to daily life the energy of the camps, who believed that the hard trials through which they had passed gave them the right to speak out louder than others in the forum. But soon Fascism lost this character. It became a band of mercenaries, backed by the great banks and industries of Italy. . . . As to the *Fascio* in Paris, we are not to be deceived by its philanthropic and humanitarian camouflage. It is here for propaganda and provocation, at once against Italian workmen who have fled their country and against French policy itself. . . . In Italy, we see Mussolini, a second king. Here, in Paris, besides the Italian ambassador, we have seen the man who controlled him, his double, M. Bonservizi. He was there to stimulate the ambassador's zeal. He was there, with the ambassador's authority behind him, to denounce to the French police – and to have expelled by order – those Italian workmen in our midst who did not agree with the Fascist system. . . .

Bonomini was indeed awarded a substantial prison sentence, but the jury found not only that there had been extenuating circumstances but also that his crime had been unpremeditated, which was absurd. Outside the Law Courts, fighting broke out between Italian fascists and anti-fascists, with French communists (of whom there were already 12,000 in Paris alone) joining in, as well doubtless as *camelots du Roi* and members of the *jeunesses patriotes*. A great deal of that sort of thing ensued, but, before we come to what may be thought its climax, I should like, if I may, just to note progress in the course of non-political mass murder in Germany.

In Berlin, Grossmann, not a butcher by profession, had been accustomed, after what appears to have been normal sexual enjoyment of the girls he picked up, to sell the fleshier parts of their anatomies for meat on the black market. In Hanover, the practice had been adopted more recently by Fritz Haarmann, who was a professional butcher, whose taste ran to boys and young men and who, with practised skill, bled them to death, so that their flesh more nearly resembled pork, leaving him also with buckets of blood for black pudding. Haarmann was brought to trial on December 4th, 1934. His method, he said, had been to bite his victims in the throat. He was sentenced on the 19th to decapitation. Two days later, a contender for the title, Karl Denke, of Münsterberg in Silesia, organ blower at his local church, split the head of a young journeyman, whose diminishingly healthy cries for help were heard, so that police called at the house and found two tubfuls of human flesh pickled in brine, as well as pots of fat and bones, the identity cards of twelve journeymen and a ledger showing name, date and weight of each of the thirty carcases, most of them those of tramps and beggarwomen, pickled during the past three years. The policemen failed to deprive Denke of his braces, so that, shortly after his arrest, he hanged himself, thus depriving us of information which might have been interesting psychologically.

My American readers may care to be reminded that, in Chicago that winter, the puritanical Dion O'Banion was killed in his flower shop and the probable instigator of that crime, Johnny Torrio, half-killed in the street, not improbably by Hymie Weiss, who was not to last long thereafter. On April 23rd, 1925, in Montmartre, *jeunesses patriotes* were marching in procession after a meeting. Unarmed and behaving in no markedly provocative manner, they were fired on, from behind, by communists with revolvers. There were many wounded and three dead.

The back is clearly an irresistible target to political zealots, not only those of the Left. Germaine Berton and Ernesto Bonomini had both got their men from behind, but then so had Raoul Villain. The identities of those who had fired the fatal shots were established by a ballistics *expertise* performed by the head of Criminal Records, Edmond Bayle. It is not perhaps even now quite generally known that this branch of criminology, though narrower in its application, is as infallible as fingerprints. If, that is to say, you have the bullet which caused death and a possible murder weapon, you can precisely determine whether the bullet was fired by that weapon. This can also be established in respect of spent cartridges. By lucky chance or sharp observation, the police arrested, during that evening's confusion, two men in possession of weapons from which bullets in the dead bodies and cartridge cases picked up on the spot had unquestionably been fired.

The trial of those two men was surrounded with a great deal of uproar in the streets and intimidation of jurors. Two lawyers for the defence were themselves among the twenty-six communist members of the Chamber of Deputies. The third was our old friend Henry Torrès. One defendant got off with three years. Torrès' client was acquitted. Those were great days for the Left in Paris.

They were not great days for that section of the Right represented by *L'Action Française*. Léon Daudet had failed to be re-elected to his seat in the House, and that summer his son, Philippe, a boy of fifteen, was found shot through the head in a taxi outside an anarchist bookshop off the Place de la République. The driver had heard nothing. The revolver lay on the seat beside the lad's body and bore his fingerprints. There seems little doubt that it was suicide, committed on the way to the shop as the cab passed through a street along which roadworks were loudly in progress. Philippe Daudet had formed a habit of frequenting that bookshop and the premises overhead for assignations with an anarchist girl, older than himself (as it might have been, but apparently was not, Germaine Berton), with whom he was having a precocious affair. The police knew it and kept an eye on the place, but sportingly said nothing to the boy's father. The latter now accused the taxi-driver of murdering his son with the complicity of the police.

The immediate result of his public insistence on this point was that a libel action was brought against Léon Daudet and that he received a prison sentence, further paying large damages to the taxi-driver. The following year, his colleague, Charles Maurras, joined him at the Santé for incitement to violence. That December, the Vatican denounced the activities of the Ligue d'Action Française, and the paper itself was placed on the Index. There followed a moment of glory. The sentence on Maurras was rescinded, and, at the time of his release, the governor of the prison was cleverly persuaded by a telephone trick that Daudet also had been pardoned. He got out and, with some hundreds of *camelots du Roi*, barricaded himself in the offices of the paper in the Rue de Rome. His surrender was smilingly negotiated by the new prefect of police, Jean Chiappe, a very smooth Corsican indeed. The *camelots* (the word simply means pedlars, hawkers or newsboys, they were the King's pedlars) were allowed to march out in military formation. Almost at once, Daudet was 'sprung' again and for a while settled in Brussels.

In the early summer of 1926, within a month of each other, were committed, in Paris, two compatriot crimes which reveal something of what lay behind the short-lived stamp-issues of Ukraine and Georgia. On May 26th, the exiled Hetman Petliura, former co-dictator of Ukraine, was shot openly, face to face, at 2 p.m., in the Rue Racine on the Left Bank, by Shalom Schwartzbard. On June 17th, a Georgian, Attendei Merabashvili, with almost equal openness, shot another Georgian, Vishapely, at that moment sitting in a taxi outside the Law Courts. For the horrors which he had witnessed six years before, Schwartzbard had always blamed the Hetman Petliura, and when the latter came to Paris he bought a revolver. Twice meeting the Hetman in the street, he had held his hand because the Hetman was accompanied by his wife and daughter. On May 26th, he saw Petliura enter a restaurant alone. From a bar near by, he sent a letter to his own wife, hitherto ignorant of this settled intention, then waited for the Hetman to finish his lunch. The Hetman emerged from the restaurant. Schwartzbard accosted him, asked him first in Ruthene and then in French whether he were indeed Simon Petliura and, on receiving an affirmative answer, emptied his revolver into the Hetman, thereafter going quietly along with the police, to whom he expressed his contentment with what he had done.

Most of the Georgians in Paris had fled from the Soviet Russian terror in their country. Merabashvili's family had been massacred by Soviet troops. Vishapely's position among the Georgians was much what Bonservizi's had been among the Italians in Paris. He was there as a Soviet agent and edited a propaganda sheet called *La Georgie Nouvelle*. On June 17th, he had been to court to give evidence against six of his fellow-countrymen after a fight at a bar in the Boulevard Voltaire. The six had been acquitted, and so we may suppose that Vishapely's temper had been only a little improved by his prompt securing of a taxi when the muzzle of big, rough Merabashvili's week-old revolver appeared through the window and emitted three bullets.

The politics of the matter would be a little obscure to all but communists and a few specially well-read Frenchmen. To the communists, Petliura had been a wicked White rightly shot by a virtuous Red, who happened also to be a Jew, while the virtuous Georgian had been Vishapely, unwarrantably attacked by a befuddled Georgian agent of the Whites. The well-informed minority would be aware that the collapse of the Tsarist armies and the murder of the Tsar had seemed to both Ukrainians and Georgians, as well as to Armenians and to Azerbaijanians north of the Aras, to be their long-desired opportunity for throwing off the Russian yoke. To Merabashvili, it was perfectly simple. He was a Georgian patriot, and (like the infamous Djugashvili, who called himself Stalin) Vishapely, a traitor to his country, had sold out to the Russians. French notions of Left and Right simply didn't enter into the matter. In his own way, Petliura had been of the Left, a republican certainly, but also a Ruthene patriot, who, when attacked by the Russians, had accepted the help of any allies to hand and so had compromised himself with Whites, while unable to check the apparently congenital tendency of Cossacks to massacre Jews wherever these were to be found. Of disposition towards Left or Right Shalom Schwartzbard seems to have been totally innocent.* He was a Jew. He had fought willingly for the French against the Germans because the French record with Jewry was better. He might nevertheless have gone back to live in an independent or even a sovietised Ukraine, had it not been for the Cossacks.

The Merabashvili case came up first, in July 1927. He was acquitted. That did not please the communists. Three months later, the Schwartzbard case came up. He, too, was acquitted. That

---

* It was, indeed, a view held on the Right that he had shot Petliura on orders from Moscow, the Hetman being in Paris to meet Marshal Pilsudsky of Poland and the Russians anxious to prevent such a meeting. This theory was to be revived in *Figaro*, five years later, in connection with Gorguloff, about whom similar views were held on the Right.

pleased all the Left. It cannot much have displeased anyone on the Right whose anti-Semitism remained below clinical level. As it happens, Shalom Schwartzbard did not look particularly Jewish. In profile, a nose anything but hooked continued the line of his forehead. His hair was thick and wavy, but it was fair. His moustache suggested the *ancien combattant* which he in fact was, with war wounds and a medal for gallantry to show. He also, as it happens, was defended by Maître Henry Torrès, but he must have appeared a sympathetic figure without counsel at all. A respectable jury of any political colour would have found it difficult to bring him in guilty. And yet he was guilty, and so was Merabashvili.

BETWEEN THEIR trials befell the execution, in New England, of Sacco and Vanzetti, an occasion curiously outside the criminal history of any country. The largely forgotten wages-snatch and double murder in South Braintree more than seven years before constitute a minor episode in American criminal history, and the execution, a few minutes before Sacco and Vanzetti, of the also largely forgotten Madeiros was the inevitable, if somewhat belated, epilogue to that. But, ever since their trial in 1921, Sacco and Vanzetti had been intermittently present to the European mind, their innocence an article of faith far beyond the ranks of any sort of militant Left, so that, even if the verdict and the long imprisonment and the rest were not thought to be part of a capitalist plot against the workers of the world, they seemed at least to show that American justice was rather peculiar, as indeed it is in the length of time which may elapse between sentence and execution or, perhaps more exactly, between conviction and sentence. For what strikes a Briton as strange about other legal systems, apart from people's behaviour in court and the lack, among lawyers, of wigs or, in America, of any ceremonial dress whatever, is that, on the Continent or at any rate in France, a man spends an extraordinary time in prison before he is brought to trial, while in the United States he is brought to trial with much the same expedition as here, but may then languish for years thereafter, whether in the end he is fried, gassed, stretched or released. This, both to us and the French, seems unjust in itself. It creates the impression that a miscarriage of justice has occurred in the conduct of the trial, when in fact it may not be so at all.

As to the case of Sacco and Vanzetti, I know that I myself had, for some thirty years, merely supposed it to be a famous miscarriage of justice, without ever troubling to look at the evidence or even discovering to what crime it was that the two Italians (anarchists, it seemed, so possibly bomb-planting or arson) were supposed to have been parties. I then read every word of Francis Russell's *Tragedy in Dedham* and have since read rather less than every word of Herbert B. Ehrmann's even weightier *The Case that will not Die*. Russell was convinced (and convinced me) of Vanzetti's innocence, a little doubtful (and left me doubtful) of Sacco's. Ehrmann (who worked on the case at the time) was convinced of the innocence of both men. In his photographs, Sacco looked totally incapable of a crime which, although it might be classed as *reprise individuelle*, did not, apart from the erratic tearing about in a car, have to my (by then somewhat practised) eye an anarchist look about it. Apart from the charm of the broken English in which they spoke and wrote, I am now on the whole for the innocence of both men. I am certainly convinced that they were convicted on insufficient evidence.

Therefore, they ought not to have been electrocuted. Responsibility for the fact that they were must lie in part with a faulty juridical system, in part with the behaviour of individual lawyers and magistrates (of certain witnesses, too) and in part with a police force which failed to establish clearly who the true criminals were (for there were certainly others, beside Madeiros). But it must also lie in part with the Communist International, which, for purposes entirely of its own, systematically devoted itself to stiffening necks already stiff. For so long now the world's most unrelenting disseminator of lies, called by the Russian word for truth, *Pravda* (a brilliant stroke, since it must have given all Russians, if not a permanent distaste for the truth, at least an ironical attitude towards it), stated prominently, on August 11th, in respect of the last twelve-day respite :

> The mighty roar of protest from the Soviet Union, together with the voice of the working classes the world over, has forced even the plutocratic American bourgeoisie to hesitate and manoeuvre.

From the moment that appeared in print, the two wretched men had no hope.

I suppose that this is a digression. It bears, certainly, on the mood of Paris in the summer of 1927, a political mood not unrelated to legal decisions in a foreign country. It must already somewhat have affected the minds of the jury which acquitted Merabashvili three months after the formal sentence had been passed (on April 9th) on Sacco and Vanzetti and while it was known that a new ballistics *expertise* was being conducted on behalf of Governor Fuller. No doubt it would incline even left-wing jurors to vote for an acquittal. By the time the Schwartzbard case came up for public hearing, Sacco and Vanzetti had been dead almost two months, and French jurors would, I fancy, simply tend to be a little more thoughtful than they might have been earlier that year or would tend to be a year later.

The excitement in Paris had been great while it lasted. I have before me as I write, a facsimile reproduction of the special edition of *Le Libertaire* for Tuesday, August 23rd, 1927. In enormous, black characters, the front page reads :

ASSASSINÉS!

Tous à l'Ambassade américaine!

There is a crudely drawn street plan showing the position of the American embassy in the Avenue Kléber, with indications of two main rallying points and the positions of the four nearest tube stations. Everyone is urged to assemble at nine o'clock that evening. The same black headline and the same exhortations appeared on the front page of a special edition of *L'Humanité*, and an appeal was similarly launched by the more respectable Socialist Party.

As Paris time is more than three hours ahead of New York time, the sheet must at least have been set up before the first cables and wireless messages reached Europe at about half past three in the morning, and indeed the other side still prints appeals, commentary, quotations and dark thoughts based on the assumption that it is still not too late to save the two men. There is, for instance, one curious article which states that the dollar-laden American tourists in Paris are 'our' hostages, that they should be greeted with shouts on arrival at the Gare St Lazare and subsequently pursued into the brothels of

Montmartre, where their champagne glasses should be broken in their faces :

> *So, in your own interest,* tell your accomplices in Boston that they had better give our two friends back to us while there is yet time.

Organised protest was then in its infancy, but Paris has always given something of a lead in the matter. A great deal of plate-glass was broken, and much looting took place. Lamp-posts were torn up and many policemen injured. The tomb of the unknown soldier was desecrated and the front of the Moulin Rouge demolished. There were similar demonstrations in other European cities, even London, the worst-affected being Leipzig, Hamburg and, of all places, Geneva, where not only American property and cinemas showing American films were attacked and in some cases burnt out but windows were broken at the Palace of the League of Nations. As a communist show of strength in Western Europe, it was interesting.

EARLY IN the morning, on May 25th, 1923, a Breton timber-merchant Pierre Quémeneur, left Rennes in the American army surplus Cadillac of his friend and business associate, Guillaume Seznec, a master sawyer. They were credibly seen some fifty miles west of Paris, and Seznec returned to Morlaix that evening, saying that Quémeneur had gone on from Houdan by train. This seemed odd. The two had apparently set off together with the idea of meeting, in Paris, an American called Charlie, with whom they hoped to conclude a deal for American army surplus vehicles. These they were selling to Russia, then short of transport.

A respectable man, a lawyer, saw Quémeneur at the railway station in Rennes two days later. That evening, lightermen serving a dredger permanently moored off the Breton coast, at a point where Quémeneur's land came down to the sea, heard two shots fired, but did not report them at the time. Quémeneur was never credibly seen again, nor was his body ever found. An inspector from the Sûreté Nationale came down to investigate. Towards the end of June, Seznec was arrested and charged with the murder of Quémeneur. For a year, he was to remain in prison first at Morlaix, then in Quimper, awaiting trial.

The case against him was flimsy, and it seems only too probable that evidence was fabricated by the man from the Sûreté. This was Inspector Bony, of whom we shall hear more, ten and again twenty years later. It seems quite certain that he planted a typewriter in Seznec's sawmill after Seznec had been taken into custody, when three previous searches had failed to reveal it and on a day when Mme Seznec was in Rennes. It seems likely enough that he had himself bought the typewriter in Le Havre on June 13th, that he there did some typing, that he destroyed the top copy, put a carbon in one of two suitcases he had brought with him, deposited this in the left-luggage office at Le Havre station and, his typewriter in the other suitcase, returned to Morlaix. This is not beyond the scope of

Bony's known deviousness. The document found in due course in an abandoned suitcase at the left-luggage office in Le Havre concerned the sale to Seznec of Quémeneur's property on the coast, and it was known that Seznec had hoped to buy this property, as indeed he admitted, at a rate advantageously lowered to take account of money Quémeneur owed him. There is the shadow of a motive here, but we often have motives for crimes we do not commit.

WHILE SEZNEC languished at Morlaix, in Lannion, twenty-five miles away, at the house of a young notary, Maître Fleury, the latter's stepfather, Count le Roux de Kerninon, was foolishly persuaded to tear up a will he had made in favour of his young mistress, Bernardine Nedellec, a typist. Count Kerninon, who could trace his noble pedigree back to the thirteenth century and whose scutcheon bore the device : *For Love or War*, had for long loved his wife, the widowed Mme Fleury, a professional singer eight years older than he, whom he had met, more than thirty years ago, while serving with the flag in Algeria, and it was he who had set little Emile up with a practice in Lannion. She had not cared for life on the family estate but had made the Count spend most of the year extravagantly in Paris or on the Côte d'Azur. As her dark, languorous physical charms raddled, he had also grown simply to dislike her. Bernardine was not only younger, she was nicer and, in her modest way, had a genuine feeling for the country. The Count was weak, however, and had even agreed to sell the Kerninon estates and live over the Fleurys in Lannion, seeing Bernardine at hotels or meeting her out of doors, as he was meaning to do in the early afternoon of September 21st, 1924.

Shortly before the appointed time, however, he was staggering downstairs at his stepson's house, bleeding from face and hands. He collapsed at the foot of the stairs and, after receiving first aid from a doctor rapidly fetched, was transferred to a nursing home. Mme de Kerninon had, she said, found her husband toying with a revolver (threatening in fact, she said later, to shoot himself). She had tried to take it away from him, and it had gone off. At the nursing home, an X-ray showed a bullet lodged in the Count's neck, which it was impracticable to remove, at any rate for the time being. Told of the dreadful accident which had befallen her middle-aged lover, Bernardine Nedellec hastened to the nursing home. Her first thought had been that the Countess had attempted to kill him, and he, recovering consciousness, said that it was so, adding that she should not report this to the police, that he himself, once recovered, would settle with his wife.

I am here simply following the account in Morain. The affair did not take place on his manor, of course, nor would he be concerned with the reports of anyone from the Sûreté Nationale, as it might have been Bony, despatched to the scene. He is not very precise about the order in which things happened, but it must have been almost at once that a doctor, either the local doctor or one from the nursing home, went round to the Fleurys' house and explained that, as it was impossible to determine from the X-ray photograph the precise calibre of the bullet in the Count's neck, it would be helpful to the surgeon if he could have another look at the revolver. Maître Fleury, who had returned from his office at the news had put it, still containing two unused rounds, in his safe. He went to get it, and it was presumably while he was doing this that the doctor found several spent cartridge-cases in the Kerninons' room. I cannot myself see that an X-ray photograph of the neck would fail to show the size of any bullet lodged there, apparently not in the spinal column, since it was not expected to prove fatal, or that a more precise knowledge of its calibre could therefore help the surgeon. I therefore assume that the doctor was doing a little detective work of his own, but doing it badly. He took away only one unused cartridge, leaving the other and the empty shells. The notary at once took these and threw them into the cesspool.

Two days later, Count le Roux de Kerninon died, and Bernardine Nedellec at once went to the police. A neighbour and a servant had heard several shots, and indeed it must have been evident from the Count's wounds that four had been fired, while of course the doctor who had been round to Maître Fleury's mentioned the spent cartridge-cases, which he had foolishly left and which had since disappeared. As Bernardine justly observed, it appeared that the Count, when he tore up the will in her favour, had signed his own death-warrant. Mme de Kerninon was therefore arrested and taken to Rennes on a date which Morain does not give us but which must have been at about the time the trial of Guillaume Seznec opened in Quimper.

THIS WAS on October 24th, a Friday (the day after Bonomini, in Paris, had received his dangerously light sentence for the murder

of Bonservizi). That forged and planted evidence would be brought
for the prosecution, we know. The affidavits of the lightermen serving the dredger (it has been said that they actually *saw* one man
shooting another) were suppressed. A main witness brought for the
defence was so obviously a liar that discrediting him became the
main incident of the trial and stood in the way of the real case for
the defence being adequately presented. Seznec was a narrow-
headed, close-eyed, wiry man (his supposed victim had had a broad
face, rather jovial in expression, and both wore moustaches, but the
latter's was turned up). He had no criminal record, but local gossip
had connected him with two fires (sawdust and shavings are inflam-
mable stuff), and this gossip was repeated in court.

Seznec had engaged Moro-Giafferi to defend him. Moro, however, had, since the May elections been a cabinet minister in the
Herriot government (it lasted a year), and his place was taken by a
younger man, Marcel Kahn. It soon becomes evident to the student
of French criminal history that miscarriages of justice, in France,
are far more likely to occur in the provinces than in Paris. To the
British or, at any rate, to the English student, the reason why this
should be so must seem to be that, in France, provincial assizes are
presided over by local judges, whereas in England and Wales a High
Court judge on circuit presides. Thus, on the one hand, local pre-
judice may affect even the president of the court, and, on the other
hand, he is likely to be an inferior judge, one who simply hasn't
made the metropolitan grade. As, in French criminal courts, the
red-robed prosecuting counsel is also a member of the magistracy,
in provincial courts he, too, is a local figure. If defending counsel
comes from Paris, he may be able to cut through entrenched local
interests and prejudices. If he is famous, the local bigwigs may try
to curry favour with him and will at least be on their best behaviour.
If he is young and perhaps more especially if he is Jewish, the local
ranks will close.

Apart from suppression of the lightermen's evidence, that kind of
phenomenon is perhaps not particularly evident in the Seznec case.
The planted evidence had a Parisian source in the abominable Bony
(not himself a Parisian, but from Bordeaux). A more intelligent and
detached presiding judge might have seen through it all. A more
practised examining magistrate might not have been imposed on in
the first place. The trial itself does not seem to have been improperly
conducted. The most discreditable witness was a witness for the
defence. It may be that Moro-Giafferi would have kept Le Her out

of court. It may be that young Maître Kahn should have. Le Her, a
bus conductor in Paris, was a Breton. He claimed to have talked to
Quémeneur, a passenger on his bus, in Paris after the latter's supposed disappearance. He remembered the occasion well, he said,
because they talked Breton, to the annoyance of the other pas-
sengers, who thought they were talking German. This witness was
to play a curious part in the sad, long aftermath of the case, the
immediate result of which was, let us simply say for the moment,
that Guillaume Seznec, found guilty of the murder of Pierre Quémeneur, was sentenced to penal servitude for life. This meant that
in due course he would depart for the penal settlements in Guiana.

On March 15th, 1925, in Marseilles, a Mme Jacques Rumèbe reported the disappearance of her husband, collector for a tile-works.
Suspicion fell on a Dr Pierre Bougrat, who had been treating
Rumèbe with injections, who, left by his wife, had notoriously
fallen into dissolute courses and who, when first sought for questioning, was found in prison for circulating dud cheques. The decom-
position of Rumèbe's body was far advanced by the time it was
found on top of a medicine cupboard in Dr Bougrat's dispensary.
He knew it was there, but said he had panicked on finding the
patient dead in his consulting room, where (he at first said) Rumèbe
had apparently committed suicide, being at the time financially em-
barrassed. There was evidence, however, to suggest that money
collected by Rumèbe had been appropriated by the doctor.

The case against Bougrat was a strong one. That, two years later,
it was to be disgracefully mistried does not prove that he was innocent, any more than Bony's planted evidence proves that Seznec
was innocent. Seznec had been, and Bougrat was to be, convicted
on insufficient evidence, and there will be that in their subsequent
careers to suggest that both were deeply wronged men, though
Bougrat's sufferings were not to be greatly prolonged. For the
moment, however, let us simply note that, in his case, the departmental magistracy employed an unfair procedure from the outset.
It was to be over a year before Dr Bougrat's own evidence was
taken by the examining magistrate. During that time, he was to
remain in a cell with a stool-pigeon or *mouton*, a one-eyed swindler
who wore a dark single eyeglass in the empty socket and who,
ostensibly in the course of judicial inquiry into his own case, visited
the examining magistrate's office at times chosen by himself, to

report his fellow-prisoner's conversation. From what transpired later at the public hearing, we know what kind of thing this man was saying Dr Bougrat said.

ON MAY 8th, at Rennes, Mme de Kerninon was sentenced to eight years' imprisonment for the murder of her husband. That was no miscarriage of justice, though we may wonder whether Maître Fleury and his wife should have got off scot-free for their undoubted attempts to pervert the course of justice. In Marseilles that summer, another lawyer, Maître Georges Sarret, *né* Sarrejani, bought, while Dr Bougrat was becoming acquainted with his one-eyed cell-mate at the Chave prison, two carboys of sulphuric acid, which he had delivered at a villa out in the country towards Aix, called, as such villas frequently are, L'Ermitage.

Born in Trieste but brought to France as a small boy, Georges Sarret had taken to the study of law only in his early forties, a few years before. Though called to the bar, he had never practised as a barrister, but set up an office at which he acted as a businessman's consultant, an enterprise at whose *louche* possibilities most of us can do no more than guess. Among the deals he'd arranged were marriages for two German sisters, Philomena and Kate Schmidt, who wanted French nationality. Philomena's septuagenarian husband died within four months. Kate, who had become Sarret's mistress, contracted a *mariage blanc* with a seedy adventurer who also died some months later. The two husbands both, it seems, died of systematic undernourishment. A business acquaintance of Sarret's, Chambon, a moneylender, had been a priest but was living in sin with a notary's ex-wife, a Mme Ballandreaux.

On August 19th, these two, invited to L'Ermitage and there arriving separately, were in turn dispatched with a revolver, the two bodies then being placed in a bath of acid. By October 23rd, the resulting sludge had been disposed of, and Maître Sarret returned the keys of the villa to its owner. He indeed noticed signs which caused him to go to the police, but nothing sufficiently incriminating was found, and the lawyer returned to his practice in Marseilles, where for the next six years he was to bring off a series of insurance frauds, helped at every turn by the Schmidt sisters and various respected citizens. It was, indeed, to be nine years before, with five of these, the sisters and he were brought to trial at Aix.

These particulars I owe to Montarron. Among matters reported from other parts of France, for the late summer and autumn of 1925, by Morain are the shooting, by a Mme Lefèvre, before her son's astonished eyes, of her daughter-in-law in a car on the road to Lille and the trials and convictions of, in Paris, Lazare Teissier, a bookmaker, and, at Versailles, three young bandits, Pierson, Bierre and Vannier. These three went to Guiana, from where, that autumn, returned to France the one attractive figure among the criminal anarchists, Marius Jacob, sent there twenty years before but unbroken by the experience. The Teissier case had resulted from clever detection and scientific *expertise* conducted upon a body found in a parcel one morning in the Bois de Boulogne. As the bookmaker admitted nothing and premeditation could not be proved, he got off with ten years.

A case in the Vosges aroused the interest of André Gide, whose writings on crime, like those of Colette and Marcel Jouhandeau, form, to my mind, an unjustly neglected part of his marvellous life's work. Gide's own comment is brief. He heads it PARRICIDE FROM FEAR OF HELL, and adds :

One of the two had to go . . . and the son kills his father to avoid suicide.

He then quotes from *Le Matin* of October 29th, 1925 :

METZ, October 26th. . . . A parricide in particularly tragic circumstances has given rise to strong feeling in the commune of Nilvange.

M. Émile Reiser, aged 50, a book-keeper at the Wendel mills, has been killed by his son Pierre, aged 23.

The murder was committed with alarming savagery. The killer crept up to his father who was resting on a settee and dealt him nine blows on the head with a butcher's chopper.

His head shattered, M. Reiser succumbed three hours later.

Questioned by the examining magistrate . . . the parricide stated that he regretted his act only in so far as it brought disgrace on his family.

'Life at home was unbearable,' he said, 'because of my father's continual criticism of my behaviour. One or other of us had to die. I did not wish to commit suicide, because then I should have gone to Hell. Now I shall be able to die in a state of grace.'

The magistrate having pointed out to him that his father might not have been in this state at the time of his death, the unworthy son replied :

'That is a matter of total indifference to me.'

A hundred and forty miles north-east of Metz, at his home in Frankfurt-am-Main, Eugen Weidmann, aged seventeen, back from his enjoyable stay at the Schloss Dehrn reformatory, had shown no sign of wishing to excel at anything but feats of juvenile daring. It was therefore decided that he should emigrate to Canada, in whose prairie provinces succeeding generations of German farmers had settled. Arrangements were made by a Catholic emigration service. The route was by train to Hamburg, from there by sea to Grimsby, across England by train to Liverpool and from there by a Canadian Pacific liner, the *Montcairn*, formerly a German vessel under the name ('if my memory serves me') of the *Augusta Victoria*, which called first at Greenock and then made for St John's. Three German boys and one Austrian shared a cabin. At first, things went well with Weidmann in Canada, but this was not to last. In the end, he would be deported, after serving a year's sentence for theft.

Arrived in England the previous year from New Zealand, a gangling youth of the same age as Weidmann, Donald Merrett, later to become better known as Ronald Chesney, moved at much the same time to Edinburgh, where in early 1926 he shot his mother in the ear but contrived to pass off her death as suicide. Remembered in the United Kingdom as the year of the General Strike, in crime it seems to have been a muted year throughout the English-speaking world. In New England, Mrs Hall, two of her brothers and a cousin were put on trial for the murders of the rapturous clergyman and his lady chorister under an apple-tree four years before. The four were acquitted, rightly as I gather from a detailed study of the case by William Kunstler, who attributes the crime to the Ku Klux Klan, indignant at the clergyman's immorality.

In Le Mans, the sisters Christine and Léa Papin, who exhibited the most alarming symptoms if they were separated, together entered the service of a solicitor, M. Lancelin, where it does not appear they were altogether happy, Mme Lancelin being a rather exacting mistress and Mlle Lancelin also a bit of a trial, but where they were nevertheless to remain for seven years. That was the year of the Schwartzbard and Merabashvili shootings. Outside the sphere of political crime, it was perhaps chiefly notable in France for the discovery of one Englishwoman, dead, and the disappearance of another. On July 21st, a Mrs Annie Gordon was murdered in bed at Juan-les-Pins. On October 6th, May Daniels, a nurse from Brighton, was last seen alive out walking near Boulogne-sur-Mer.

A Guiana escape in December was that of Eugène Dieudonné, a survivor of the Bonnot gang, to many people's minds wrongly convicted.

After weathering the winter on a hill near a Napoleonic monument, Nurse Daniels's body was discovered in February 1927, but the mystery was never to be solved, nor was that of the death of Annie Gordon. On the last day of February, in the suburbs of Paris, a roadmender called Nourric clubbed a bank messenger to death, parcelled up the body, trundled it out in a handcart and dumped it in the Marne. On March 13th, at Nancy, an electrician called Vermandé strangled his wife and stuffed her body into the furnace at the printing works where he was employed. Ten days later, the case of Dr Bougrat at last came up for hearing at Aix-en-Provence. Him, it may be remembered, we left, almost two years ago, at the Chave prison in the eastern suburbs of Marseilles, sharing his cell with a one-eyed swindler who wore a black monocle and had been planted there by the examining magistrate as a stool-pigeon or *mouton*. Papered over on top of a cupboard in Bougrat's dispensary had, I hope it may also be remembered, been found the body of a former patient of his, Jacques Rumèbe, an industrial debt-collector and former Army comrade.

PIERRE BOUGRAT was now in his middle forties, well made, with regular features, dark hair brushed smoothly back, a closely clipped moustache first grown in the Army, the lips indeed sensuously full. Completing his studies with distinction at Lyons in 1920, he had put up his plate in Marseilles, married the daughter of an established doctor, had a daughter by her, taken over part of his father-in-law's practice and become also a consultant in skin diseases. Then he had become moody (the effect, it was said, of head wounds received in the war), had neglected his practice, been divorced, taken a mistress in to live with him, contracted debts and drug habits. The mistress had been a whore, and Bougrat had not merely paid her ponce or bully a lump sum down but continued to pay him a monthly subsistence. That had been the situation when Rumèbe had disappeared and Bougrat, first arrested for passing dud cheques, had been brought out of prison to stand by while the police searched his premises and discovered Rumèbe's body.

Aix is not a big town even now, though it has grown. In 1927, its population was 23,000. There are good historical reasons why departmental assizes should have been held there rather than in Marseilles, then well over twenty times larger (the ratio now is more nearly twelve to one). The court house in Aix is a massive, rather flat, rectangular, almost square, eighteenth-century building in neo-classical style, with a bespired clock tower jutting off it towards one corner. The trial of Dr Bougrat opened there on March 21st, 1927. The regional magistracy solidly presumed his guilt and listened without belief to the defendant's account of what had happened on that dreadful Saturday.

BOUGRAT : For four years, Rumèbe and I had messed together in the Army. He came from Marseilles, and we met again when I had set up in practice there. He had been my patient for some five years past. I treated him without payment. Latterly, he had been coming to me once a week for injections. He came that Saturday morning, at about nine o'clock as usual. Later in the day, he returned. That was at about half past one, as I was finishing my midday meal. He was very upset. He told me that he had been robbed. He did not explain. He simply asked me to get him a sum of between seven and eight thousand francs. Added to what he possessed, that would make up the amount that was missing from his money-bag. I reminded him of my own financial difficulties, but I offered to see whether I could borrow money elsewhere. I installed Rumèbe in my surgery, on the couch, and went out. I could not find the person I had in mind, who might have lent me the money. I returned. Rumèbe was no longer where I had left him. He was stretched out on the floor of my dispensary, near the sink. He was dead. Beside him were fragments of broken glass, and on the table stood a number of bottles, some of them containing toxic preparations. I had not given my old comrade much reason to hope that I should be able to borrow the money he needed, and I thought that he had committed suicide. I thought he had poisoned himself and that I should be accused of poisoning him. Do not forget that, forty-eight hours previously, I had been summoned to the examining magistrate's office and that I faced charges of passing unsupported cheques. Money was missing from Rumèbe's bag, my number was up. My first thought was to conceal Rumèbe's death for two or three hours. My mistress had gone to Nice. I no longer had any friends. When I returned home at about seven o'clock in the evening, I found myself in a situation from which there was no way out. I saw that I was lost. And it was not until I had been in prison for sixteen months that I was told what a medico-legal expert had said : Rumèbe might have succumbed to a therapeutic hazard. Had that crossed my mind, I should have gone straight to the police. It was the one hypothesis I had not thought of. That is the extent of my crime.

The *accident thérapeutique* suggested by autopsy would, presumably, be some unexpected side-effect of the course of injections which Dr Bougrat had been giving his friend Jacques Rumèbe and more specifically of that morning's injection (of what substances and for what ailment, I have failed to gather). The information had no doubt been divulged eventually and reluctantly, with the entire *dossier*, to Bougrat's counsel, Maître Stéphan Martin. At any rate, court and prosecution, hand in glove, meant to discount it. They preferred to listen complacently to such witnesses as the one-eyed swindler, with his black single eyeglass. He indulged in a rhetoric of his own.

WITNESS : When I went to prison, I did not leave my conscience at the gate. . . . I drew a cheque on justice : it is up to you to honour it. . . . I stood sentinel before the tomb of Rumèbe: the court must relieve me. . . . I was chosen by Rumèbe to present the bill. . . . I have only one eye, but I see clearly with it. For Bougrat, it was a matter of proving that Rumèbe was a gambler and a rake who frequented a certain bar in the Rue de la République. He also had to find somebody who had robbed Rumèbe. For a long time, I played that part myself, but it was in order the better to unmask Bougrat's villainy. You understand, I was the last shot in his locker. I know how hard it is to accuse a man who has the Legion of Honour, that red ribbon so small and so great and so venerated by me. . . . Mr President, allow me at this point to pause briefly, in view of the gravity of what follows. . . . I bring you the truth. Bougrat killed Rumèbe. His crime was premeditated, as was the false witness he has borne. It was not to an injection that Rumèbe succumbed. Bougrat wiped his mouth with a wad of prussic acid. He died at once. It was he himself who told me that that was the poison he used. And he did not hoist the body on to the cupboard unaided : he was helped by a man who was waiting on the pavement outside and to whom he had given 4,500 francs, half the money contained in the collector's bag.

On the fourth day of the trial appeared, as a witness for the defence, Professor Barral of the medical faculty at Lyons. The court treated him with less courtesy than it had extended to the one-eyed swindler.

FOR THE DEFENCE, PROF. BARRAL : I examined the internal organs of the deceased. I found in the body no more than minute quantities of arsenic and mercury, the remains of therapeutic injections. What we are considering was one of those accidents of which several have been brought to notice in recent years and whose cause remains unexplained.

PRESIDENT (*angrily*) : You have exceeded your commission. You were not asked how Rumèbe died. You did not see the body, in any case. How can you estimate the cause of death?

BARRAL : My opinion is based on fact.

PRESIDENT : In reality, you know nothing.

COUNSEL FOR THE PROSECUTION : If Rumèbe succumbed to what you call a therapeutic hazard, how do you explain that Bougrat, an intelligent man, should have papered over the body on top of a cupboard, where it was found three months later, quite by chance?

BARRAL : That is outside my competence. I am not a specialist in mental disorders.

PROSECUTION : I am going to put a delicate question to you. Did you know Bougrat and his family?

BARRAL : I do not know the family. I know that Bougrat attended my lectures, but I was not personally acquainted with him.

FOR THE DEFENCE, ME MARTIN : If you were told that a witness, who moreover has a long criminal record, had stated in this court that Bougrat murdered Rumèbe by causing him to inhale prussic acid, what would be your reply?

BARRAL : I should say that it was a lie.

ME MARTIN : Professor, before these men who are called upon to judge Bougrat, I am going to ask you to join with me in contradicting the examining magistrate who wrote that, out of friendship for the family, you falsified your report so as to make it favourable to the accused, because he comes from the university world of Lyons to which you yourself belong. That is a thing you cannot have done. . . . I beg of you, answer in the name of justice and truth. . . .

Here broke out a demonstration so favourable to the accused and to his counsel and the witness that the reply of this last was not heard. In a fury, the presiding judge adjourned the hearing until next day. That day, an eminent forensic scientist from Paris, Professor Desgrez, appeared in evidence to confirm the findings of Professor Barral.

DESGREZ : The deceased could have succumbed to an injection given the previous week. . . . Analysis of the viscera showed no trace of aconitine, cyanhydric acid or mercury cyanide.

PROSECUTION : Be that as it may, do you consider it natural that a doctor should stow away on top of a cupboard a patient who had died as a result of therapeutic hazard?

DESGREZ : Bougrat is not the first to whom such a thing has happened. I remember a doctor in Paris who stuffed a patient who had died in similar circumstances into a trunk. What do you expect? When a terrible thing like that happens and there are other patients waiting in the next room, a doctor may well be excused if he loses his head. . . .

That got a laugh, of course.

The sixth day's hearing was entirely taken up with the concluding speech for the prosecution. The red-gowned prosecutor was clearly bent on impressing journalists from Paris. He went on for seven hours and perorated thus :

> . . . There were fair pages in your life, doctor. That was when you wore the uniform at Verdun and Salonika. Then you encountered a heartless gutter prostitute, whom we should like to see treated as were the ribalds of the Middle Ages and whipped in a public square. As we have heard from that Don Quixote of the prisons who stood here before us, that was enough to capsize you, to cause you to descend every step of the circles of Hell. For, apart from sloth, Dr Bougrat, all the vices are yours : that is why you killed Rumèbe.
>
> Shade of Rumèbe, come among us, rise up before this individual. Appear, pitiful spectre whose mortal remains were, by this coward's fault, for three months deprived of sepulture. Forgive the law its inevitable delays. Turn to this man who was your comrade in arms, your friend, towards this man who, to satisfy his filthy passions, did not hesitate to suppress you. Then turn to the jury and crave justice of them. Gentlemen of the jury, I demand sentence of death!

Until very recent times, the French have always been a rhetorical people by Anglo-Saxon standards, but, even as long ago as 1927, I cannot imagine that kind of thing going down in Paris. Perhaps it did not really go down in Aix, but the jury were convinced of Bougrat's guilt and came back in half an hour to say so. They allowed extenuating circumstances, in general an empty formula,

which in this particular case may simply have meant that they did
not like to think of a war hero, once a good doctor, literally losing
his head. And so Pierre Bougrat was marked down for a lifetime at
the Guiana settlements.

Getting there always took time. For a crime with which he was
first charged four years before and of which he had finally been
convicted (also with extenuating circumstances, since the body of
his business associate had never been discovered) at Quimper assizes
in October 1924, Guillaume Seznec, for instance, did not sail until
the month after Pierre Bougrat's conviction, that is to say in April
1927. Dr Bougrat, in turn, seems to have spent rather less than a
year more in prisons on French soil before, finally, on the Île de Ré,
he was formed up, in the appropriate uniform, with a contingent
embarking on the convict ship *La Martinière*. I should like to think
that the reader retained Seznec's name, as also that of the Inspector
Bony who planted evidence on him. Not that the fact proves
Seznec's innocence, any more than the disgraceful conduct of the
trial at Aix proves Bougrat's.

A YOUNGER man, Marcel Petiot, born and brought up in Auxerre,
early in trouble with the juvenile courts and a great nuisance to the
Army, had nevertheless qualified medically and taken a practice
in Villeneuve-sur-Yonne. In 1927, a Socialist, he was elected mayor
of the commune. This was odd, for although many liked him, ugly
rumours circulated about the disappearance the previous year of a
servant girl pregnant by him. Also in 1927, he married a woman
from a neighbouring village, Georgette Lablais, who did not long
delay conceiving a son.

Among the *faits divers* noted that year by André Gide, most
concern suicides (in two of which the dying man carefully noted his
last sensations) or happenings in remote parts of Russia (fourteen
people burning themselves alive in a little church, the discovery of
a village in which the women had murdered all the men). He also
notes, however, with an Italian parallel eight weeks before, the
following item from *Le Temps*, the precise locality being un-
specified.

MURDER BY A BOY OF 15. On August 31st, a little girl
aged 6, Jeanne Mullier, was reported missing. After a search
had gone on for several days without result, the child's body was

Fernande Segret at the witnesses' bar, November 22nd, 1921

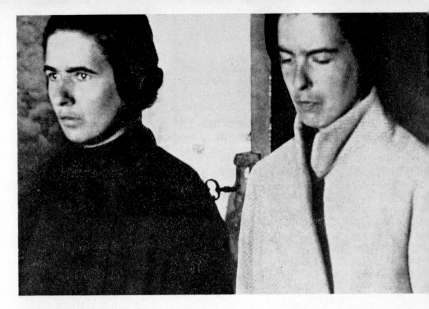

4 Léa and Christine Papin

5 Schwartzbard

finally discovered at the bottom of a disused stone-pit near her home. A boy of 15, Florimond Robitaillie, who lived in the neighbourhood, was arrested by the police on September 15th. Questioned all that day and into the night, he made a full confession at two in the morning. This was his account:

'I had arranged to meet little Jeanne in the quarry. We played there, but when she hurt herself by falling, I was afraid she would tell everything to her parents, and I took her through the dark workings to where I knew she would fall down the pit. As I expected, she slipped into the water, and I shone my pocket-lamp on her to watch her die. It took ten minutes. When I saw she was dead, I left the quarry, and since then I've been to work as though nothing had happened.'

Gide's principal reaction was to record disbelief of the boy's supposed motive ('I was afraid she would tell everything to her parents'). Either, he suggests, the lad was prompted to this reply by the police, or some journalist or news agency has inserted these words to make the crime seem rationally explicable in terms of a commonplace psychology. It was, that is to say, what many psychologists call a rationalisation.

For the United Kingdom that year, the chart on my wall shows only the John Robinson trunk murder and the shooting of P.C. Gutteridge by Browne and Kennedy, both crimes in the London area. For the United States the prominent names are those of Tom Dreher and Ada le Boeuf, who murdered the latter's husband in Louisiana, an autumnal *crime passionnel*, and Earle Nelson, who, nearing the end of his spectacular career, made for Canada, where he was arrested and where no doubt Eugen Weidmann, in prison, would at least hear of him. He would perhaps hear, too, of the terror that year already stalking Düsseldorf, its author still woefully far from being known to be Peter Kuerton.

D

7 | DECADE ENDING

A JEWELLER by the name of Mestorino had premises on the fifth
floor of a building in the Rue St Augustin, off the Avenue de
l'Opéra in the direction of the Stock Exchange, a very rich neighbourhood indeed. There, on the morning of February 25th, 1928,
at 10 a.m., a man in the same line of business, Gaston Truphène,
called on him to request payment of a bill for 35,000 francs and
perhaps to show him a few interesting new stones. It is to be presumed that Mestorino found it difficult to meet the bill, that he
knew to what extent Truphène's wallet bulged with notes and his
side-pockets with gems on Saturday mornings and that he did not
particularly care for the man. At any rate, he picked up a mandrel
or triblet (a cylindrical rod on which rings are placed for working)
and struck his visitor forcibly on the head. Despite a skull immediately cracked, Truphène did not at once lose consciousness but,
as he staggered about the office and fell to his knees, protested
noisily and cried out for help, also saying : 'There are 300,000
francs, you can take it all!' To Suzanne Charnaux, aged twenty-one,
Mestorino's sister-in-law, who was in the office, he called : 'Suzanne,
I have a sister like you, take pity on me!' But Mlle Charnaux stood
and watched as her sister's husband repeatedly struck with the
mandrel, until Gaston Truphène lay stretched on the floor, his brain
largely exposed, still demanding pity, and expired before the eyes
of Mestorino's workpeople, curious at the commotion. There were
four of them. They were M. Moncey, the *sertisseur* or setter, a
polisher, Suzanne Langlois, aged seventeen, an apprentice, Pierre
Lefèvre, fifteen, and another.

This anonymous workman was sent out to buy pack-cloth, while
his employer and Mlle Charnaux went through Truphène's pockets,
removed rings from his fingers and tied him up. When the workman returned with pack-cloth, she had sponged up the blood and
was washing the parquet floor. Young Suzanne Langlois was given
a pendant for herself and a small parcel of other jewels to keep at

94

home for the moment. The silence of the others was variously ensured. As to the story they were to tell if questioned, it was agreed
that M. Truphène had indeed called that morning, that a bill had
been paid and that he had then departed. For the moment,
Truphène's carefully packed body remained in Mestorino's office.

At nightfall, he and his sister-in-law returned to it. She preceded
him with it watchfully down five flights of stairs, then called on the
caretaker and engaged the woman in conversation while he took it
to his car. This he then drove to the garage where he kept it. There,
with the bundle inside, it remained for the rest of the night and all
day Sunday. On Sunday evening, Mestorino took his car out again
and, alone, drove first to Brie-Comte-Robert, somewhat less than
twenty miles south-east of Paris. At a petrol station there, he bought
four cans of petrol, then drove on to the Armainvilliers woods,
where he disembarked all at a point clearly not overlooked. Laying
Truphène's wrapped body on the ground, he emptied the four cans
of petrol over it and with due care set the petrol alight. He drove
back to Paris, returned his car to the garage, asked the garage-
owner to have it cleaned, paid him well and instructed him, if
questioned, to say that it had not been out at all on Saturday, Sunday or the Monday which had not yet dawned and would dawn
late, as it was February.

Not long after the said dawn, delivery-men with a van saw smoke,
stopped and, investigating, discovered the smouldering body. They
reported their find to the police at Brie-Comte-Robert, who traced
the petrol cans back to their source. The petrol-station attendant
remembered his customer of the evening before, the colour and
make of his car and even, at least approximately, its registration
number. It was a Paris registration, and, given also colour and make,
the car was promptly traced to its owner. *Post-mortem* examination
further established the identity of the victim, whose disappearance
had been reported. Mestorino was summoned to the Quai des
Orfèvres, while a search was made at his premises in the Rue St
Augustin. His sister-in-law and four employees were questioned. So
was his wife, and so were the owner of the garage at which he kept
his car, and a mechanic.

Mestorino appeared untroubled. He admitted seeing Truphène
on Saturday morning in his own office and in the presence of his
sister-in-law. A bill had been settled, and Truphène had gone. As to
the car, he had not taken it out at all that day or the day after or
the day after that. This story was confirmed by sister-in-law, four

employees, garage-owner and mechanic. Confronted with Mestorino, the petrol-pump attendant from Brie-Comte-Robert now stated that he did not recognise him. Mestorino was deeply grieved, he said. Truphène had been his dear friend. No doubt the crime had resulted from Truphène's homosexual frequentations, his one weakness. Mestorino attended his late friend's funeral with every sign of deep grief.

His questioner at the Quai des Orfèvres had been Chief Superintendent Nicolle's secretary, M. Massu, in effect second-in-command of what was then not the *brigade criminelle* but the *brigade spéciale*. The job did not preclude action outside, but was sedentary in so far as the man who held it had passed examinations which made him an expert in procedural and administrative matters. The interrogation of suspects in serious criminal cases normally fell to his lot. It is commonly said that Massu was the original of Simenon's Maigret, and the conspiracy of false witness in the Mestorino case certainly called for Maigret-like qualities. Over a fortnight had gone by without result when, on March 14th, Mestorino was summoned again to the Quai des Orfèvres and there took place one of those epic questionings into the night, with sandwiches and beer sent out for and the rest, the story gone over and over until contradiction appears.

A fact difficult for Mestorino to explain away was that the bill he said he had settled with Truphène had been found unreceipted on his premises. All right, so he hadn't paid the bill. As to the car, yes, he had taken it out and disposed of the body. Gaston Truphène's death had occurred accidentally in the course of a quarrel. He had been paying attentions to Mlle Charnaux, who was Mestorino's mistress as well as his sister-in-law. The two men had come to blows, and Truphène, falling, had struck his head on the corner of a desk. Then, of course, panic when Truphène was found to be dead.

The true story came out at two o'clock in the morning. Mestorino was remanded in custody. The garage-owner admitted that the car had been taken out, but said that he had understood it was in the pursuance of an affair of the heart and that Mme Mestorino must not know. The whole thing is beautifully recounted by Lucien Zimmer, who had it from Massu and who further relates it both to its more immediate and to what may be thought its long-term legal consequences. For, when the case came up for public hearing, Mestorino himself was to be given a life sentence for manslaughter, and Suzanne Charnaux two years for concealing a body and receiving stolen property, but no punishments at all were to be awarded either for perjury or for standing around while a man was battered to death. The perjury had been committed in the examining magistrate's office, where the witnesses were on oath. Proceedings could only have been taken against them had they repeated it in open court. At the public trial, even Suzanne Charnaux would appear in the first place only as a witness, to be arrested and separately charged after she had given her evidence.

Ever since 1861, if I understand this matter correctly, she and the four employees would, in the United Kingdom, all have been charged as accessories after the fact, she at least also as an abettor, which would have made her liable to the same penalties as Mestorino. The French idea of complicity requiring, it seems, actual participation in the crime and French ideas of conspiracy having no legal warrant, nothing could have been done at the time or for almost twenty years more, until a court ruling of 1945 was upheld, legislation nine years later further creating that famous criminal offence, non-assistance to a person in danger, still unknown to us, embodied in Article 63 of the Penal Code.

I have dwelt somewhat on this point because, as it seems to me, for lack of some knowledge of it, a significant work of modern literature, Albert Camus's *The Fall*, which is widely read in translation, has quite failed to be understood in the Anglo-Saxon world. Necessitating as it did mention of a book by Lucien Zimmer and of Massu and what his job was in 1928, the Mestorino case also provides occasion for a glance at the French police world of the time, a number of its key personnel having recently changed and being due to remain more or less in place during the greater part of our remaining period.

As HEAD of the crime squad or *brigade spéciale* in the Quai des Orfèvres, René Faralicq had been removed in 1925, apparently in consequence of disquiet created by Léon Daudet's wild allegations of police complicity in the death of his son (he himself merely tells us that it was 'because of political spite directed against me'), and, having applied for his pension rights to be commuted, had withdrawn into non-official life, where he wrote poems and annotated Dante. Morain recalls Faralicq, in his younger days, as a man of Herculean strength, effortlessly heaving doors off their hinges. As prefect of police, Morain had been replaced by Chiappe in the spring of 1927, in the normal course of retirement, and was engaged in writing his memoirs, in which he notes, as a horrid warning to those who betray their mothers, that Paule Jacques, daughter of Mme Bessarabo by her first marriage, had recently been found destitute. Jean Chiappe had been head of the Sûreté Générale, a move to the Paris prefecture of police, Belin tells us, being regarded as promotion. Jean Belin himself had never got on with Chiappe and was glad to see him leave the Rue des Saussaies, where his own promotion to the rank of *commissaire* was not slow to follow.

These ranks are difficult to translate, in part because not only they but their English equivalents are renamed intermittently. At the Rue des Saussaies, Belin's *commissariat* would make him equivalent, in British terms, to Superintendent or Chief Superintendent, as, at New Scotland Yard, it would Nicolle, replacing Faralicq, Guillaume after him and presently the former *secrétaire*, Massu, in due course replacing Guillaume, while for the time being M. Benoist, as director of the *police judiciaire* for Paris would no doubt be Assistant Commissioner. Subsequent secretaries at the Quai des Orfèvres, of whom Massu's first was to be Emile Casanova, a Corsican, would presently be designated *officiers de police* (a particularly awkward term in the United Kingdom, where every policeman is a police officer) and subsequently themselves first *commissaires adjoints* and finally *commissaires*, while detective-inspectors would then be *officiers de police* (but this is outside our period). At the Sûreté, Zimmer had been and, moving with him, would for the next six years be in the Boulevard du Palais (round the corner from the Quai des Orfèvres) *chef de cabinet*, which in ordinary contexts would be no more than head clerk, to Chiappe. I shall hope that the British reader need not worry, but there are American differences with which I dare not attempt to cope, despite assiduous reading of the novels of Ed McBain, from which, however, I learn that American detectives are bulls. When they are not *flics*, French ones are merely chickens or, a little braver-sounding, pullets.

THE YEAR's unsolved murder of an Englishwoman in France was that of Florence Wilson, aged fifty-five, whose husband was at the time not far away, on the golf course at Le Touquet. She had died of strangulation, but subsequently (a corpse, however fresh, does not appreciably bleed, and this one's carotid artery was severed) been stabbed fourteen times. Of this crime we are lucky enough to have accounts by both Greenwall and Morain. At least it is luck if we do not crave certainty. The two agree that Mrs Wilson's handbag lay some little distance away and that she herself lay on her back with knees raised, skirt pulled up and no knickers. According to Morain, however, the handbag was empty, while according to Greenwall there was money in it and jewellery on the victim's person, so that robbery cannot have been the motive. According to Greenwall there were, but according to Morain there were not, the usual indications of recent sexual intercourse, which gives or does not give us an alternative motive. From both accounts it appears that Mrs Wilson had been on her way to meet someone, not her husband, at a dance, so that the knickers need not have been forcibly removed. Mrs Wilson was a grand-daughter of Charles Cammell, founder of Cammell, Laird, the firm of shipbuilders, of which Mr Wilson had been a director. Successively under suspicion but released after questioning were a deaf mute and the band leader at the casino.

The man on the spot from the Sûreté Générale was Inspector Mariani, as great a rogue in his different way as Bony. In Paris, nothing of equal importance occupied those at the Quai des Orfèvres, though a 'masked bandit' was burgling great houses (and in due course turned out to be a Serbian gang). Dr Bougrat had reached Cayenne, where his medical qualifications eased his lot from the outset and five months later facilitated his escape, for by the end of August he had collected, while employed at the prison hospital, not only the right tropical medicines but a mariner's compass. He departed with seven companions and by October was in Caracas, where his medical qualifications again stood him in good stead (for your reception by the Venezuelan authorities was always very dodgy). In Paris, on the 28th of that month, appeared the first issue of *Détective*, founded by the novelist Joseph Kessel and his brother Georges.

This weekly magazine still exists. Its appearance is now repulsive in the extreme. When you get behind the shock headlines and cheesecake, the low-grade drawing and the advertisements for virility, big tits, life-size inflatable rubber dolls and blank-firing automatics and revolvers, you still find three or four pieces of crime-reporting of a kind which British journalists cannot attempt because of the rules here governing comment on matters *sub judice*. In its early days, *Détective* was published by Gallimard and enjoyed the collaboration of such writers as Pierre Mac Orlan, Léon-Paul

Fargue, Francis Carco, Marcel Achard, the ineffable Paul Morand and a young barrister who was to become a member of the Académie Française, Maître Maurice Garçon. On the editorial staff was a young crime reporter, Marcel Montarron.

For the moment, there was not much local stuff of great interest to report, and the first issue features the shooting of Al Capone's man, Lombardo, in Chicago. In November, a bank cashier was obligingly killed in a raid in Marseilles, and a young man, found unaccountably dead in the Bois de Boulogne and buried at public expense, turned out to be the son, just over from England, of a South African millionaire. Crimes of the year elsewhere had been the Lainz zoo murder in Austria, the young Bruno Lüdke's first effort on the outskirts of Berlin, the inscription on the British roll of the uncharacteristic name of Chung Yi-miao and, at Dobbs Ferry in the state of New York, the strangulation, decapitation, cooking and eating (with carrots and onions) of little Grace Budd, not until six years later to be known as the work of the remarkable Albert Fish.

A DECADE of great individual German sadists ended, on May 24th, 1929, with the arrest of Peter Kuerten, sometimes known as the vampire of Düsseldorf, though his actual blood-drinking seems to have been confined to that of a swan in his youth. At the time, Superintendent Guibal, O.B.E., of Marseilles, was failing to solve the mystery presented by the death of Olive Branson, forty-four, a well-connected and not unsuccessful painter, who also had briefly been a Mrs Wilson, at Les Baux, where she was found standing upright, wearing a nightdress and stockings, in a water-tank, with a hole in the head.

The police in Paris were not doing very well, either. Since April, they had been failing to find a lead to the killer of a Mme Blanc, caretaker, abortionist and friend of anarchists who met in a room over her lodge. On September 9th, the body of her son, Frédéric Rigaudin, a crooked speculator, was found in a trunk at Lille, where it had been sent by rail from the Gare du Nord. On the 16th, the head of Criminal Records, Edmond Bayle, was murdered in the staircase leading to his office by one Philiponnet, who gave himself up without struggle, declaring that he had killed an evil man. For the murder of Rigaudin, a number of clues pointed towards an Armenian tailor, Almazian, and these were improved upon or simply misread by the experts of Bayle's former team. Although he was in fact innocent, it was not absurd to pull Almazian in for questioning or even to arrest him on suspicion, but at the Quai des Orfèvres, under Superintendent Nicolle's orders, he was questioned and kept without food for a quite inordinate time, over forty-eight hours, being subjected to the *passage à tabac* or generally knocked about with extraordinary brutality, in the hope of a confession. *Détective* boldly printed his account of these proceedings, and Guillaume was promoted to take Nicolle's place.

In early December, the police in Strasbourg received a telephone call from Leipzig, asking them if they could find and hold a man believed to be travelling with false papers in the name of Stranelli. This the Strasbourg police efficiently did. The man's real name was Tetzner, and on November 25th what his wife identified as his body had been found calcined in a crashed and burnt-out car, the body in fact being that of a young journeyman to whom he had given a lift. The real detective work had been done by an insurance company from whom Frau Tetzner was claiming money on a policy recently taken out on her husband's life. They had discovered that she was receiving telephone calls at a neighbour's house from a M. Stranelli in Strasbourg.

AMONG CASES, generally unsolved, of Britons murdered in France, Greenwall collected six for the 'twenties, and we have found a seventh, a Mrs D., in Faralicq. Six out of the seven were women, all but one of them either living alone or footloose in a strange land. When everything else has been taken into consideration, I am inclined to think that the circumstance which principally accounts for these distressing facts and for the fact that during the same period there was no similar slaughter of Frenchwomen by the English or other Britons is that the Frenchwomen in the United Kingdom were in general either respectably married and well protected by the walls of family life or were concentrated in Soho and Mayfair under the professional protection of ponces either of their own or of other continental nationalities, while a favourable rate of exchange encouraged Englishwomen, perhaps of a more independent disposition anyway or less family-tied, to live cheaply in France or to take inexpensive holidays there. It is true that, statistically, the average Frenchman has always been twice as murderously inclined as the average Briton, that those middle-aged spinsters or widows in their villas seemed eminently worth robbing, that good-looking girls found walking or cycling alone about the countryside were commonly British and that, when either type of Englishwoman was found dead, there was some lack of that local outcry which drives even the least conscientious police to make arrests.

There seem to have been fewer cases of these kinds in the decade which followed. Among those collected by Greenwall, the one mysteriously dead young woman cannot with certainty be said to have been murdered. This was Pamela Raper, again an artist, found in a fisherman's net off Toulon as late as 1938. His only three other 'thirties cases were concentrated in the first years of the new decade, and the victims were all men. Let us therefore briefly notice them before considering matters which seem more truly characteristic of the next ten years. Reginald Arthur Lee, acting British consul-general in Marseilles, was last seen on July 5th, 1930. Six months later, on January 6th, 1931, John Albert Drinan, aged eighty-three, was found murdered in a house on the outskirts of Nice. Neither was Lee ever traced nor the murderer of Drinan discovered. On September 17th, 1932, a Scottish businessman, Donald Ross, was found dead and tied up with wire in his villa at Maisons-Laffitte, twelve miles west of Paris. Three years later, three men, two of them Swiss, were indeed to be sentenced to Guiana for this crime.

A PIMP is a pander or procurer, and men who pursue this avocation are the more despised in that the job may be done at least as well by old women and small boys. A ponce lives on the immoral earnings of a woman or women whom he protects, for prostitution is a dangerous trade outside controlled State or municipal brothels. No doubt many a ponce has descended to pimping in hard times, and no doubt many a young pimp has later achieved poncedom, but a ponce's day will generally be spent in some favourite bar near one or another of his women's beat, drinking a little, gambling a little, keeping an eye on clients and seeing that all goes well, occasionally pursuing some other encounter likely to yield easy money. Except in the highly emotional sense given by Protestants to this expression, it is a man's job.

In any large city, there will be at least one centre of prostitution, which, among other facilities, will need to contain many bars. In any such centre, a hierarchy will develop. There will be men who, from modest beginnings, have risen to positions of wealth and power, with bulk control of that commodity with which God or Nature has so abundantly supplied women. Where the competition is fierce, they will, among their subordinates, employ men who are not reluctant to injure or even kill those whom their employer points out to them for such treatment. These will use such weapons as the technology of the time permits and local circumstances require. The ponce or bully on a smaller scale must deal in his own way with those who intrude upon what he regards as his territory, which may be only a few yards of pavement and a small room. If his rivals are armed, so will he be. On the outskirts of such a world, there will also be men who do not quite make the full ponce grade, who aspire to it but who must, in the meantime, help themselves and their unestablished girls out with petty theft and other more ardous, unrewarding, anxiety-creating practices or even an honest job. Such a *demi-sel* may also be a police informer, not because that is what he wants to be or proposes to be all his life, but because at the moment a charge hangs over him which the police will not press so long as he tells them what he knows about the activities of the larger game on whom they are keeping their eye.

Throughout our period, the vice centre of Paris was Montmartre and, more specifically, the area, of less than a square mile, unofficially designated Pigalle. The characteristic fauna of this neighbourhood were known, by a word which has larger connotations even for us, as *le milieu*, though indeed a *milieu* (or *mitan*) might flourish anywhere. In that or any similar French context, the prevailing type of culpable homicide is known, by an expression which also has larger connotations, as a *règlement de compte*. This simply means the settling of an account, any account, by means however peaceful, but French has no other widely current expression for gang shootings or gang warfare in general, and indeed a *règlement de compte* need not involve whole gangs but may occur between two soloists, without so much as a brother involved. As in the different worlds of lawyers and policemen, there are linguistic difficulties here which I beg the reader to believe I am not raising out of mere pedantry.

French has no words of its own for a hold-up, a bank-raid or the protection racket. French journalists to this day use the terms 'hold-up' and 'raid' and 'racket'. And yet, whatever may be the origin of the protection racket, street hold-ups and bank-raids, with get-away by car, originated in Paris, in 1911, with the Bonnot gang, who were anarchists. Displaying modesty of a similar but non-linguistic kind, the French also call (have long called) confidence trickery *vol à l'américaine* or American-style theft. In general, we may say that these linguistic signs are not to be trusted. In modern times, urban gang warfare had never attained such heights as in Chicago in the 'twenties. The circumstances were highly artificial. As a result of the 18th amendment to the Constitution, the illicit sale of beer had become more remunerative than that of cunt. There were high-minded gangsters, like Dion O'Banion, who never dealt in this latter commodity, but his Italian rivals continued to do so, and that was where they had started. Basically, the great American gangsters were ponces. A majority of them were Latins, specifically from the mainland half of the former kingdom of the two Sicilies.

It was to be through islanders of Italian background and language that gang warfare on a notable scale would presently reach Paris, via Marseilles, where they already had a *milieu* of their own. In a moment, we shall have to glance at that little Chicago and its forays elsewhere. For the moment, we must consider a minor piece of culpable homicide in Montmartre. Later in the year, Paris would notice one effect of the Wall Street crash six months before, but the holiday season had not yet got under way, and the absence of American visitors cannot to date have been very evident. For almost ten years past, a fair proportion of these had come to Paris for good liquor as much as anything, but they had also wanted women. No doubt they would be seen around Pigalle again that summer.

At three o'clock in the morning on March 26th, 1930, shots rang out at the corner of the Boulevard de Clichy and the Rue Germain-Pilon, Montmartre. An unknown passer-by went to the assistance of a man who was staggering and clutching his belly. He stopped a taxi, driven (as so many were in Paris at the time) by a Russian exile, and got the wounded man in, then told the taxi-driver to wait and went into the Clichy *bar-tabac* near by, emerging with two women. These got into the taxi, and he walked away. The taxi drove to the Lariboisière Hospital, a mile or so to the east, in the Boulevard de la Chapelle.

As his papers showed and as the two women were able to confirm (and as the passer-by must have known), the man with one or more bullets in his guts was Roland Legrand, aged twenty-four, described as a pork-butcher, having indeed worked briefly at various *charcuteries*. One of the two women was his mistress and principal support, Eugénie Verne, known as big Nini. Shortly after his arrival in hospital, four men called to ask about his condition but did not give their names. In the operating theatre, a laparatomy was performed, but the bullet or bullets could not usefully be removed. Legrand's condition was declared desperate, and his mother was sent for from Melun. Police from the 18th district, 69th ward or quarter, were joined by Inspector Grimaldi from the Quai des Orfèvres. At first, Legrand refused to name his assailant, but, urged to do so by his mother, said that it was Papillon, Roger, and that Goldstein knew him. Goldstein was one of the four men who had called at the hospital earlier. Roland-Maxime Legrand lingered all that day, but died shortly after midnight, general peritonitis having quickly set in.

Georges Goldstein, twenty-two, had no criminal record. He lived with his father in the Rue Pigalle, had received a secondary education and travelled as his father's sales representative, frequenting those of *le milieu* for their glamour and prestige. In due course, he was to be the prosecution's chief witness, but his first statement to the police says very little. A search was made for Henri-Antoine Charrière, twenty-three, known as Papillon because of a crude butterfly tattooed on his chest, but also perhaps because he commonly wore a bow tie, for which the French expression is *noeud papillon*. He had left his last known address in the Rue Tholozé. Described as a barman, he seems in fact for the past seven months to have lived wholly on the immoral earnings of Georgette Fourel, known as Nénette, nineteen, who, in addition to casual earnings, received a small monthly allowance from an Englishman. She was questioned on March 28th at the Quai des Orfèvres and allowed to leave but kept under observation. Big Nini lay low. Charrière was in hiding at St Cloud, on premises kept by a friend of his called Orsini, a former policeman. He was arrested on April 7th and charged with murder. He denied the charge and pointed out that there were others in the *milieu* who bore the same nickname as himself, while 'Roger' was certainly no part of his name.

Henri Charrière, *dit* Papillon, was the only son (he had three sisters) of the schoolmaster at St Étienne de Lugdares, a village of 700 inhabitants in the uplands of Ardèche, which is northern Languedoc in the historical sense. Inapt for study and indisposed to any of the manual occupations available, he had joined the Navy at eighteen, after a year on shore duty at Toulon received two months' detention, been thereafter shipped (his only sea voyage) to the disciplinary station at Calvi in Corsica, there been tattooed with a butterfly, there ensured his premature discharge by crushing his left thumb between two stones. After failing to make any headway in the Marseilles *milieu*, he had reached Pigalle at the end of 1927, then aged twenty-one. Within a year, he had been awarded a four months' suspended sentence for receiving and attempting to dispose by sale of stolen goods (445 francs' worth of postage stamps). In January 1929, he had again been questioned by the police, been detained for a few days but then been released, over a further matter of theft and receiving. In the course of that year, he had first met Georgette-Jeanne Fourel, lived with her at various addresses in Montmartre, taken her with him on trips to Montélimar and Marseilles, Brussels and Ostend, in connection, it was believed, with a modest enterprise in drugs, and, it seems to have been quite certain, shown his gratitude to the police by supplying those in his own neighbourhood with regular and valued information. It appeared that, in March 1930, Roland Legrand had been overheard talking about Charrière's relations with the police, and it was supposed that this indiscretion had led to his death. The murder weapon had been a 7.65 automatic, though not the one found in Charrière's possession, with which he had occupied himself in the main by firing into the plaster of bedroom walls.

Georges Goldstein was questioned again. With Charrière in custody, he spoke more freely. The statement he signed on April 18th reads as follows :

On the night of the tragedy, I was walking along in the company of a friend when we met Papillon who asked me if I knew where Roland Legrand was. I told him that he was in the bar at No. 48 in the Boulevard de Clichy, where he often went. Papillon was with two individuals unknown to me. Papillon left me.

I then went to warn Legrand that Papillon was looking for him. While I was talking to him, one of the men I'd seen with Papillon came into the bar and asked Legrand to step outside with him. I myself left shortly afterwards.

On the pavement outside, I saw Papillon and Roland Legrand having a discussion. I didn't wait, but walked home with my friend. Later, returning to the Place Pigalle, I again met Papillon who said to me : 'Go to the Lariboisière hospital and see what condition Legrand is, I've just shot him. If he's still alive, tell him whatever he does not to talk. . . .'

Two days later, warned that friends of Charrière's would be after him, Goldstein packed his bags and went on a business trip to England, where he remained until the end of July.

ANOTHER HANGER-ON in the *milieu* of Montmartre, a son of well-to-do parents who frequented low bars for the glamour and excitement and the girls, was Georges Gauchet. The champagne flowed when he was around, but in the end he had spent all his inheritance from his father, and his mother grew tired of giving him money. He then took the obvious step and in 1930, at the age of twenty-five, set himself up as a ponce, but that summer's absence of American visitors made itself felt, and by autumn he was broke and desperate. In November, in the early evening, he walked into a jeweller's in the Avenue Mozart, in Auteuil, where his father had formerly had a pastry-shop, attacked the jeweller with an adjustable spanner, followed him into the back shop and hit him with a mallet, finishing him off with a revolver, then stuffed his own pockets with watches, pendants and such and took a taxi back to Montmartre. He did not take the stolen goods to a regular fence, but hawked them around bars and was observed so doing by an informer, so that he spent Christmas, a fateful season for him, in a cell at the Santé prison.

A more specialised hanger-on around Pigalle was a young, bespectacled barrister with a little Hitler moustache, Maître Biffaure, who had been briefed for the defence of Henri-Antoine ('Papillon') Charrière. No doubt he also sought glamour and excitement, but it was the male prostitutes he went for. He had also found a taxi-driver who was willing to swear that, at the time of the shooting of Roland Legrand, he had seen Charrière in a specific bar, the Iris, drinking with the owner and his manager. Owner and manager denied this, but it was hoped that they could be persuaded to change their testimony.

Two young Americans whom Montmartre still glimpsed that winter were Emily Verbeech and Richard Wall, the former a dancer of some kind, the latter wanted by the police in New York for questioning in connection with a matter two years old. Towards the end of January 1931, they moved out to a villa at Bougival, ten miles west of Paris, on the Seine. On February 6th, Wall reported to the local police not that the girl had left him, which was no concern of theirs, but that, knowing him to be out, she had returned with two young men who had broken into the house and stolen three suitcases in which, among other things, were 10,000 dollars in cash. Emily Veerbeech and the two men were traced to Chamonix and taken into custody. The three suitcases in their possession contained no money, and Richard Wall failed to establish that he had ever had 10,000 dollars, so his complaint was dismissed. He left Bougival, lived at various fashionable addresses in Paris, finally took a room near the Invalides and stole cars, which he found means of selling. Among his new French friends was Guy Davin, another wastrel of good family who had become a *demi-sel* around Montmartre.

The date originally fixed for the trial of Papillon Charrière was July 27th, but the proceedings were halted at the request of the prosecution, to whom new, if unpromising, evidence had been offered. The defence also thought they had found an alternative suspect. The trial eventually took place in October, and on the 28th Charrière was sentenced to penal servitude with hard labour for life. The case against him was defective, but certainly his alibi had been rigged and did not stand up for a moment. Both *Détective* and *Paris-Soir* wondered whether there might not have been some miscarriage of justice, and it was thought even at the Quai des Orfèvres that the sentence was heavy. The case did not arouse much public interest. *Règlements de comptes* in Montmartre were not uncommon. The victim had not been an estimable person.

Unlike the jeweller in the Avenue Mozart, whose undoubted murderer had, moreover, been more popular than Charrière round Pigalle. The trial of Georges Gauchet came up in early November, and sentence of death was inevitably pronounced. While Gauchet lay in the death cell at the Santé and Charrière out at Fresnes, on December 14th, Wall stole a car parked in a main street of Paris. That day or the next, he telephoned Guy Davin and asked whether, in order to spare him a visit to the bank, Davin would change 300 dollars for him into French currency. Davin said he would see what he could do, arranged to meet Wall on the 16th, went out and bought a gun and practised firing it in the Bois de Boulogne. On the 16th, the two went out together in the new car, Davin driving. In woods to the north-west, he stopped, saying that his hands were cold and that he must put gloves on. He then shot Wall three times in the back of the head. Thereafter, he drove around for several hours, going as far as Magny-en-Vexin some thirty miles to the north-west, where he pitched out a folding seat. Twice, he stopped to make purchases, of petrol and of a pair of scissors. He stripped Wall's body and dumped it in the Seine at Triel, cutting up the clothes, sprinkling them with petrol and attempting to burn them. Then he went back to Paris. Next day, he drove out on the eastward side and staged an unconvincing car crash near the racecourse at Vincennes.

The lucky policeman was Superintendent Belin. The clues had been widely distributed, but there they all were, as for a treasure-hunt, and there were witnesses, including a roadmender who had seen a young man in a car with an older man's head resting on his shoulder and who had thoughtfully noted the number of the car, while, back from Chamonix, one of the two men who had absconded with Emily Verbeech and the suitcases had been with Wall on the 16th at a club which the latter left to keep his appointment with, as he distinctly said, Guy Davin. And so, after a textbook investigation lasting no more than five days, Davin was being questioned, not at the Quai des Orfèvres but in the Rue des Saussaies, as, at Fresnes,

Henri Charrière prepared for his marriage next morning. After some little delay, Davin confessed. Charrière's elaborate strategy was designed to postpone, if not to cancel, his eventual departure for Cayenne. The marriage was but a first step.

On the morning of December 22nd, 1931, he was brought to the 1st district town hall in the Place du Louvre and there joined in civil wedlock to Georgette Fourel (Nénette). The bride wore navy-blue. After the wedding, Papillon was taken back to Fresnes, and Georgette left Paris to work in the provinces, at Vals-les-Bains, near her husband's birthplace and site of a brothel at which he had once been a favoured client. On Christmas night, Anatole Deibler and his assistants came to set up the guillotine in the Boulevard Arago, and the police erected barriers to keep back a crowd largely composed of prostitutes who had come over the river in their night finery. The weather was exceptionally mild for the time of year. At first light on Boxing Day, Georges Gauchet was brought out, hands tied behind him, feet hobbled, the collar cut away from his shirt. When the barriers were removed, the girls from Montmartre surged forward to dip their handkerchiefs in the blood.

In the Chave prison on the outskirts of Marseilles languished Maître Georges Sarret, né Sarrejani, the company lawyer, while Kate and Philomena Schmidt were accommodated either in a women's wing there (for I do not know the prison) or elsewhere. Sarret's career in insurance fraud had drawn to a close in spring. Two elderly clients had died too abruptly, one after bedside jollity with champagne (hers laced with salts of zinc). Philomena had first been pulled in, and the other had given herself up. They had talked, and acid-bath dissolving had come into the conversation.

Me Sarret had nothing, so far as I have discovered, to do with the flourishing Marseilles *milieu*. He had moved only in the most respectable circles. It was in large part through mingling with those of the *milieu* that his personally more interesting or at least more attractive predecessor, Dr Bougrat, had got himself into such very dreadful trouble, though it could not have happened without that *nostalgie de la boue* (itself inexplicable and not properly *nostalgie*, since he had not been brought up to it) which caused him so to mingle. But here we should perhaps consider that southern *milieu* for its own fragrant sake. For, despite its advantages as a favoured part of a peculiarly delightful capital city, Montmartre merely paralleled Marseilles and was already in danger of being engulfed by its rival, which it never equalled for sheer monotonous violence except when men who had reached it by way of Marseilles were involved.

The criminal pre-eminence of Marseilles has survived the destruction by German occupying forces of that area to the north of the Old Port in which, between the wars, it bred. During that period, it perhaps deserves better of us than that we should describe it as a little Chicago. The town itself was smaller, certainly. Its population even now is under a million, whereas by 1930 Chicago had already topped three million. Marseilles is the second largest city of a country whose total population is only a quarter that of the United States and which until recently was far less industrialised and thus also less urbanised (even today, it is less urbanised than the United Kingdom). It had, however, the advantage of being also France's chief sea port, a town always full of foreign sailors with money in their pockets and one or the other of two thoughts in their heads, the port from which white slaves had been shipped at first to the Near and Middle East and North Africa and later to South America, the port of entry for narcotic drugs and, of course, the point for which restless and ambitious Corsicans, or Corsicans on the run, made automatically, once Ajaccio had supplanted Bastia, from which they might have made rather for Genoa, itself a town of some criminal note.

American criminal history is a subject in which I have read far less than I could wish, but, despite a healthy native tradition of banditry and feuding farther west, it seems beyond all question that urban gangsterism in the United States was the creation of Italian ponces, especially those from the two Sicilies. Though French nationals for 150 years, the Corsicans also were a kind of island Italians and to a decreasing extent still are, and *vendetta* was rather specially their idea. In Marseilles, their criminal activities were protected by a political boss, at once mayor and deputy, Simon (or Simone) Sabiani. Here, too, according to what I have read, there is some kind of parallel with Chicago.

The question is whether Marseilles imitated Chicago, and I do not think it did. French novelists were affected by Hollywood films and, when these appeared in translation, by the work of American novelists, but then French novelists did not know the underworld of Marseilles and would not have understood its language in any case, however well they might know the *argot* of La Villette, Belleville and Montmartre. For that language was Italian. In Chicago, there were soon enough non-Italian gangsters for a *lingua franca* to develop, no doubt containing some Far West elements, and this could be readily adopted by novelists and movie-actors. It seems to have been otherwise in Marseilles. The gangsters there were and still are likely to bear such Christian names as 'Ange' or 'Sauveur'. Though gallicised, these are quite un-French. They are clearly 'Angelo' and 'Salvatore'. The two great *caïds*, big shots or super-ponces in the Marseilles of the early 'thirties were a Neapolitan, Spirito, a Francesco who had become a François, and a Corsican, Paolo or Paul Carbone. Though we should read of them in our newspapers, over twenty years later, as Antoine and Mémé Guérini and though no doubt on their birth certificates they were Antoine and Barthélemy Guérini, we may assume that, in the Corsican village of Calenzana, the Guerini brothers had been Antonio and Bartolommeo and that abbreviations of those names would be used for them in the underworld of Marseilles, where they were already flourishing, though not yet on a scale to challenge the supremacy of Carbone and Spirito, who were Sabiani's intimates.

The American Depression at once increased the importance of the drug trade and favoured a Corsican take-over in Montmartre. Paris had been deprived of rich foreign customers for the natural commodity of women. Once things had begun to pick up again in the United States, the end of Prohibition would have made it unnecessary for rich Americans to go to Europe simply to drink good liquor. Meanwhile, not only had the trade in white powders assumed its own importance, but the footsore, hungry prostitutes were themselves on drugs. This gave the Corsicans of Marseilles a double advantage, in that they were able, with their readier access to the stuff, to tempt the girls away from their former protectors. This led to bad feeling, and there were *règlements de comptes* in every turning off the Boulevard de Clichy. Presently, the Corsicans began to shoot each other.

Two of the Corsican gangs were led by Ange Foata and the Stéfani brothers. They had been friends and colleagues, but became first rivals and then deadly personal enemies, to their common detriment, as well as to that of a child, the seven-year-old son of Foata's mistress, who, taken out for a Christmas treat and clutching a Father Christmas, was just kissing Uncle Ange in gratitude when a Stéfani brother came into the bar and started firing at the latter, wounding him and killing the child. Things went from bad to worse, and there were to be prison sentences, sealed lips in court and such dramatic scenes as that of Foata, armed with a rifle, waiting all night in a frozen cemetery and firing at Jean-Paul Stéfani, just out of prison, beside his wife's grave. A point would be reached at which Foata was in Guiana and the Stéfani brothers reigned supreme among the night-clubs of Montmartre, Jean-Paul himself being conspicuous for a big, chauffeur-driven Mercedes which he summoned with a blast on a whistle. This was not to save him from being eventually shot down while on foot. But, in the winter of 1931-2, it all lay in the future. For the moment, the activities of all three concerned rather the vice and narcotics squads than the crime squad.

This chapter shall end with what we may describe as Papillon's last throw. In March 1932, Mme Charrière left Vals-les-Bains for Paris on instructions from her husband at Fresnes. In her handbag were a revolver and letters in her own fair hand to various newspapers. It is clear that the devoted girl (a second woman had worked for Papillon, but had deserted him soon after his arrest) had been meant to post these before she went to Fresnes to see her husband (in them, she accused herself of the murder of Roland Legrand). On the morning of March 31st, husband and wife faced each other in the parlour at Fresnes. Nénette pulled out her 7.65 and, with strong and evidently practised first finger, discharged all six bullets in the general direction of her husband, carefully missing him. She was arrested, of course, and taken to St Lazare, where she remained until the beginning of July, when a sensible judge acquitted her of all but unauthorised possession of firearms, for which she received a sentence of two months, already served. That was the last of Henri-Antoine ('Papillon') Charrière's stunts in metropolitan France. He was transferred to the central prison at Caen, where he was to spend a year before embarking for Cayenne.

IN EARLY 1931, Julia Wallace was brutally battered to death in Liverpool. The trial of Alfred Arthur Rouse, the bigamist, who had burnt his unknown victim in a car, took place at Northampton assizes, and on the day of his conviction, near Berlin, Sylvestre Matushka began his short but spectacular career as a train-wrecker. In May, at Regensburg, was executed the Tetzner whose crime Rouse's had so closely copied. Also executed that year (in Cologne, by guillotine) was Peter Kuerten. In Frankfurt-am-Main, Eugen Weidmann, whose parents had welcomed him back from Canada and bought him a car, apparently in the hope that he would use it as a taxi, raided a villa at Sachshausen and tied up two women, for which he received a prison sentence of five years and and eight months, to be served at Preugesheim near by. Despite his previous convictions, the sentence seems heavy if all that happened was what Weidmann was later to describe in a red exercise book. His conduct, as always, seems to have been exemplary in prison, and he was presently made librarian.

Not for six years more would he appear in France. Pavel Gorguloff had first appeared there the previous year, leaving Czechoslovakia pursued by abortion charges. Though given a *permis de séjour* for no more than a fortnight, he had contrived to live for six months on the outskirts of Paris and there to contract a fourth marriage, subsequently installing himself in Monaco, where he gambled and continued to write, not only pamphlets but a long novel, *The Story of a Cossack*.

On March 1st, 1932, in New Jersey, a German, Bruno Hauptmann, abducted the son of a national, indeed a world hero, Colonel Lindbergh, and of his poet wife, Anne Morrow. On April 21st, in Marseilles, the police, tipped off, were waiting in ambush when a raid was made on a post-office by a gang of four who had previously specialised in robbery from moving trains, one of the four being a railway worker who pitched parcels out of the guard's van to the others waiting beside the track with a lorry. This had been accomplished without fatal or even serious casualties, but that post-office raid left three policemen dead. Two of the gang of four were quickly caught, a third traced to Spain and there held for extradition by the Spanish police. The fourth, Camille Maucuer, a short-sighted man in his early forties, was known to have gone to Avignon looking for a former mistress and an old friend of his father, an anarchist, who, however, had moved to Paris, where Maucuer might be expected to follow. Although two of its members were Corsicans, that little gang did not belong to the Marseilles *milieu* in the word's more specific sense.

On May 3rd, having finished *The Story of a Cossack*, Gorguloff posted its 636 manuscript pages to the Universitäts Verlag in Berlin, granting the publisher full rights without payment. Next day, he bought two revolvers and took a night train to Paris. Though no doubt mad enough by then, he showed method. Knowing that it was unwise for him to book into a hotel on his own, on the night of the 5th he picked up a prostitute, went with her to the kind of hotel where names were not asked for, was shown to a room and at once kicked the prostitute out and locked the door. Then he got out an exercise book, filled it, in Russian, with a wild account of his life and, at dawn, wrote, in French, on the cover : 'The Memoirs of Dr Paul Gorguloff, President of the Fascist Republican Party, who killed the President of the French Republic.' With this in one coat pocket and a loaded revolver in the other, he left the hotel and for the next six hours roamed the streets of Paris.

The President of the Republic at that time was Paul Doumer, aged seventy-five, a sufficiently active and pleasant old man with a white beard. His principal engagement on May 6th, 1932, was to inaugurate book week, the *journées du livre*, devoted that year to writers who had served in the Great War. Stalls had been set out in the Salomon de Rothschild hall in the Rue Berryer off the Avenue de Friedland, and one of them was devoted to the works of Claude Farrère, who was himself in attendance.

Like the more famous Pierre Loti, Claude Farrère was a naval officer who wrote exotic novels. Like Loti's, his name as a writer was a pseudonym, his real name being Frédéric-Charles Bargone. Though not much read now, his books had been very successful indeed in the years before the war. At 2.45 p.m. on May 6th, 1932, he cordially autographed one of his books for a big, powerfully-built man, clean-shaven, with wavy hair and a foreign accent, who gave his name as Paul Brade and said with truth that he was a Russian writer and an old soldier. At that moment, the presidential car drove up, and presently the head of State, with his entourage, had reached the Farrère stall, where the proud author gave him a *de luxe* copy, suitably inscribed, of *La Bataille*, a novel first published in 1909. For this gift the President just had time to thank him in gracious terms.

That, at any rate, is Montarron's account. *Figaro*'s, at the time, lays more stress on the fact that Claude Farrère was president of the *écrivains combattants* and formed part of the entourage. *Figaro*, then in a five-year phase of appearing without the definite article and transferred more than six years before to its present premises at the foot of the Champs Elysées, also called the pseudonymous big Russian Paul Brède, not Brade. However, when this last began firing at the neatly white-bearded president of the Republic, it is agreed that the novelist acted bravely, Montarron stating that he attempted to shield the President and *Figaro* that he grappled with the assailant. He was wounded in the arm by the last of four bullets, the second and third of which had struck the President with fatal effect, one of them entering behind the left ear and emerging from the right cheek. The old man died at a quarter past three the following morning.

The assassin, who was none other than Gorguloff, had by then been installed for some hours in a cell at the Santé prison. In the next cell, in which the light burned continually, lay a young man called Eugène Boyer, convicted in January, with his elder brother, of the murder of a widow for her savings. The elder brother, Alexandre, had been reprieved by the President because of his war record and would go to Guiana for life. Eugène had not been reprieved and was, had he known it, due to be topped at first light. The temporary shallow grave was ready for him at Ivry cemetery. The *bois de justice* had already been set up in the street. He slept uneasily, dreaming, he was to say later, that he was hammering long nails into the floor. Had the President lived two hours longer, Eugène Boyer would have gone to the guillotine. Having already reprieved the elder brother, it was unlikely that he had been minded to reprieve the younger, but a last-minute reprieve is always possible, so long as the Republic has a president, and, at Boyer's last minute, it had none. So the machine was dismantled, the shallow grave filled in.

President Doumer never knew that he had been assassinated.

Enquiring, while in a state of consciousness, how he came to be where he was and in such a state, he had been told that it was the result of a road accident and had murmured, as though satisfied, 'Ah, a road accident, a road accident. . . .' He was succeeded by President Lebrun, to whose notice the matter of a reprieve for Eugène Boyer would presently be brought, with happy effect (at any rate, Boyer thought so). It assured him of a quarter of a century in Guiana, ten years alongside his brother whom he hated, for at their trial each of the two had lied to save his own skin at the other's expense.

At his first session with the examining magistrate, M. Fougery, Gorguloff stated that he had killed President Doumer because the French ought to have driven the Bolsheviks out of Russia. He had previously thought to kill Presidents Hindenburg and Masaryk for similar reasons. The real nature of his relations with the Bolsheviks was obscure, and *Figaro* was convinced that he had acted on orders from Moscow, as, they continued to imply, had Shalom Schwartzbard six years before. Information came in from Interpol headquarters in Vienna, and some of it was consonant with Gorguloff's own account. He came from the Caucasus and had indeed served with the Russian armies in the Great War, receiving a head wound. After the Treaty of Brest-Litovsk, he had studied medicine for a while at Rostov-on-Don and there contracted the first of his four marriages.

Presently, there came forward a former Cossack officer in Denikin's army, Lazareff, who said that, under the pseudonym of Mengol, Gorguloff had for a while been head of the Cheka in Rostov, that he had been responsible for the shooting of 200 people there and that he, Lazareff, had personally been tortured by Gorguloff (there were details of finger-breaking and so on). The judicial inquiry lasted under three months, which is very short indeed by French standards. Gorguloff plagued the examining magistrate, his warders and the two lawyers appointed to defend him with rambling talk about an 'idea' of his, whose rejection would lead to the ruin of Europe. The trial opened on July 25th and continued for three days. From the dock, Gorguloff ranted on about his idea, but also railed first at the doctors who said that he was mad and then at those who insisted that he was sane and therefore responsible for his actions. On the last day of the trial, tribute to Farrère's bravery was paid by the retiring Minister of Defence, M. Pietri, who, with various senior policemen, had formed part of the entourage on May

6th and who spoke of the novelist leaping boldly on the big, armed man. The jury were out for no more than twenty minutes.

As predicted, Camille Maucuer came to Paris to see his former mistress and his father's old friend, and there, after a wild chase by car, he was arrested on August 10th and sent back to Marseilles to await trial in Aix, which would result in death sentences on him and another and the dispatch of two Corsicans to Guiana. During his statutory six weeks in the condemned cell, Gorguloff did not cease to write, his 'idea' gradually losing all political tinge and becoming pantheistically mystical, with laws which specifically forbade the taking of any form of life in May. His own was taken on September 14th at first light. Because of his height, bull neck and massive shoulders, there were difficulties with the guillotine.

It is uncommon for an established writer to be so closely involved with a murder that he is called in evidence at the trial. Paul Bourget was present in the next room when Mme Caillaux shot Gaston Calmette, editor of *Le Figaro*, in 1914, and extracts from his latest novel were read out in court, for they had a curious relevance to the case. The only writer in English I can think of who appeared in a murder case was Oliver Wendell Holmes. That was in 1850, at the supreme judicial court of Massachusetts, when Professor John White Webster was found guilty of the murder of his colleague and benefactor, Dr George Parkman. Dr Holmes was Parkman professor of anatomy and physiology in the medical school at Harvard, and, although he had known both Webster and Parkman and might well have given evidence about the relations between the two and their movements on the day of the crime, it was as an expert witness that he was called, for he had examined the savagely stabbed and hammered body by way of autopsy.

In a case I hope to touch on in a future book, Joseph Kessel, in 1953, was to give evidence on behalf of a friend and fellow-Latvian, Michel Gelfand, who in 1932, after four years of Parisian debauch and a stay at a sanatorium in the Alps, settled in with the owner of a hotel at Megève in that health-giving climate. Murders by women that year and the next were later to receive important literary attention, which is a kind of testimony, though not given in court. The first of these was the poisoning of both her well-to-do parents by a Left Bank tart, Violette Nozières, who contentedly declared that it had been about time. This revolutionary sentiment greatly endeared her to the *surréalistes*, who seem to have been partial to young murderesses, for the first issue of *La Revue Surréaliste*, eight years before, had been illustrated with a photograph of Germaine Berton, the killer of Marius Plateau on political grounds. When in due course Violette Nozières came up for trial, the occasion was to be celebrated in a poem by Paul Éluard.

She was already in prison at the Petite Roquette when, on February 2nd, 1933, occurred the provincial double murder which was to inspire a play, *Les Bonnes*, by Jean Genet, himself a minor figure in criminal history, a male prostitute and thief, whose attachment to the case may have originated in direct counterpoise to the interest the *surréalistes* were taking in that of Violette Nozières. Here, he may well have felt, was meatier stuff. The murder took place at Le Mans. Christine and Léa Papin did what, one supposes, confined and harried maidservants have often thought of doing. They killed their mistress and their mistress's daughter. It was truly a deed of darkness, for it took place during a light failure in the house, for which, the sisters subsequently claimed, they thought they would be blamed. Afterwards, they huddled together, with a candle, on a bed at the top of the house and waited for the police. The murders themselves were committed with blunt instruments, including a pewter pot. Then the sisters attacked the bodies with knives and gouged the eyes out. The sight of an eye on the staircase, in the light of an electric torch, first intimated to the police, when they broke in, what kind of thing had happened in the house, that of the respectable solicitor by whom the girls had been employed for seven years past.

Less than a fortnight later, at Miami, by firing at their president elect, Giuseppe Zangara reminded Americans that the criminal gifts of Italians were not confined to organising brothels and booze in Chicago. In Berlin, twelve days later again, the gutted Reichstag marked a further step in Hitler's final accession to power. On April 7th, the end of Prohibition disorganised gang life in the United States. The replacement, however, of speakeasies by smart new premises openly selling good liquor at first led frustrated gangsters to wreck these and then suggested to some wily Italian that their proprietors might be willing to pay not to have them wrecked, whence protection was added to prostitution as a basic means of livelihood.

On October 27th, André Gide, at his family home in Normandy, noted in his diary :

Stupefying article by Morand in the front pages of *1933*, the new weekly launched by Massis. Others have called for 'more light'. Morand wants more air. *Give us Air! Give us Air!* is the title of the article, in which he explains what he means by this. He ends with the sentence : 'We want clean corpses.' I had to have this explained to me. The allusion is, it seems, to the recent murder of Dufrenne. Does Morand, then, want only respectable people to be killed?

Manager of the Casino de Paris and a leading figure in the theatrical world, with, also, some pretensions to respectability as a city councillor and parliamentary candidate, Oscar Dufrenne had been murdered and robbed in his office by a male prostitute, who was later extradited from Spain but never convicted, the homosexual *milieu* having its own rules of silence. No doubt Dufrenne's scandalous death increased the already well-developed and fully justified public sense of corruption in high places.

The day after Gide's note, the Papin sisters were brought to trial at Le Mans. The elder, Christine, was sentenced to death, the younger, Léa, to ten years with hard labour. Death sentences passed on women had been a dead letter since 1887, though a reform of the previous year, whereby the jury had a say not only in the verdict but in the sentence, might conceivably have quickened it. Christine Papin's sentence was in fact commuted to twenty years with hard labour, but in a very short while she went demonstrably mad and was committed to Rennes asylum, where she would live on for little more than a year. Also that October, Henri-Antoine ('Papillon') Charrière, transferred from Caen to the Île de Ré, embarked on the *La Martinière* for Cayenne. With him, so far as I can see, must have sailed Guy Davin, murderer of the American Richard Wall. Davin's case had aroused far more public interest, and a photograph of the time shows his mother, in what look like expensive furs and presumably having found a privileged place away from the mob which commonly assembled to watch embarkations of convicts, sitting alone, on a low stone wall, waiting for the convoy which included her son to shuffle along the quayside, wearing fezlike caps and flanked by helmeted soldiers, rifles at the slope on the right shoulder and with bayonets fixed. It might console her to think that, in Guiana, Guy would be under his father's eye, for, after a financial scandal, her husband had gone out to join the prison service there.

Arrived that year in Paris from Villeneuve-sur-Yonne, the former mayor of that town, Dr Marcel Petiot, had put up his plate in the Rue de Caumartin and issued a prospectus in which he described himself as 'using the most up-to-date equipment, with X, UV and UR rays, faradisation, ionisation, diathermy, ozonotherapy, aerotherapy, *et cetera*', and which further stated that Dr Petiot restored lost youth, would spare future mothers the pains of childbirth, soothe those of cancer, ulceration and neuritis, relieve constipation and cure nervous patients of drug addiction. Petiot had left ugly rumours behind him on the Yonne, including those which related to two missing women and the sudden death of a patient who would have been the chief witness in a threatened action over the later disappearance. These did not prevent him from soon acquiring a list of respectable patients in that not unfashionable part of Paris, and for three years he was to attract no unwelcome attention from the police, let alone from the Faculty. A man not yet forty, with a son, Gérard, aged five, he was neatly made, rather good-looking, almost swarthy in colouring but clean-shaven, with nicely waving hair and well-spaced eyes. There is no reason to suppose that he then showed any of the defiant cynicism he was to display in court thirteen years later. His bedside manner was, we may feel sure, exemplary, his social manner charming and such as to inspire confidence on all hands.

The *La Martinière* docked at Cayenne on November 6th, and among the five or six hundred who went ashore were Henri Charrière and Guy Davin, the latter to be greeted by his father. Among others there at the time was still the Breton master sawyer, Guillaume Seznec. They would presently be joined by the Boyer brothers, with the younger of whom, Eugène, Seznec was to find himself engaged in a notorious and bloody feud, while, after years of preferential treatment, Davin was to come to a very sticky end indeed. Dr Bougrat, remarried and with the first of a series of daughters by his Venezuelan wife, must already have been installed as the treasured only doctor on the island of Margarita. A yet earlier escaper, Émile Courgibet, who had got away in 1922 and spent seven years in reaching Caracas, had by 1931 got as near home as Spain, where it was his misfortune to meet the small but deadly Émile Buisson. By the end of 1933, he was in Paris but found the city unwholesome.

IN THE afternoon of January 9th, 1934, died the crooked financier, Alexander Stavisky, with a hole in the head and less than two pints of blood in his veins. He had been found, stretched out on the floor of a locked room in which none of the furniture was disturbed, by men from what for the moment was still not the Sûreté Nationale but the Sûreté Générale, led by Superintendent Charpentier, sent to arrest him. Jean Belin, of the Sûreté, a man of the Left, and Lucien Zimmer, of the Prefecture, a man of the Right, agree that it was a genuine suicide, and we can only accept their joint conclusion, while admitting that there may nevertheless have been signs of some *mise en scène*, the oddest (and the most interesting to criminalisticians) being that the small 6.35 bullet, which had passed through the dead man's head, was found in the wall at a height of less than four and a half feet, while Stavisky was a man of almost six.

At any rate, the extreme Right claimed that Stavisky had been murdered by the police in order to prevent disclosures damaging to left-wing politicians, of which no small number were nevertheless made. Demonstrations organised by both the extreme Right and the communists culminated on January 27th with the resignation of the Chautemps government and the formation of another by the supposed strong man Daladier. The prefect of police, Jean Chiappe, hated by Belin, idolised by Zimmer, was dismissed by Daladier on February 3rd, and it was this treacherous action, as much as anything, which produced, on February 6th, riots which brought France once more to the brink of revolution. The communists joined happily in these, just to cause trouble, but what seriously threatened was a take-over by the extreme Right, more particularly by the Croix de Feu organisation led by Colonel de la Rocque, whose nerve seems to have failed. All this is, luckily, historians' history, and I am not required to sort it out, for neither the Croix de Feu nor the Ligue d'Action Française, nor yet the *jeunesses patriotes* and other right-

122

wing organisations then active, were murderous or otherwise criminal in a sense which concerns the present volume. From my specialised point of view, I would like to say, however, that at scenes of riot and revolution no witness is likely to be so exact as that of the police and that orthodox historians would be as foolish to ignore Belin and Zimmer on February 1934 as, on July 1832, for instance, they are to pay so very little attention to Canler and Vidocq.

Daladier went, and in came a former President of the Republic, Doumergue. Within a fortnight, there took place another death in curious circumstances, which again we must probably take as suicide, that of M. le Conseiller (this makes him the equivalent of what in England and Wales is a High Court judge) Albert Prince, who had studied the Stavisky files, was upset by what he found there and had been called on to give evidence before the *premier président* of the Court of Cassation (his, as we might say, permanent Lord Chief Justice), but had postponed the occasion with the excuse that his wife in Dijon was ill. On February 20th, his mortal remains were found by the railway track near Dijon. There were signs of him having been tied to the rails by his feet, and the clamour on the Right was that Stavisky documents had been with him in his brief-case and that this had been stolen. Hotfoot from the Rue des Saussaies, Belin convinced himself that it had indeed been suicide, but a colleague who did not agree was the Pierre Bony whom, ten years before, we saw planting evidence in the form of a typewriter on Guillaume Seznec. Betweenwhiles, Bony had made a fool of himself over a wholly imaginary murder of the American film star Jeannette MacDonald, in which, he had claimed, Maurice Chevalier was involved. This, however, had not stood in the way of his career, and in the Prince affair he was given a free hand and described as France's leading policeman, a marked case of pride going before a fall.

Bony's belief was that the crime was connected with the Marseilles *milieu* and specifically with Carbone and Spirito. It is at least of literary interest that, among Parisian crime reporters, one who had been hoaxed into sharing Bony's belief was the Belgian we know and admire as Georges Simenon. In his column, he named names. One evening, a group of these and their friends caught him in the entrance hall of the Carlton, where he was staying, and debagged him. Carbone and Spirito were in fact arrested, but the case against them was quickly non-suited, and they returned from Aix to Marseilles amid scenes of popular rejoicing. Bony himself was arrested on blackmail charges and, after being held on these and others for over a year, would, discharged the service, be released with a suspended sentence of three years hanging over him. That was not, however, to be the end of Bony.

At Aix, meanwhile, were belatedly brought to trial the insurance trickster, acid-bath dissolver and champagne-poisoner, Maître Georges Sarret, with the two German sisters, Kate and Philomena Schmidt. Kate Schmidt was defended by Moro-Giafferi. The two women were sent for ten years to the prison at Montpellier in which Marie Lafarge had spent much that length of time almost a century before. Sarret was executed on April 10th, 1934, in Marseilles.

The year's most spectacular political crimes were committed on German-speaking territory and thus in German, a language whose barked orders and satisfied grunts, the dreadful gasping of whose glottal stops and the sentences groping towards the false climax of their verbal endings we may fancy we hear throughout the night of June 30th, the Night, as it is called, of the Long Knives, oddly, since most of its victims were shot, a hundred and fifty of them in a line, Hitler's old friends, Nazis of the wrong faction, Nazis of the Left, or when, on the afternoon of July 25th, that number of S.S. in Austrian uniforms pushed their way into the Viennese chancellery and shot Dolfuss or when, within a week, Hindenburg died *de sa belle mort* and Hitler finally came to power. In view of all that was to follow, it is interesting to recall that Mussolini, meeting him six weeks before in Venice, had thought Hitler a poor thing and that he had 60,000 troops on the Brenner to prevent the *Anschluss*. It was to him that the Croat separatists, the Ustachi, and their Macedonian counterparts then looked for help and money, which the Italians willingly supplied in manoeuvres against France.

The French foreign minister, Louis Barthou, aged seventy-two, last (but for his old enemy, Caillaux, and, for the moment, Poincaré) of that generation of French statesmen, had visited Dolfuss earlier in the year. In early July, he had been in London, getting no sense out of Sir John Simon and Ramsay MacDonald. In September, he realised one of his ambitions when the U.S.S.R. was admitted to the League of Nations, greatly to the annoyance of the Swiss. The following month, in furtherance of his Mediterranean plans, Alexander I of Yugoslavia was to pay a State visit to France. While the Queen travelled by train from Belgrade to Paris, the King would be brought by cruiser, the *Dubrovnik*, to Marseilles, where, landing in the Old Port from his own naval launch, he would be welcomed to

Interpreter taking the oath, Gorguloff and below him Maître Géraud

7 Weidmann shortly after his arrest

8 Versailles, June 16th, 1939

French soil by Barthou and General Georges, with whom he would drive triumphantly up the Canebière in an open Delage. The crown prince was at the time a schoolboy in England.

This, too, is historians' history, but the security precautions may somewhat concern us. In May, the Sûreté Générale had changed its name and become the Sûreté Nationale, but this was not to improve its performance under M. Berthouin, who was perhaps a little young for the job and who is known to have had brought to his attention in August a Serbo-Croat paper, published in Berlin, in which the Ustachi openly proclaimed their intention of assassinating King Alexander at the time of his French visit (to do it on French soil would serve Mussolini's turn, alienating Yugoslavia from France). There is an account in English, in Belin's reminiscences, of his own subsequent investigation, together with the statement, under interrogation, of one of the conspirators, who was to have made a second attempt by bomb in Marseilles, had the first attempt by revolver failed. Others were variously deployed, for further alternative attempts, in Paris and at Versailles, their headquarters being outside France, at Lausanne. From Paris to Marseilles, to inspect the preparations, went police top brass in the person of Assistant Commissioner Sistéron. To a close escort of police he preferred the more decorative Garde Mobile on horseback. The local police were overworked as a result of municipal elections, for which, in that excitable, corrupt and violent neighbourhood, a strong *service d'ordre* was needed. In Aix, during the night of the 8th-9th, the sub-prefect, Albert Sauvare, dispensed his tired men from the usual small-hours hotel check, which would have revealed the presence, at the best-known hotel in the town, the Moderne, of a group of named suspects, who at dawn were able to take the road for Marseilles, an hour's drive away.

The King duly landed and was taken to the car, with its broad and convenient running-board. The police stood with their backs to the crowd. Barthou sat beside the King, both wearing pince-nez, facing General Georges. The Garde Mobile pranced, swords drawn, led by Lieutenant-Colonel Piollet. Cameras whirred or clicked. Opposite the Café Glacier, a man ran forward, jumped on the running-board of the Delage, shot the King through the heart and turned his revolver on Barthou and General Georges. On his head descended Colonel Piollet's sword, and the crowd surging forward finished him off, but also blocked the car's progress for so long that, by the time it reached the prefecture, Barthou, who had been shot

E

through the arm and needed only a tourniquet, was so weak from loss of blood (I here adopt Ragon's account, not Belin's, which at a number of points it contradicts) that he died almost at once, murmuring : 'I can't see what's happening now. My eyeglasses? Where are my eyeglasses?' The more severely wounded General Georges recovered. There had never been any hope for the King.

It is said (by Ragon) that the crew of the *Dubrovnik* were barely restrained from shelling Marseilles. Goering obtained a film of the occasion and, visiting Belgrade for the royal funeral, had it shown there to demonstrate to the Yugoslavs how little care France had taken of their King's safety. Three of the conspirators were caught and would be tried and sentenced in France, but the ringleaders had escaped to Italy and were not extradited, though Mussolini found it advisable to imprison Ante Pavelitch for a while. Heads of course rolled administratively in Paris and Marseilles, at the Sûreté Nationale those of Berthouin and Sistéron, in the Marseilles area notably that of the sub-prefect at Aix, M. Sauvare, who throughout the remaining thirty-six years of his life would not cease to proclaim that it had all been his fault. The Minister of the Interior or, as we should say, Home Secretary, Sarraut, also went. At the Quai d'Orsay, Louis Barthou was succeeded by the disastrous Pierre Laval.

THREE DAYS after the assassination, Violette Nozières was sentenced to death, a sentence automatically commuted to one of life imprisonment. In prison at Vannes was Michel Henriot, a silver-fox farmer, the son of Morbihan's chief prosecuting magistrate. In May, he had attacked his lame and almost speechless wife, married the previous year, with a poker, then shot her six times with a .22 rifle. The telephone having been knocked off its rest at the outset of these proceedings, the prolonged and noisy murder had been heard at the nearest post-office, whose switchboard-operator did not report the matter, it being common knowledge that the oddest things went on in that house. In prison at Mulhouse was Jean-Baptiste, elder brother of Émile Buisson. 'Mimile' had not grown much since we first saw him, three days after the Armistice, before the juvenile court at Paray-le-Monial in Burgundy. At thirty-two, he stood no more than five feet three, though he was neatly made, with regular, unsmiling features, haunting eyes, dark complexion, thick black hair brushed back. For a reason unknown, 'Mimile' called his elder brother 'le Nus', but to the underworld Jean-Baptiste Buisson was *Fatalitas*, having this Latin word tattooed on his chest.

The younger brother went to see the elder in prison at Mulhouse and suggested an escape plan. The fractures ward of the prison hospital was on the ground floor, with unbarred windows opening on to a garden. Le Nus must break something, get himself transferred there and at once make his way out. Mimile would be waiting with a car, false papers and a new friend, Émile Courgibet. From Mulhouse to Bâle was barely twenty miles. In his cell, Jean-Baptiste Buisson propped one leg up on his bed and bashed at the shin with a stool until it was broken. His leg in plaster, he was put to bed in the fractures ward. Within an hour, according to Montarron, he got out of bed, took a neighbour's crutches, shouldered a nurse aside and joined his brother and Courgibet, who got him into the car, into Switzerland and to Genoa, where, after a convalescent pause, they took ship for China.

Émile Buisson was never a *milieu* man in the proper sense, but an altogether different type of gangster, happier with a bank-raid or anything carefully planned, short and violent in the execution, a little man with a gun to add to his height (if you risk gunfights, it is also a practical advantage to be small, since you present less target). The brothers bought an old crate of an aeroplane, and, with an American pilot as mad as themselves, they went in for gunrunning to one or another of the Chinese bandit factions. With the money they made from this, which was to Mimile's taste, they bought Jean-Baptiste a smart night-club in the French concession in Shanghai, profitable in prostitution and drugs. This also suited Émile Courgibet, a comparatively mature-minded, patient man who liked a steady job (this is suggested by his later history). They were to stay some two years in Shanghai, but in the course of the drug trade were made responsible for the body of a Chinese, who had cheated a Maltese friend of theirs, being found floating in the Whangpoo, so that it became advisable to return to Europe.

WHEN A murder is being investigated, discovery of the murderer is held to require the establishment of motive, means and opportunity. When the case against him is presented in court, in the United Kingdom at any rate, the question of motive may be quite disregarded. Attempts, by writers on the subject, to classify murder are commonly made in terms either of motive or of means, though opportunity is clearly in part an explanation of what has been so often pointed out, viz. that people more frequently murder close acquaintances than perfect strangers. Questions of opportunity, too, figure largely in many of the best fictional detective stories.

Among the French cases so far noted here (French cases in so far as the crimes were committed in France and so fell within the jurisdiction of French courts) have been eight in which murder was committed (by Villain, Germaine Berton, Bonomini, Merabashvili, Schwartzbard, Gorguloff, the Macedonian who killed Louis Barthou and King Alexander, and the communist anti-demonstrators in 1925) for some kind of political reason; eighteen or more (Landru, Train 5, Girard, René Jean, the Boyer brothers, Gauchet, Davin, Mme de Kerninon, Mestorino, Nourric, Sarret, Seznec and Bougrat if they were guilty, the murder of Oscar Dufrenne and most of the cases of British citizens murdered in France) in which the motive was more or less unambiguously gain; four (Mlle du Bot de Talhouët, Violette Nozières, the Papin sisters and Charrière if he was guilty) crimes of revenge; a double case (the murders of Mme Blanc and her son) for which motive was never established; what we may think a true *crime passionnel*, with jealousy as the prime driving force (Courgibet's murder of his mistress); from four to seven (Bessarabo, Burger, Dervaux, the young Reiser and Petiot's presumed early murders) in which the purpose was what Fryn Tennyson Jesse would have called 'elimination' (only in the case of Petiot's male patient that of a potentially dangerous witness); and two in which murder was incidental or, as we should once have said, 'constructive' (the Maucuer post-office raid and the death of a child when the intended victim was Ange Foata), while, at the point in time we have reached, the police were looking for a man called Auguste Méla (known as 'Gu le Terrible'), doubtless of remoter Corsican origin but born in Marseilles, who in 1933 had killed a sentry while raiding an air-force base. As to means, firearms were much in evidence, with some use of knives, none of explosives or burning alive, some poisoning, perhaps strangulation in the case of Landru. As to propinquity providing opportunity, it was consanguineous only in the cases of Violette Nozières and Pierre Dreiser, marital or at least sexually intimate in those of Mme Bessarabo, Dervaux, Mme de Kerninon, Mlle du Bot de Talhouët, Landru and Courgibet; and a matter of prior association in business or some degree of social intimacy with René Jean, Mestorino, Davin, Petiot, Seznec, Charrière and Bougrat if they were guilty, Dufrenne's murderer, Sarret, Girard and (with a difference) the Papin sisters. The political murderers all knew who their victims were, but had never previously met them. The victims of the Train 5 gang, the Boyer brothers, Gauchet, Nourric and the 'constructive' murderers were either total strangers or slight acquaintances, their identity a matter of more or less total indifference to those who killed them.

To most of us, I fancy, crimes arising out of some form of personal association, a strong feeling being assumed to exist between murderer and victim, are more interesting than crimes of perfect indifference, more interesting even than political crimes seen purely in terms of their criminality. Political crimes are fraught with consequences, often incalculable. Murder at random is socially dangerous, whence, in our foolish Homicide Act of 1957, murders committed 'in the course or furtherance of theft' and 'by shooting or causing an explosion' were alone regarded as capital irrespective of victim or serial number. About the guilt involved in a political murder, few of us can be assumed to be wholly proof against a tendency to estimate it by whether our own political views more nearly resemble those of the victim or the murderer. Among crimes of propinquity, special condemnation was formerly given to parricide and to the murder of a husband by his wife. This was petty treason, while indeed the extreme form of high treason was also parricide, since a king was the father of his people, as some other heads of State have been felt to be, while to Villain, we may guess, Jaurès, though by no means a head of State, was symbolically a wicked father, flauntingly unfaithful not to a wife in the madhouse but to young Raoul's greater mother, France.

I do not propose to venture far into this field, but further possible classifications do suggest themselves. Like the class war, the sex war is largely symbolic. In the sphere of culpable homicide, it becomes real. Murders of men by women and vice versa are, we might say, *l'amour* continued by other means. If, among the cases we have listed, we bracket off those (the majority) in which men killed men and a few in which women killed or helped to kill women, and view our period to date as a phase in the sex war, we shall find, on counting casualties, no strategically important victory for either side. From a male point of view, the peerless hero was Landru, but, him apart, Mmes Bessarabo and de Kerninon, Mlle du Bot de Talhouët, Germaine Berton and Violette Nozières were more than a match for René Jean, the Boyer brothers, Courgibet and Dervaux. It is true that Violette Nozières killed her mother, too, and that fact, together with young Reiser's real and what I have suggested may have been Villain's symbolic parricide, ought perhaps to remind us that, as I began by saying, the oldest of our *dramatis personae* were victims. The trend has been maintained. For the most part, Landru killed within his age-group, and so did young Courgibet. In general, husbands and wives are much of an age, Mme de Kerninon being indeed older than her husband but killing him only when he was involved with a woman younger than herself. The tendency otherwise in domestic crime is for the old to be killed for their money. The victims of political crime are commonly older than their murderers. At least in one sort of killing, the ambitious young are eliminating the old. If Freud was right, there is a parricide hidden in most young men.

There is one type of crime, in most of the accepted classifications, in which the victim is commonly the younger, and that is the sadistic sex crime, of which (such are the aberrations of sexual desire) the victim may even be a child, female or male. To date, we have noted, in passing, remarkable sadists in Germany and the United States, but none in France, unless it were the murderer of Nurse Daniels, whose body, by the time it was discovered, had been too long weathered to show the obvious signs. Within our period, there had been sex murders in the United Kingdom, those, for instance, of Burrows, Allaway and the undiscovered murderer of eleven-year-old Vera Page. France had not been in the past, nor was to be in the future, free of this blight, several of its most notable carriers being priests, which tends to support the view that repression is its breeding-ground, but whatever outbreaks there had been in our period did not make *causes célèbres* during the first fifteen years after the Great War.

The Breton fox-farmer, Michel Henriot, was in fact a sadist, as soon appeared after his arrest. His murder of his wife (who was, incidentally, much of his own age) was not at all the typical sex crime and might not have struck anyone as the crime of a sadist, had not her letters to her sister been presented in evidence before the small court of assize in Vannes and printed in *Détective*. From these it appears that the foxy-faced, chinless, wispy-moustached, pale epileptic was not quite impotent sexually, but that he had married this lame and almost speechless young woman mainly because he wanted someone to beat and torture and that, fond of shooting other game, he shot her in the end to obtain a new excitement.

His case came up for trial in Vannes in late 1935, shortly after
the discovery at Chaumont, three hundred miles to the east, of the
body of a child, Nicole Marescot, who had been abducted and killed
six months before, on Good Friday, by a prematurely bald young
transvestite, Gabriel Socley, who liked either to wear false beard
and moustache or to dress and pad himself out as a woman before
interfering with little girls and who was sent to the special prison at
Château Thierry, then perhaps more nearly equivalent to our
Broadmoor. Henriot might have benefited from a similar disposition
on the part of his jury, but there had been too much method in his
madness. Shortly before treating himself to the sensation of shooting
his wife, he had taken out an insurance policy on her life and had
already made a move to collect when he was arrested.

AFTER THIRTY years of ups and downs in the white slave traffic, Riga-born Red Max Kassel, aged fifty-six and with a badly scarred face, was living in London, where he had first had a Frenchwoman on the streets in the early years of the century. When, around 1928, the road to Buenos Aires had been somewhat blocked by League of Nations pressure and a new Argentinian government, he had gone to Montreal, where he was dogged by misfortune. Back in London, he had a small jeweller's shop as cover for his activities as a fence, with one Frenchwoman on the streets. He was known by the name of Allard and understood to be a French Canadian, as was another Monsieur Georges, who lived in Great Newport Street and also had world-weary proxenete, known as Édouard or Charles Lacroix or one woman on the streets, by name either Paulette Bernard or Suzanne Bertron. To or from Lacroix, whose real name was Robert or Roger Vernon and who had escaped from the Guiana settlements in 1927, Red Max had lent or borrowed either £100 or £25. The question of repayment led to a quarrel on the evening of January 23rd, 1936. It ended with Kassel dead on the floor of the flat in Great Newport Street, with wounds in his belly made by from one to six bullets.

In essence, what happened to 'Max le Rouge' or 'le Rouqin' (also known, in his later years, as 'Max le Balafré' or 'Scarface') is clear enough. It was some kind of *règlement de comptes* in an expatriate *milieu*. It occurred in a world in which real and assumed names vary and fluctuate unusually, and, as the matter concerned the police in two countries, there was also some likelihood of mishearing and mistranscription. There are three accounts of the matter in books on my shelves, respectively by a senior French policeman who was administratively involved, a French journalist who covered the case both in Paris and in London at the time and a young English writer who does not state what his source was but who clearly felt every confidence in it. Some discrepancies between the three accounts seemed to yield to a little commonsense. Two of the three writers agree that the murder was committed on January and not May 23rd, 1936, while Belin also mentions the winter weather (in connection with the fact that Max's body was to be discovered without overcoat) and Montarron's assignment to the case was somewhat delayed. I state, as Belin does, that the flat was in Great Newport Street and not (with Rickards) Soho's Little Newport Street or (with Montarron) simply Newport Street, because in present-day London, while there is indeed also a Newport Place, there is a Great Newport but no Little Newport or plain Newport Street.

There is no significant disagreement about the discovery, on the morning of the 24th, of Max's body by a Mr Sayer, a carpenter cycling to work, in a ditch or under a hedgerow in a country lane outside St Albans, Hertfordshire. Name-tabs and makers' labels had been removed from his clothing, which was not mass-produced cheap stuff. Into one jacket pocket had been stuffed a collar and tie neatly folded. There was no money in any of the pockets, but an expensive ring still encircled the little finger of the left (Belin) or right (Montarron) hand. A safe-deposit key was also found. Marks on the face and knuckles suggested that the dead man had fought for his life. Tyre-marks had trespassed on the grass verge. From these signs or clues a Chief Inspector Sharpe from Scotland Yard made a number of intelligent deductions and thereafter took a sensible course of action. A pathologist's report took care of the time of death. The folded collar and tie suggested that a woman might have been involved. The safe-deposit key led to the customer known as Émile Allard. According to Rickards, the dead man's fingerprints and description were immediately flashed to the police in every major city in Europe. According to Belin, Chief Inspector Sharpe suspecting that the dead man's claim to be a French-Canadian was simply a cover to his being French, Scotland Yard telephoned Belin directly, and he asked them for a photograph, a set of fingerprints and a full description of the dead man. At any rate, the *service d'identité judiciaire* soon came up with an answer to who he was. By means which Belin circumstantially but, to my mind, not quite adequately describes, Scotland Yard got on the trail of Vernon and his girl-friend but found that they had left Great Newport Street. They were arrested at a hotel in Paris.

Members of the C.I.D. and the Sûreté Nationale had a pleasant

time visiting each other's manors, and we hear of a British Inspector
Lander who spoke French, including underworld *argot*, like a
native and who, to great applause, stood up in a Montmartre night-
club and sang folk songs from the Auvergne. As the murder of Red
Max had taken place in England, it was thought here that his
alleged murderer, though a French national, should be extradited,
but the French kept Vernon, by most people's reckoning luckily for
him, since here he would most certainly have been hanged. For the
moment, he remained at the Santé.

On April 14th, 1936, Dr Marcel Petiot was arrested for the theft
of a book from a bookshop in the Boulevard St Michel, the students'
familiar Boul' Mich' on the Left Bank. He said that he had taken
it absent-mindedly, its interest for him being that he thought it
might help his researches into the possibility of a pump for extract-
ing hardened faeces from the constipated. In court, psychiatric
grounds were again invoked, and Dr Petiot was confined at Ivry,
for how long seems obscure, though, when we see him again, in
1940, he will be found still or again in practice in the Rue de
Caumartin, without a stain on his medical character and not in the
least short of money.

Raoul Villain was to be found, twenty-two years after his murder
of Jean Jaurès, living on Spanish territory. He had settled in the
village of San Vicente on the coast of the island of Ibiza, which lies
midway between Majorca and the mainland. Now turned fifty, he
lived in a weird house built by himself, devoted to a cult of the
figure of Joan of Arc and assiduous in his attendance at church,
where he was more than once observed to weep. They were not,
however, tears of contrition for the crime which had gone so re-
markably unpunished, for he continued to affirm that what he had
done was duly chastise a man engaged in acts of treason.

On July 18th, 1936, the Spanish civil war broke out at last.
Among the incidents of its first two months was the bombing by
some of General Franco's aircraft, whether from the mainland or
from Majorca, on September 13th, a Sunday, of Ibiza, which had
remained in loyalist hands. By way of reprisal, the loyalists shot 239
political prisoners and then, to make the number round, went looking for Raoul Villain. On Monday morning, he was found with

two bullets in him on the beach at San Vicente. He was still breathing, but died later that day.

In PRISON at Preugesheim, near Frankfurt-am-Main, two young Parisians had served the greater part of their sentences for currency fiddling. Their names were Roger Million and Jean Blanc. The latter, fair in colouring, nervous and thoroughly stupid, was the son of prosperous shopkeepers, led astray and never quite comfortable about it. Million was sharper, a corner-boy, ill-spoken, his father a waiter. Among the German prisoners were Fritz Frommer, in for a political offence, and Eugen Weidmann, who had already served five years for armed robbery with assault but who, for good conduct, general brightness and a comparative literacy, including a knowledge of English and, as presently appeared, some aptitude for French, had been appointed librarian. Frommer was a dull stick, but Weidmann was outwardly cheerful, lively and enterprising. He was rather good-looking, especially in profile, rather tall, dark for a German, darker than either of the Frenchmen. He was also left-handed. Wholly masculine in manner, there is some evidence to suggest that, as might be expected with his history, he had been versatile in his choice of sexual partners and that, at twenty-seven, he was tending to settle for his own sex. There is no suggestion that either Million or Blanc was other than normally heterosexual, except in so far as the latter lacked all masculine pride.

A point of general interest in what Weidmann was later to write about his first dealings with Blanc and Million is its sidelight on the German metal shortage in 1936 and how even this could be turned to individual advantage. A job given to some of the less ham-fisted prisoners was dismantling old telephones for the sake of the nickel, copper and iron which they contained. The ear-pieces remained, and from these it appears that small receiving sets were able to be made, on which, when these were connected to the light, the prisoners could listen to Hessische Rundfunk, thus, for example, in the spring having been able to follow the progress of the Abyssinian War. As librarian, Weidmann moved about freely, distributing books, and had been able to fix his French friends up with a 'musical bug'. They would be released before him. They promised to keep in touch. He might join them in France. On release, Frommer also meant to go to France, where he had Alsatian relations, a M. Schott, a businessman in Strasbourg, and a M. Weber in

Paris, who, it seemed, even had some connection with the police.

BEFORE THE court of assize sitting in Aix, Auguste Méla, forty-one, known as 'Gu le Terrible', was sentenced to death in his absence, on October 28th, 1936, for shooting and killing an air-force sentry three years before. The sentence did not impede his activities in 1937. On February 28th, he badly wounded a bank messenger. On May 31st, raiding a Marseilles post-office, like Camille Maucuer and his friends five years before, he left an employee dead. Gu Méla was to remain at liberty for two years more and, during that time, to carry out a train robbery on a massive scale, without, however, serious casualties and thus outside my field.

As IN the United Kingdom, political uniforms were banned in France in 1936. The *camelots du Roi* and the momentarily danger-ous Croix de Feu disbanded themselves. Neither had been in any proper sense a criminal organisation. This was not true of their successors, known to themselves as the Comité Secret d'Action Révolutionnaire or CSAR but to other as *les cagoulards* or *la Cagoule*, mocking names first given them not by the Left but in the pages of *L'Action Française*, in the belief, not wholly unfounded in the early days of the conspiracy, that they wore ku-klux-klanlike hoods or *cagoules* at their meetings. They were indeed organised very much as a secret army, with military ranks and their own courts martial. Their 'executions' were carried out with cut-down bayonets, and their victims could be recognised by the triangular stab-wounds these made. Influential among the commissioned and *sous-officier* ranks of the real Army, they were for the moment anti-Nazi but not averse to Italian money or, more to their point at that time, Italian arms. Their leader, Eugène Deloncle, had, in Novem-ber 1936, been received in interview by Marshal Pétain, but too much has been concluded from that occasion.

The most famous of the *cagoulard* murders was that of the Rosselli brothers, Carlo and Nello. It was not the first. There had been, in October 1936 and February 1937, those of two traitors to the organisation, whose improbable surnames were Jean-Baptiste and Juif, dispatched respectively in Paris and outside Nice. On January 24th, the body of a Soviet agent, Navashin, was found in the Bois de Boulogne. On May 17th, Whit Monday, Letitia Tourneau (Belin) or Toureaux (Bourdrel), Italian-born mistress of one of the leaders, was stabbed with exceptional speed and dexterity in a first-class compartment on the Underground. The Rossellis were killed at Bagnoles-de-l'Orne in Normandy, on June 9th. Carlo Rosselli had been a leader of Italian anti-fascism in exile, editing a paper, *Giustizia e Libertà*, which he hired aeroplanes to scatter in Italy. His blood had been demanded in return for a consignment of arms, which the *Cagoule* was stock-piling in a variety of hidden retreats. According to Belin, the Pierre Bony of whom we keep hearing was himself a *cagoulard*. According to Bourdrel, he offered his services and was to be successfully employed as an informer.

It was a year of strikes and demonstrations in northern France and around Paris. An International Exhibition, due to open at the beginning of May, was in fact not opened until the 24th, and even then some of the pavilions were not yet ready. The Popular Front government of Léon Blum was on the point of falling. Even so, Paris had more summer visitors than it had had for years, including a great many Americans. Two non-American newcomers, neither of whom was ever to leave France again, were Fritz Frommer and Eugen Weidmann. Weidmann had crossed the frontier between Saarbrücken and Forbach, where he was met by Roger Million with a motor-bike. By June 12th, with papers in the name of Karrer, he was installed at a hotel in the Rue St Sébastien, near the Winter Circus, in an easterly district which otherwise contains no public buildings of greater interest than the Petite Roquette prison. A few days after his arrival, he met Frommer in the street. Thereafter, with Million and Jean Blanc and with money provided by Blanc, he rented a tiny villa out at St Cloud, west of Paris. Jean Blanc's mother provided china and cutlery. Blanc himself further provided a mistress, a married woman, Colette Tricot, whom Million presently took over, without more complaint from Blanc than her husband had ever made about her absence from home. Nor, indeed, does she seem to have been much of a prize, though she made herself useful in various ways.

It is not clear what the group as a whole meant to do at La Voulzie, as the villa was called, though apparently there was talk of manufacturing some beauty product. Relations were established with people near by, notably a M. Mouly, a man with a little moustache, no regular occupation and a daughter, a dressmaker, who played chess with Weidmann. Mouly also had been engaged in currency smuggling and knew Million's father, so that it seems likely he was the man who had found the villa empty and to let. Frommer was invited to the place and appeared there more than once as a guest, to the disapproval of his uncle, M. Weber, who knew from connections in Frankfurt that Weidmann was, as his nephew was not, a common criminal. It may have been for this reason, to disarm his uncle's suspicions, that Fritz Frommer appears to have known Weidmann by the name of Siegfried Sauerbrey. But there may in fact have been a Sauerbrey as well. All this was to remain mysterious, as was the usual source of M. Mouly's income.

THE NUMBER of foreigners in Paris that summer was doubly an advantage to Eugen Weidmann. It made him less conspicuous, and it offered him a wealth of strangers whose language he could speak. The first American whom he tried to lure out to the villa at St Cloud, with the idea of kidnap and ransom, was, by his own account, one Michael Stein of Baltimore or Philadelphia, who was staying at the Continental in the Rue de Rivoli and for whose release $25,000 were to be demanded. Stein took fright in time, though it seems already in a car on its way to La Voulzie, with Weidmann at the wheel and driving fast. This episode was not to come out at the time or until very recently, and it may be that Mr Stein died peacefully in Baltimore or Philadelphia without ever learning what other criminal enterprises were launched from the headquarters at which he came so near to being illegally restrained. It could, of course, be that some comparative criminal historian in Philadelphia or Baltimore might yet trace Mr Stein, might even find him still alive and ready to be at once astonished and informative.

A young American dancing instructor, Jean de Koven, over for the Exhibition with her aunt, Mrs Sackheim, was not to be so lucky. The two women stayed in the Rue du Vieux Colombier, where the hotels are not smart. It was, however, in the lounge of the Ambassadeur, a hotel which, if it is not quite *de grand luxe* like the Continental, is yet *de luxe*, in the Boulevard Haussman, near the Opera, that, on July 24th, Miss de Koven noticed a personable young man reading an English-language newspaper and, when he put it down, asked him if she might borrow it for a moment. Two days later, she was strangled at La Voulzie. Fully clothed, even to coat, hat and gloves, her body was buried at the foot of the front steps, where it was to remain undiscovered for some four months.

During that time, Weidmann further dispatched the driver of a hired car, an estate agent, an aspiring theatrical impresario, Fritz Frommer and a Strasbourg woman who had come up in answer to an advertisement for a companion-help on the Riviera. These five were dispatched with shots in the nape of the neck. The woman, Janine Keller, was buried in a sightseers' cave in the forest of Fontainebleau. In the murder of the aspiring theatrical impresario, Million certainly took part. In the back of that neck, there were two bullet holes of smaller calibre, one fired by a right-handed, one by a left-handed, man. It is probable that Million also helped bury the body in the cave. Mme Tricot was kept busy cashing Jean de Koven's travellers' cheques. What Jean Blanc was doing meanwhile is unknown. It seems likely that others were involved, including M. Mouly. The police were first led to the villa through a visiting card in the name of M. Schott and the suspicions entertained by M. Weber.

La Voulzie lay within the jurisdiction of Versailles, in what was then Seine-et-Oise and is now Yvelines. There Eugen Weidmann was held, and there he would be tried after a judicial inquiry which lasted eighteen months. He confessed by stages. Million, Blanc and Mme Tricot were also pulled in, not in the first place incriminated by him. To begin with, he was disposed to take everything on himself, but, when he found Million too eager to take advantage of that disposition, he turned on Million. A woman lawyer at the Versailles bar, Renée Jardin, was *commise d'office* by her local *bâtonnier* to defend Weidmann, and she arranged that at the public hearing she would be led by none other than Vincent de Moro-Giafferi. She was sorry for her client, and, as he seemed to show genuine remorse, she started him off both on a course of religious reading and on keeping a diary in a red exercise book which she got him. As he had been brought up a Catholic, the choice of his reading may seem a trifle odd, but it was no doubt limited by the fact that his first language was German. At any rate, he seems to have concentrated on the New Testament and on the *Imitation of Christ* by Thomas à Kempis.

Some of the religious had at once been attracted by Weidmann. In a letter which is undated but which may be deduced to have been composed on about Thursday, December 16th, 1937, a leading Catholic novelist wrote to Maître Jardin as follows :

L'Hermitage
Boulevard Louis-Sorel
Toulon

Madame,

I do not have the honour of knowing you, and the feeling which leads me to write to you is one of those whose expression is commonly limited to a small circle of friends. What matter! I also do not know whether you ever chanced to open a book of mine, or indeed if my name is known to you. Again, what matter! What worries me far more is finding the few simple words without which this approach to you could only seem ridiculous or affected.

I have no romantic prepossession in favour of murderers. But it seems to me that, once a certain degree of horror is passed, crime begins to resemble the extremes of poverty – as incomprehensible, as mysterious as utter destitution. Equally, they put a human creature outside and as though beyond life.

I know nothing whatever about the poor wretch whom you are helping. But it is impossible to look without a kind of religious terror at the admirable photographs in *Paris-Soir*, especially one in the issue for Tuesday, the 14th, which makes him, between the faces of two doubtless worthy but ordinary policemen, the very image of solitude, of a supernatural abandonment. I was dining that evening at a monastery near Toulon, and to the monks who were in my company and who knew nothing of this dreadful news item I repeated the words which journalists – wrongly of course, it may be – put into the mouth of Eugène Weidmann ('It is because you speak to me gently. . . .'). I shall not recount our conversation to you, though it went on till late in the night. That a child could have come into the world with this invisible sign already printed on its forehead, that should provide a pretext for many ingenious theories on the part of psychologists or moralists. I am not a psychologist and far less a moralist, being a Christian. The thought simply arouses in me the heartrending sense, heartrending to the point of anguish and beyond, of a barely conceivable hope : the solidarity of all men in Christ.

To you, Madame, I leave the decision whether or no to convey to Eugène Weidmann what I and those friendly monks thought. For my part, I know that I can offer little. I should like to think him able to understand that men of religion, in their solitude, are doing more than merely feeling sorry for him, are now fraternally bearing a part of his frightful burden.

G. Bernanos

At that time, Georges Bernanos was at the height of his fame.
Even in English, his *Diary of a Country Priest* had been rapturously
received, and, while Weidmann remained in prison at Versailles
awaiting trial, his account, the following year, of the massacres in
Majorca, was to delight the Left and to shock the Right. It is
perhaps true that he was not predisposed to romanticise murderers,
but he was interested in murder. *The Crime* (translated the year
before) is about a murder committed by a woman who disguises
herself as a priest. There was murder in *La Joie* and *Sous le Soleil
de Satan* (both earlier, but not yet translated). There was to be
murder in *Monsieur Ouine* and *Nouvelle Histoire de Mouchette*.
And what Bernanos wrote to Maître Renée Jardin was not
idle sanctimoniousness to him. He really did believe that priests
could take other people's guilt on themselves, sometimes dying
of it.

Among multiple murderers, Weidmann is not unique in the fact
that, after some years of milder criminality, he suddenly took to
murder and committed all his major crimes within a few months,
as though unable, once he had started, to stop. He was not, I would
say, a sadist in any meaningful sense. He murdered for money,
though he made very little (so did Landru). And he seems to have
been glad when he was stopped. He is perhaps unique in the variety
of angles from which we may glimpse him. In Belin, we have the
investigating policeman's worry about a series of men shot in the
back of the neck, with which the disappearances of Jean de Koven
and Mme Keller were not yet connected in anyone's mind. In due
course, there would be the usual and some unusual variety of
reactions by journalists and others at the trial and afterwards.
There are the eventual contents of the red exercise book. There are
letters from a German farmer in Canada. There is no such detailed
clinical study by a psychiatrist as Dr Karl Berg was able to devote
to Peter Kuerton, though indeed there are Dr Furstenheim's findings
on the boy Weidmann at fourteen, including the comparative in-
sensibility of the young delinquent's right side to a neurologist's
pin-pricking.

And yet I am bound to say that I do not find Eugen Weidmann
less opaque than other murderers. For one thing, he was (like, I
think we may say, not merely all murderers but all criminals) something of a mythomaniac, a compulsive or pathological liar. In the
red exercise book, as later at his trial, he did what looks like his
best, at times an agonising best, to tell the truth, and yet quite

demonstrable lies creep in, as do unconvincing fantasies which yet cannot be checked. Among these, we could no doubt find clues worth picking up. I fancy that some of them might be such verbal clues as my German is not adequate to discover, had I the German text (had *we* the German text, for I don't think it has been published). I picked up one while translating Bernanos above. The reader may have noticed that I there left Weidmann's Christian name in its gallicised form as 'Eugène'. That is the form in which we most commonly see it. Although we are not so readily given to anglicising foreign names as the French are to gallicising them, it is not merely to be supposed, it is known, that, among English-speaking Canadians, Eugen had been Eugene, pronounced in the English way, and therefore, familiarly, Gene. To English speakers, 'Gene' is homophonous with 'Jean'. The suggestion is that the murder of Jean de Koven, the first murder, may have been, symbolically and unconsciously, an act of self-destruction. It is a widely accepted notion that homicidal and suicidal impulses are in general ambivalent and largely interchangeable. In this case, a simple homophony of names may have been enough to bring to the surface or just below it a painful wish to die which found itself with a substitute to hand.

I dare say that this is unimportant. I am not a committed Freudian, and I don't offer the thought with any great solemnity. I do find murderers opaque. That is a reason for me to write about them. In a series, it is clearly the first murder which counts. Like stealing cars, to go on shooting people in the back of the neck is showing off. In the case of the neck with two holes, it looks like a matter of Weidmann letting Million have a go and then saying to his side-kick : 'Not like that, silly! Like this!' But the murder of Jean de Koven was very odd and private. The idea was kidnap and ransom, which indeed all too frequently leads to murder, the name given to a factor presumed common to all such cases being 'panic'. The material evidence suggested, both to police and subsequently to prosecution, that, having reached the villa in St Cloud, Jean de Koven was immediately strangled, her back being turned to Weidmann so that he might help her off with her coat. His written account is that he put veronal in her coffee, that he tied her hands and feet when she went to sleep, that he himself then went to sleep and that he awoke to find her untied and in possession of the key and the loaded revolver he had placed under his pillow, that she shot him in the leg and that he then strangled her in a rage. If the story is not quite past all belief, that at least is the best that can be said for it.

It certainly occurred to Weidmann that the name 'Jean' was interlingually ambiguous. The problem of cashing travellers' cheques arose.

It was the Christian name 'Jean' which gave me the idea of using the dancer's passport. The name 'Jean de Koven' could be a man's name in France. No sooner said than done. I detached Jean's photograph and stuck my passport photograph in hers. Then I applied myself to imitating her signature.

If this were true, its hint of the murderer's identification of himself with the victim would be unimportant because it served a practical purpose. It seems to have been the purest fantasy. The travellers' cheques known to have been cashed were cashed by Colette Tricot, who sufficiently resembled the passport photograph of Jean de Koven to get by in the crush of Exhibition visitors.

Two incidents in the course of the judicial inquiry seem worthy of note. The murder about which Weidmann showed most compunction was that of Janine Keller, but also the reconstruction of that crime was attended by circumstances of crude commercial exploitation which, though they might have flattered the vanity common to murderers, must have made the comparatively sensitive Weidmann wonder whether this was quite the kind of success he had aimed at. It was summer. There was a crowd of sightseers. Beside the brigands' cave in the forest of Fontainebleau, refreshment stalls had been set up, and hawkers sold postcards of Weidmann, which those who bought them pushed forward and begged him to sign (it is said that he did sign some, but it also appears that his signing hand, the left, was handcuffed to the right hand of a gendarme). Before the police cars and those of the journalists and of sightseers who had driven out for the occasion from Paris started up for the return, Renée Jardin tells us that for a moment her client was almost alone, that he sat on a rocky outcrop weeping and that she asked him what he was thinking about, to which he replied : 'Meine Mutter!' We may, of course, knowingly and cynically say that we know all about murderers and their mothers. His seems to have been remarkable in what we may think a partly explanatory way.

If, indeed, his disposition was homosexual, we shall find in his early years the classic situation of a father absent otherwise than because he was dead, a mother who was in any case the dominant parent, himself the only son. Frau Weidmann was in fact brought to Paris during the inquiry. Her son tried, but was not allowed, to refuse even the briefest confrontation with her. She, for her part, loved being in Paris. A woman journalist, Claudie May, who spoke German, took her in tow :

> I could see I'd let myself in for a sightseeing tour. We bought scent – Frau Weidmann was very anxious to get some French scent, she was sorry she hadn't been able to come to the Exhibition last year. I wanted to take her to a quiet restaurant, where we shouldn't be noticed, but Frau Weidmann wouldn't have any of that. She wanted a copy of *L'Intransigeant* because there was a photograph of herself in it. A boy brought it. She said : 'Oh, I don't call that good of me at all !' She said Eugen was a good boy and couldn't possibly have done what they said. Then we had to go to a cinema. It was a Marx Brothers film. I couldn't concentrate on it, but Frau Weidmann laughed like anything.

EUGEN WEIDMANN had arrived in Paris three days after the murder of the Rosselli brothers in Normandy. Between the dates of Weidmann's first two murders, the surviving head of the Corsicans in Montmartre, Jean-Paul Stéfani, had been shot dead in the street by a *demi-sel*, a butcher from La Villette, whose woman the superponce had taken without paying the customary compensation. Between the dates of Weidmann's second and third murders, there were synchronised *cagoulard* explosions near the Place de l'Étoile, and General Miller, leader of the militant Whites in Paris, vanished, not the first Tsarist Russian general to be successfully abducted in Paris by Soviet agents. Between Weidmann's third and fifth murders, an elderly eccentric called Pluvinage, in a sudden rage, shot three women neighbours dead on the sixth floor of a house in the Rue Condorcet and was not to be discovered for six years. A *coup d'état* planned by the Cagoule was frustrated by the police in November, before Weidmann's fifth and sixth murders. The Buisson brothers and Émile Courgibet were back from China. On December 29th, 1937, the two Émiles, with four accomplices, took part in a carefully planned bank-raid in Troyes.

Émile Buisson was arrested on April 6th, 1938. The other four were already in custody, but Émile Courgibet succeeded not only in taking passage on the *Normandie* but in staying and settling in New York, where, under the name of Fernand Châtelain, he was employed as a cabinet-maker. That summer, the butcher who had killed Jean-Paul Stéfani 'got his' in Cannes. Pamela Raper, twenty-six, of Battle, Sussex, a sculptress, was found in a fisherman's net off Toulon, while, at a modest hotel in Paris, the Rev. James Cecil Howard, forty-seven, of Farnham, Surrey, was found shot in a locked room. On November 9th, the murder by a young Jew in Paris of Ernst von Rath, a minor German diplomatist, was made the excuse for those pogroms throughout Germany poetically known as the *Kristallnacht*.

In early 1939, the public executioner, Anatole Deibler, died of a heart attack and was succeeded by Henri Desfourneaux, whose family had been longer in the trade than the Deiblers. The trial of Eugen Weidmann, Roger Million, Jean Blanc and Colette Tricot opened, at Versailles, in mid-March. In its outcome, it was to make penal history. It was also, had anyone known it, to be the last *cause célèbre* under the Third Republic, the last tried in France before a jury of twelve.

AMONG THE journalists were the great Colette, a frequenter of
criminal trials for twenty-seven years past, covering this one for
Paris-Soir, and, from London, for the *Daily Mail*, the novelist and
woman criminologist F. Tennyson Jesse. But there were journalists
from as far away as Japan and Argentina. According to Marcel
Montarron, there were twice as many journalists in that small courtroom as there had been, eighteen years before, for Landru. They
did not fail to note Landru parallels. Weidmann's cell had been
Landru's. There had been a villa. One victim, Janine Keller from
Strasbourg, had hopefully answered an advertisement. Maître Jardin
(photographed posing with Maurice Chevalier) was not the only
woman barrister. A novelist's daughter, Lucile Tinayre, represented
the estate agent's family, a pretty blonde the Frommers. On the
defence benches below the dock, one of the two bearded gentlemen,
for Roger Million, was Maître Henri Géraud, who had defended
Gorguloff, the mad assassin of President Doumer. With Moro-
Giafferi for Weidmann, in addition to Me Jardin, were the leader
of the Versailles bar, M. le Bâtonnier Planty, and one of his young
men. Moro was tubby now, hair and moustache white.

The presiding judge was Councillor Laemmlé. In the horse-box
to his right sat the regional attorney-general, M. Balmary, and a
substitut. In the dock stood, from left to right, Weidmann, Million,
Jean Blanc and Colette Tricot, a dumpy little woman (as, indeed,
was bespectacled Me Jardin). Million was charged with murder and
complicity to murder, Blanc with harbouring criminals, Mme Tricot
with receiving stolen goods. These three sat down. In reply to the
many charges with which he was faced, Weidmann said that he
pleaded guilty and did not wish to be defended. M. Laemmlé told
him to sit down. In France, you had to be defended. A plea of guilty
simply meant that among the evidence to be heard was your con-

146

fession. The only question was whether he wished to confirm his choice of counsel. This he did. The clerk to the court read the indictment.

The first day's hearing closed with police evidence of arrest. This was given, saltily enough, by Inspector Bourquin of No. 1 flying squad of the Sûreté Nationale, who had gone to St Cloud and called at La Voulzie, in the company of Inspector Poignant, with *gendarmerie* in the offing and, at Vaucresson town hall, Superintendent Primborgne, directing operations from a safe distance.

BOURQUIN : We've tried the villa twice, and there's nobody there. The second time, we're just going away when a well-set-up young fellow turns out of a side-street. He's playing with a dog. He sees me and Poignant, leaves the dog, comes over and says can he help us : I ask him if he knows a M. Karrer. He says he is M. Karrer, and what do we want? I tell him we're from the rates office and just want to check the lease. Poignant takes his card out. The chap has obviously spotted it says POLICE, but he doesn't show much sign of being fussed and invites us to follow him in. We go into a very small room. Karrer's asked to see our papers, so now I ask to see his. Polite like. Fair exchange. He puts his left hand into his right coat pocket, quite natural in his manner otherwise. Then his hand comes out quick. There's a gun in it. He says : 'Here are my papers, damn you!' and fires. I jump at him. Poignant's been hit and collapses on the couch, holding his shoulder. I grab the fellow. Two more shots at the level of my face. One bullet grazes my forehead, just over the right eye. The other goes through my hat (a new hat, I was wearing it for the first time). I get hold of his wrist, but he goes on firing. There's bullets bouncing off the wall. I don't let go. He's an athletic type, you can tell. He twists round, and he's butting at me with his backside. I've got hold of his head. Just then, lying about on the table, I see a small hammer, the sort they use for laying carpets. Of course, there'll be my seventeen stone behind it. I let go of his head and hit it three times. A matter of stunning him, I didn't want to do him any damage, or he'd be complaining of police brutality. Poignant said something. That was a relief. I thought he'd caught it bad.

PRESIDENT OF THE COURT, M. LAEMMLÉ : Didn't you get a chance to use your revolver?

BOURQUIN : I hadn't it with me, Mr President.

PRESIDENT : And Inspector Poignant?

BOURQUIN : His was still buttoned up in his holster.

M. LE BÂTONNIER PLANTY : Mr President, I should like to

point out one thing which is all-important from a psychological
point of view. It appears that Weidmann pulled the trigger of
his pistol without having been threatened in any way.

PRESIDENT : He was threatened with being arrested.

(*Laughter.*)

BÂTONNIER : Weidmann, why did you fire?

WEIDMANN : There was a person in the bedroom sleeping. I
fired to warn this person.

PRESIDENT : What was the sex of this person who was enjoying
an afternoon nap in your house?

WEIDMANN : He was of the masculine sex.

PRESIDENT : Well, tell us his name.

WEIDMANN : I cannot do that.

ME TINAYRE : Mr President, can Weidmann inform the court
whether this mysterious sleeper was the man who killed my
client?

WEIDMANN : I killed him.

That ended the first day's hearing.

On Tuesday, March 14th, Dr Paul described the pathologists'
finding. One exhibit in a jar was almost a yard of discoloured linen
which had been pushed down Jean de Koven's throat during the
course of her strangulation. Then came the first of a procession of
psychiatrists, who were to take up several days' hearings. When
they had finished, Moro-Giafferi got to work on two of the more
eminent among them.

MORO : In his statement, the learned specialist stated that he
had discovered nothing, no stigma, no hereditary taint. There
were, he said, nevertheless undoubted anomalies. That seems
neither black nor white. The learned doctor *finds nothing* but
notes anomalies. If he found them, he must have found *something.* Here is a book. Do you know it? *The Prevention and Cure
of Nervous and Mental Disorders* by Dr Génil-Perrin. Ah, you
wrote it? Let us look at Chapter 2 : 'Affective Disorders'. These
include, it seems, hyperemotivity, anxiety and obsession, difficulties in sleeping, energy variations, perversions of instinct.
Twenty pages on a form of madness of which in court you deny
the existence. . . . And, dear Professor Claude, here is what you
teach. It is set down in your *Medico-Legal Psychiatry*, page 77.
I summarise. 'The criminal may be considered as a being who

shows psycho-moral defects which will impel him to commit anti-social acts.' And you go on to the 'degenerate' and the 'moral madman' with his set of instinctual perversions. Most instructive. Thank you, Professor! That is the line I shall be following when I plead my case. Thank you, Mr President.

In effect a plea of insanity, then, for, although a kind of Macnaghten madness was, the idea of diminished responsibility was not yet (and wouldn't be for another fifteen years), enshrined in the Penal Code.

Million's line of defence was to deny everything. Jean Blanc said he hadn't realised what was going on, Mme Tricot that, in cashing travellers' cheques, she had acted under duress, as indeed in accepting a fur tippet, a belt, a watch and various good clothes. One of her replies might have come straight out of *Gentlemen Prefer Blondes*.

> PRESIDENT : How did you explain these presents to yourself, when at the time you were all very poor?
> TRICOT : It is not interesting where money and presents come from, so long as they arrive.

For the most part, Weidmann serenely acquiesced, insisting only on the complicity of Million in the murder of the house agent, Leblond, and the burial of Mme Keller. The prosecution had not called the mysterious M. Mouly. The defence insisted, and he was fetched from Lisieux in Normandy, where he may well have hoped to be out of the way. He was indignant at being called, and it seems likely enough that police and 'public ministry' or Parquet had promised him that he wouldn't be, having no doubt been helpful during the investigation. His evidence is not mentioned either by Montarron or by Jardin-Birnie (i.e. Renée Jardin in later life). It is made great play of by Tennyson Jesse, who seems to have been affected by the chatter of uninformed French journalists, who (having perhaps more reason to do so) have always been much inclined to suspect politics, secret policemanship and so on. M. Montarron and Weidmann's junior counsel must have understood very well what the position was. Mouly was, we may say, in a very minor way, being 'protected'. He did not want to appear. It would make him an unpopular figure. There was no good reason why he *should* appear, except in so far as the defence might gain from spreading vague suspicion widely. To so excellent an analyst of English criminal cases as Fryn Tennyson Jesse, it must have been clear that such 'protection' was far less than is afforded, in the United Kingdom, to anyone who 'turns King's (or Queen's) evidence'. It seems to me that, on this occasion, Tennyson Jesse was naïve. What I find particularly interesting, however, is that, when reporting British cases (he was, for instance, at the Moors murders trial in 1966), M. Montarron, who takes a bit of discreet police cover-up in his stride, reveals astonishment at our formally recognised immunity for prosecution witnesses against whom charges of aiding and abetting might have been brought. It reveals a deep cleavage between the criminal proceedings found acceptable in our two countries, not, I suggest, entirely to British advantage.

All but one of the victims, Janine Keller, were represented by *parties civiles*. Only lawyers spoke for the Frommers and De Kovens, these last having returned to the United States. The aspirant impresario's mother, the widows of the chauffeur and the estate agent, Leblond, also spoke. What is remembered as the great scene occurred during this middle part of the trial. Leblond had been shot with a pistol of smaller calibre than the rest, a 6.35 mm., and twice, from different angles, once therefore, it seemed natural to think, by a right-handed and once by a left-handed person. On March 22nd, Weidmann had insisted that it was Million who had fired first. At the opening on the 23rd, Weidmann asked to be heard :

WEIDMANN : Yesterday, Mr President, during evidence in the case of Leblond, when Million and Maître Géraud were protesting about some point which I cannot remember, I caught a glance from a side from which I least expected it. From Madame Leblond. That gave me a shock and also a feeling of joy. There was at least one person who believed that I was speaking the truth.

It is not that I wish to see Million convicted. I shall be very pleased if he saves his head. But I wish the truth to be known. I wish, if it is possible, to be forgiven as much as I can. You know the remorse I feel for what I have done. For what I have not done I wish to be forgiven. You can hardly know how important this is to me. To understand it, you would need to find yourselves in my situation.

You are going to punish me with the utmost severity of the law. But you see before you a man who is ready to accept that redemptive sacrifice and will await it courageously until his last minute. Do not refuse my last request. This prayer, it is a cry which comes to you from the depths of my soul. I stand before

you in all confidence. Do not repulse me. Grant me as a last
consolation your belief in the sincerity of my feelings. My
mother. . . . Forgiveness. . . . Ah, yes, her forgiveness. . . .

At this point, he broke down and wept, head in hands on the front
ledge of the dock. There was a commotion, in large part unfriendly
to the prisoner. An Italian voice was heard baying : *'Commediante!
Tragediante!'* The presiding judge ordered a brief adjournment.

Colette knew Renée Jardin and bore down on her. 'From up
there,' she said, 'I saw everything. I didn't miss the batting of an
eyelid. He was crying, and he suffered. It's true, then, this story of
a conversion? *I* don't mind, it's O.K. by me. Pity he's got to be
guillotined. He's a good-looking kid.' Then Colette left the courtroom and wrote for *Paris-Soir* :

> It goes without saying that Weidmann, loaded with crime, re-
> mains abominable. The law has never been called upon to judge
> anything blacker. But, to move their auditors, the public con-
> fession, the avowals cried out to the four winds of heaven,
> needed only the accent of a moral abandon borrowing its stut-
> terings, its tears, from physical weakness. We cannot have been
> the victims of a collective hallucination, the playthings of an
> exhibition almost of genius. Weidmann, word by word, effort
> piled upon effort, shivering and sweating profusely, said in sub-
> stance : 'Million killed Leblond, but all the other murders are
> mine. If there were any pardon for me, I could only hope for it
> from God and elsewhere than on earth.' Then, as though choked
> by regurgitation, he finally lost the power of speech and crum-
> pled. They said he'd fainted, he hadn't. From where I was sit-
> ting, I could see the abundance of the tears so long denied him,
> the deep-drawn spasms which make a man's sobs so very striking
> a sight to us women. The power of confession is a torrent which
> bears everything with it. Weidmann, freed of his gag, is now a
> straw in the wind. Day after day, night after long night, he will
> drift to join those, the dead, whom he already resembles.

Understandably, the journalists felt that they'd had their money's
worth, and few returned after the adjournment. They missed a little
more of the same kind of thing.

> WEIDMANN : I said just now that I asked for forgiveness. It
> was true. For that forgiveness I am offering my life, and I want
> to say why. This is why. In my cell, I have found God, the God
> of my childhood, Him of whom my mother used to speak to me

at night as she tucked me into my little bed. That is why I feel regret and shame. That is also why I did not wish to offer any defence.

MME LEBLOND : *I* believe you, Weidmann! And I am ready to forgive you, as the Lord will certainly do!

ME TINAYRE : Monster! Filthy clown! You're just repeating a lesson, taught you by my colleague, taught you by Maître Jardin!

ME JARDIN : Answer her, Weidmann.

WEIDMANN : Some will believe me, and some will not, it doesn't matter. I am guilty, I am dreadfully guilty. I offer you my life. It is all I can offer, my remorse and my life. I hope I shall be allowed to write to my mother that I have been condemned, but also that I have been forgiven. It is all I can give her now.

That last spring of peace, the late-March weather was lovely. With all moderation, red-robed M. Balmary demanded the heads of Eugène Weidmann and Roger Million. For the defence of the former, Bâtonnier Planty spoke first, then his young *protégé*, then Renée Jardin, who concluded as follows.

ME JARDIN : . . . Gentlemen, there is a word which comes naturally to women's lips when a possible effusion of blood is in question. I shall not pronounce it. Ah, gentlemen, enough of killing, enough of these abominations, no more slaughter! Other civilised countries have abolished the barbarous penalty you have been asked to impose, according to the ancient *lex talionis*. Every fibre of our woman's flesh rebels against the inhuman vision I evoke.

You will do what you think just. Weidmann is prepared. But you will remember the circumstances which permitted that satanic life to unfold, and that life is all hazard for those who were born perverse and evil. If, from this dark soul, you wish that light should spring, that time should enable it to rediscover God with a new conscience, then you will allow that word to sound on your lips which, out of respect for so much present grief, I did not utter. Be assured, if you grant him the boon of life, it will be so that, during years of confinement, there shall germinate in his heart the bitter fruit of repentance.

MORO-GIAFFERI : Mr President, gentlemen. This trial is approaching its end. Forgive me if I postpone its termination with a speech I should like to keep short but which will have to be long, because I must try to make it complete in order to appease my conscience and yours. I can hear you say : 'To what purpose? The man killed. Let him die!' Then what are we here for? Why am I wearing this gown, and why are the judges wearing theirs? Why all these forms and ceremonies? Because this is a court of law and not a slaughterhouse.

The man before us was born with a certain heredity, which he could not escape. . . .

A large part of Moro's concluding speech was devoted to the psychiatrists. He began with the past record of some of those who had been heard.

> . . . Truelle, for instance. Was it not he who certified 'on his honour and his conscience' that the Papin sisters were fully responsible and in their right minds? Now both of them howl with raving madness behind the bars of a cage in the asylum where they had to be shut up on the night of the verdict?

Not quite accurate, as the reader may remember. Shut up indeed, the elder, Christine, had died four years ago, while the younger, Léa, was in prison, where she was to remain for two years more, after which there were still at least thirty years of tolerable life before her. But *causes célèbres* of the past were to be much heard of in the course of this one.

> . . . And Génil-Perrin, didn't he examine Gorguloff and declare him fit to plead? That man was utterly mad, but had to be executed for reasons of State. My dear friend Henri Géraud will remember, though for the moment he sits quietly here and says nothing. . . .

Moro must have enjoyed his onslaught on the psychiatrists. What would be remembered as his main point was more immediately telling, if rather tricky.

> . . . Very carefully measuring my words, I say that the crimes committed by Weidmann are German crimes. A nation's politics are reflected in the consciousness of individuals. I am pleading the cause of a child who was taught that might is right, a young man who grew up among murderers and witnessed a rebirth of the barbaric Middle Ages. The question of my client's normality faces you in an exceptionally acute form not only because of the number of his crimes but because he is German, because in his veins flows the poison of this evil.

Yes, Weidmann is the victim not of his own nature, but of all that he received at birth. And now you will understand why I dare to pronounce before you the word which, having admirably suggested it, Renée Jardin dared not pronounce : the word 'pity'. I ask you to be pitiful, not for Weidmann's sake but for your own. Members of the jury, do you not feel to what a height this trial has borne you? To those who sat on those benches before you, it has been customary to say that they were the representatives of society. You are more than that. It seems to me that you are the delegates of humanity.

You won't allow yourselves to be confused by words. With a cheap facility unworthy of him, your regional attorney-general said : 'Abnormal? Well, of course! Good heavens, all murderers are abnormal, and let us rejoice that it is so, that they are not like us!' When you said that, my learned friend, you knew that you were evading the essential truth. I am not speaking of the differences which may exist between members of a species. I, who know Weidmann, and know what my colleagues have told me, I say that he is a being who was cast into this world in different conditions from those which attend the birth of other men. Of certain blessed souls it has been said that they took the trouble to be born. In fear and trembling, I tell you that *there* sits a man who committed the crime of being born.

In the teeth of the world, and whatever clamour is raised by a public avid for bread and circuses and blood . . . you, my countrymen, my country's judges, I say this to you . . . to this fallen creature of another race, here, today, you must offer the lofty, the magnificent spectacle of a justice which knows that true greatness lies in balance, in reflection and thoughtfulness, in pity.

The applause was perhaps deceptively great and prolonged.

Maître Géraud, arms hitherto folded, cap on head, long-bearded (an Elijah, says Tennyson Jesse, to the Elisha of less-impressively bearded Me Zevaès for Tricot and Blanc), now rose to speak for the defence of Roger Million.

ME GÉRAUD : Mr President, gentlemen. My client, I know, is no favourite with the public. His face, it appears, lacks grace and harmony. In the great juridical drama here taking place, he is not the best type of defendant, he is devoid of elegance or charm or the dazzling smile of a juvenile lead. In this trial, it is Weidmann who takes the part of the truly sympathetic character, the prince charming; Weidmann whose soft-spoken words and obsequious gestures are savoured, whom the respectable fair view with a tender eye; and who, at the same time, is the prosecution's essential auxiliary, its accredited prompter, its chief witness.

When the prosecution case falters, Weidmann is called to the rescue. He will provide all the information my learned friends opposite need. In reality, it is not by the State but by Weidmann that we are indicted. Let us at least ask ourselves what his word is worth, what are his credentials. For he has contradicted himself often enough, and yet his is the only testimony, if we except a few equally contradictory words from the lady in the dock, whose memory seemed as variable as her favours. Not a trace of material proof. Not a fingerprint, not a single disinterested witness, no admissions! Everything rests on the importance we attach to the testimony of Weidmann, sufficiently motivated by hatred of his old prison companion.

Ah, gentlemen, what an astounding play-actor he is, that man whose hands are red with blood! With what art, with what calculated slowness, he rose to his feet! With what a carefully studied gesture he wiped his brow! With what affected humility he called for silence and begged not to be interrupted during that theatrical monologue! And he got silence, profound silence, a religious silence. People held their breath. They were all eyes, all ears, anxious not to miss a word, a syllable, a comma, of that dreadful murderer making his confession, begging forgiveness of the families of his victims, calling upon his mother and grandmother. My great colleague said that his crimes were German crimes. I think we may give a different sense to that. I will remind you of the performances given in court by two other German murderers.

Between 1921 and 1924, in Hanover, a butcher, Fritz Haarmann, killed twenty-eight young men and boys. When he appeared on trial, he also confessed, in these terms : 'The charges against me are heavy. I denied some of them at the time of my arrest. I shall make amends. But any man in my situation would have denied these charges. Not that I am a coward. Death will seem to me a form of redemption. I have a conscience, after all. I've confessed. I haven't confessed everything. What good would that be? I beg the jury to put an end to my tribulations. I am about to appear before my Maker, and my mother is waiting and praying for me already.' So Weidmann's tune is an old one. He uses monsters' language. There was another nine years ago, Peter Kuerten, known as the vampire of Düsseldorf. He was charged with twelve murders and eighteen miscellaneous crimes, mainly rape with grievous bodily harm. During the preliminary inquiry, he said to the examining magistrate : 'You may believe what I say, I am sincere. The consequences of what I say matter little to me. I seek neither to excuse nor to justify myself, but simply to make the truth known, to declare the infinite distress of my existence.' Then, at his trial, in June 1930 : 'My crimes, the crimes I have committed, seem so horrible to me now that

I shall not try to excuse them. What I feel at the bottom of my heart is an inexpressible bitterness, and I should like to explain to you the so-very-confused impressions which overwhelm me. It is in youth that a man's fate is decided. It is regrettable in this connection that the family spirit is not more fully developed and that atheists are not more openly despised. The families bereaved through my fault inspire me with great pity. I shall allow myself to beg forgiveness of all those whom I have made weep. I know that I shall be called on to expiate my fault. I have indeed already made some expiation, for, in the solitude of my prison, I have suffered a hundred times over the tortures of a condemned man : a hundred times have I imagined my death.' Three great German criminals and three times the same language!

But of course what principally concerns us is to know whether Million killed Leblond or whether Weidmann has accused him out of spite – revenge, no doubt, to his own mind, on a poor accomplice, a bad friend. Well, we've heard from my eminent colleague a great deal about Weidmann's psychology. That he *is* a monster seems to be his defence. The medical reports insist on the fact that he is a liar and that his feelings are perverted. And yet the prosecution relies on his word. For my part, I say that the man who strangled the young and charming dancer, Jean de Koven, and committed all the other crimes we know about – and those we don't – is perfectly capable of telling lies to convict an innocent man. . . .

And Géraud perorated about classic miscarriages of justice, in particular mentioning Peter Vaux, Dreyfus and Christ.

Followed Me Zevaès for Blanc and Tricot. The prisoners were removed. The jury retired. They were away for a long time. It was midnight when they returned. On his honour and his conscience, before God and before men, the foreman of the jury informed the court that, by a majority of more than seven to five, they returned an affirmative answer to all the questions concerning Weidmann and Million, who were found guilty of all the facts alleged against them, with aggravating circumstances of premeditation and lying in wait. For the prisoner Blanc they found extenuating circumstances. They exonerated the prisoner Tricot. Accordingly, the prisoners were brought back. Weidmann and Million were informed that they were to have their heads cut off in a public place, Jean Blanc that he had been awarded fifteen months' imprisonment but that he must be considered to have served these already and was therefore discharged, as was Colette Tricot.

The conduct of the trial revealing no defect of form and no new

Dr Petiot

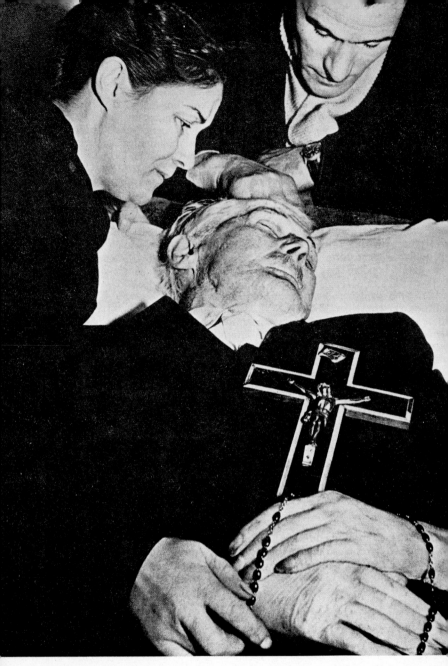

10 Seznec dead, February 1954

evidence having come to light, the *pourvois en cassation* were rejected. The date for Weidmann's and Million's execution was fixed for June 16th. The previous day, President Lebrun signed Million's reprieve, but not Weidmann's. Accordingly, during the night, Henri Desfourneaux and his assistants set up the timbers of justice on the pavement outside St Peter's prison, Versailles. A crowd began to assemble, and the bars and restaurants stayed open. In his lighted cell, Weidmann would hear the music and the hammering and the laughter.

At 4 a.m., some forty privileged persons were allowed into the prison. They included the lawyers for the *parties civiles* and Weidmann's advocates. The chaplain was shut in with the prisoner, who made his last confession. They came out of the cell, Weidmann dressed in his own clothes, arms and hands free. The clerk to the court appeared with a cablegram in English. It read : FACE TO FACE WITH GUILLOTINE ADJURE YOU SPEAK TRUTH STOP DID YOU RAPE JEAN DE KOVEN QUERY. We must, I suppose, assume that it did indeed come from Jean de Koven's family and not from some newspaper-reading busybody, though anyone fully apprised of the proceedings would know that evidence had been heard to the effect that sexual intercourse had not taken place at all recently before the young woman's death. Weidmann himself could presumably have read the cable, but it had to be read aloud to him in French, and there was no accredited translator present. As his defending counsel, Maître Jardin, was not allowed to do what was needed. It should have been one of the magistracy, but none of those present knew English. Eventually, the lawyer who at the trial had represented the interests of the De Kovens and Sackheims was allowed to translate and read the splendid example of transatlantic delicacy. When it got out to the journalists, the irony of Weidmann's reply was to be richly savoured. It was : 'No, I did not touch her.' This was taken down in longhand and signed by him. There followed Mass and communion in the parlour, matters commonly skimped. There were further signatures, quibbles about personal possessions, handing over of sealed envelopes, trimming of the back of the neck and cutting away of the shirt collar, a mouthful of rum, a few pulls at a cigarette, fastening of hands behind back, hobbling of feet, jacket dropped. By then, it was so light ouside that the street lamps had been switched off.

It was more than a hundred years since executions had been as public as they once were, when they took place on a raised scaffold

F

in the middle of the Place de Grève, thereafter named (as it still is) the Place de l'Hôtel de Ville, and in the afternoon. Dr Guillotin's improved decapitator now stood on the pavement at ground level. Some two hundred people stood in a half-circle, and barriers extended across the tramlines. Despite police checks, two cameramen were installed at upper windows in buildings near by. The new executioner's long and distinguished career did not get off to a good start. The *bascule* or see-saw plank to which the patient is strapped and then tipped horizontal had been badly adjusted for height, so that Weidmann's neck did not lie neatly in the *lunette*. The assistant known as *le photographe* had to pull him forward by hair and ears, and even then his chin would be chipped.

Among those in the half-circle was Tennyson Jesse. My appetite for guillotine horrors is small, but I quote her for one interesting detail which I have not seen recorded elsewhere.

> The great blade crashed down and rebounded from its own force and weight. The voice that had been so beautiful, so soft, so gentle in the courtroom, was stilled for ever. There only came as a last exclamation from Weidmann – and that was involuntary – the whistling that always sounds when a head is cut off. For the neck gives a gasp as the last breath of air leaves the lungs, though the head be already in the basket. It is the man's windpipe and not his tongue that protests.

Marcel Montarron speaks of 'a geyser of blood'. Renée Jardin noted the staring eyes. Vincent de Moro-Giafferi exclaimed : 'He lived like a monster. He has died like a saint.' Women pushed forward to dip their handkerchiefs in the bright arterial blood before it was hosed away and the pavement strewn with sand.

IT WAS the photographs, taken in broad daylight, which caused the outcry. As it was not known that they existed, the authorities did nothing to stop their publication, with reports on the crowd's behaviour. People were reminded of realities they had long contrived to ignore. Two kinds of strong feeling were also aroused by the fact that the man executed had been a German, while a Frenchman had been reprieved at the last moment. On the one hand, this was considered unsporting. On the other hand, at a time when relations between the two countries were strained, it was feared that the Germans might resent Frenchmen executing one of their male citizens of military age. It was in fact Moro's blood that the German press bayed for. At any rate, there were to be no more public executions in France. By a statute of June 24th, all death sentences would thenceforward be carried out inside prison walls as in England, before nine specified officials.

On August 23rd was signed, between greater Germany and the U.S.S.R., a pact which presumably meant that, when the two presently invaded Poland, the United Kingdom and France would find themselves automatically at war with both, because of the guarantees we had given to Poland. A short while before, there being a shortage of English for them to murder at home and most of us being preoccupied with these larger matters, the I.R.A. had set up a headquarters in unsuspecting Coventry, where, two days after the Hitler-Stalin pact, they accounted for five of the hated race with one explosive charge in a shopping street.

On September 1st, the Germans alone invaded Poland. On the 3rd, war on Germany was declared by the United Kingdom. France declared war on Germany twenty-four hours later with understandable reluctance, since it was clear that neither we nor they could help the Poles directly and since the speed of the German advance was such that the invasion would probably be completed before either of us could do more than make threatening noises in the West. It was in fact all over in three weeks, the Russians having occupied their part of Poland unopposed. On them neither we nor the French declared war, though many would have liked to do so when, that winter, they pushed a rabble of their unwanted Orientals into Finland. Of the principal sad events of the following year I suppose that even the young are sufficiently informed in the United Kingdom and in France. The one that obviously concerns us most in this volume is that, less than a year after the execution of Eugen Weidmann, there were German troops in Paris, where some of them were to remain for a little over four years.

THE RUE Le Sueur lies in a residential area to the west of Paris proper, as it might be the better parts of Bayswater, with Marble Arch taking the place of the Arc de Triomphe. No. 21 had once housed the famous actress Cécile Sorel. It was up for sale in the latter half of 1940, when property values in Paris were low. It was bought, in the name of his son, by the Dr Marcel Petiot of whom we have twice heard and who, after the bit of trouble about a book theft and a period in a mental home, had returned to his practice in the Rue de Caumartin, nowhere near the Rue Le Sueur, where he intended to start a clinic. In the difficult circumstances of the time, certain structural alterations were indeed carried out the following year. A wall was raised at the back and a surgery built there, with double doors and soundproofed partitions. The yard was full of planks, cement and lime. The twelve windows on the street remained shuttered, however, and the new owner was rarely seen.

During that first year after the fall of France, we in the United Kingdom had time to notice the running amok with a shotgun of a Mrs Ransom in a Kentish orchard and, in Mexico, the murder of Trotsky. Then we kept being bombed, and we missed such American penal episodes as the electrocution of Blazek, while the Nazis kept dark even from neutral correspondents the adventures of their train murderer, Paul Ogorzov, who was a Party member and therefore not supposed to kill German women. After all, if he had confessed his sadistic urges to some responsible person, he could have been found useful employment elsewhere, such as, for example, was being offered to French convicts, released from Fresnes as early as August 6th, 1940, and incorporated in the Abwehr.

Early promulgations of the Vichy government were that abortion should be made a capital offence and that capital sentences passed on women should no longer be automatically commuted, as they had been for over fifty years. The first of five to suffer under the new rule was a Mme Ducourneau of Bordeaux, who had poisoned her mother and husband. Awakened in the small hours on January 8th, 1941, and told by the public prosecutor that the time had come to pay her debt to society, she grumbled that there was money of hers kept in the office. When the head wardress explained to her what the gentleman had really meant, the prisoner kicked up such a hullabaloo that they could not even get her dressed, so that, yelling and struggling, she had to be strapped to the *bascule*, tipped and topped in no more than a few torn scraps of night attire.

Among the prisoners released from Fresnes for service with the Abwehr were some of the more violent and dangerous members of the pre-war *milieu*, prominent among them Henri Chamberlain, a man in his late thirties with a long criminal record and due for Guiana. With our old friend Pierre Bony, who, it may be recalled, had eventually been dismissed from the Sûreté, he, under the name of 'Lafont' by which he is commonly remembered, had been given premises and authority to run what became known as the Gestapo of the Rue Lauriston. Another member of the original team was one Estébétéguy, Adrian the Basque, of whom we shall hear again. In due course, the Gestapo (soon known in underworld jargon as *la Carlingue*, the word being a colloquial term for cockpit or cabin) was to offer a home to other French gangsters, some of whom would make individual names for themselves in the sphere of common-law murder after the war. Two such were Abel Danos and Pierre Loutrel. In 1941, Danos, a big man known as the Mammoth, then still free-lancing, performed, on February 24th, the first bank raid of the Occupation, leaving one cashier dead and another wounded and collecting a very large sum indeed.

With him on this occasion was Émile Buisson. Imprisoned at Troyes to await trial in connection with a hold-up there, 'Mimile' had escaped in the confusion caused by the rapid advance of the German armies, ten months before the bank raid in Paris with the huge Danos. He and *le Mammouth* must have made an odd, Mutt and Jeff pair, and the fact may well briefly have amused the cashiers until the shooting started. From later form, it seems likely that it was the little man who fired. There is a Freudian explanation for little men with guns, though Émile Buisson seems to have been virile.

In April, German troops entered Belgrade. In May, Hitler's closest friend, Rudolf Hess, landed in Scotland and was pointedly ignored by Churchill. In June, the Germans invaded Russia, and the same elderly statesman decreed that the monstrous Stalin must therefore be treated as a friend and ally. The main effect in France of that invasion did indeed seem, both to silly us and to many decent Frenchmen, to be good. The Communist Party in France, seeing it all till then as an imperialist war and favouring the Germans on account of the Hitler-Stalin pact, had done all they could to bring about the French defeat and to get the German authorities in Paris to admit themselves to useful collaboration. The Germans had treated them with marked coldness, and of course Vichy had banned them. Already organised as an underground movement, they soon became the backbone of the Resistance, to nobody's advantage ultimately, though it was to give them some years of doubtless enjoyable wrecking, pillage and massacre on a scale denied even to those who allied themselves with the Germans.

It was, apparently, *cagoulards* who blew off the head of Marx Dormoy, former Minister of the Interior, then living under house arrest at a hotel in Montélimar. This took place on July 26th. The operation was successful, but it cost the lives of the three who had placed the time-bomb under poor M. Dormoy's bed. Going into his room, they had found under the bed what they took to be a deed-box. This they removed. It blew up on them at Nice. It was another time-bomb, cleverly disguised, which a group of their fellow-conspirators had placed there earlier that evening.

IN THE Rue de Caumartin, at No. 69, three doors away from the premises mainly used by Dr Marcel Petiot, was a furrier's, Guschinow & Gouédo. Towards the end of 1941, Joachim Guschinow, a Polish Jew, consulted Petiot about a shameful disease. The really bad time for Jews in France had not yet started, but Guschinow was anxious, and Dr Petiot said that he knew of an organisation which, for a consideration, would get anyone in danger first into the so-far-still-unoccupied southern half of France, then into Spain and thereafter to South America. On January 2nd, 1942, Joachim Guschinow packed his clothes and some valuables and, taking plenty of money, including dollar bills sewn into the shoulder-pads of his jackets, from which any identification marks had been removed, set off for a mysterious appointment in a street off the Rue Le Sueur. He was never to be seen again, though messages convincing to his wife continued to reach her through the intermediary of the doctor.

On February 19th, a former prostitute and her well-to-do and comparatively respectable gentleman-friend, Jean-Pierre van Bever, were arrested on a drug charge, she being a recognised heroin addict who, however, had been getting prescriptions from five doctors, of whom Petiot was one. Van Bever was conditionally released on March 15th. Next day, another young woman addict was arrested, the daughter of a Mme Khait, not herself Jewish, though her third husband was. The girl also was a patient of Dr Petiot's. Van Bever disappeared on March 22nd, Mme Khait on March 25th. Nobody enquired after the former, and Petiot contrived to allay M. Khait's suspicions with supposed messages from the unoccupied zone until such time as M. Khait was arrested and sent to a concentration camp where he died. On May 26th, Petiot himself was called in for questioning about the two drug cases, but released. The reader may care to be reminded that a death in Villeneuve-sur-Yonne, while Dr Petiot was mayor of that town, had also been that of a person expected to give evidence in a case pending against him.

On June 5th disappeared a young married woman from the country south-west of Paris, Denise Hotin, on whom Petiot had performed an abortion the previous year and who had come to see him again for what reason we know not. On June 20th, a Jewish colleague, Dr Paul Braunberger, in hourly expectation of being forbidden practice, was last seen setting off for an appointment outside the Étoile underground station, the nearest to the Rue Le Sueur. On July 20th, a family of three Knellers disappeared, Jews of course. Then a new type of customer appeared and disappeared, ponces and their women. There were five of them, two men and three women, all friends. They disappeared in two batches in July and August 1942. It is uncertain whether the trouble they had been in was with one or other police or with colleagues and competitors in the *milieu*.

On September 12th, Mme Braunberger reported her husband's disappearance to the French police, with no immediate consequences. Next to go were the Wolffs, three of them. They were followed by the Basch, Ansbach and Stevens couples. That was in October. I take all these dates from the excellent little book by Ronald Seth which is listed in my bibliography, rearranging them in chronological sequence. Mr Seth gives a fair amount of circumstantial detail in each case. One item in this puzzles me. The Ansbachs and the Stevenses, says Mr Seth, 'were living in Nice'. Perhaps it was simply that they wanted to get back to a home they had in Nice, for it seems unlikely that they would come from the Italian zone to German-occupied Paris in order to be got to, say,

Bordeaux. The lack of simple chronological sequence in his narrative also leads Mr Seth to ignore the event which divides these earlier disappearances from a smaller group of later ones.

On November 8th, the Allies, mainly American, invaded North Africa to meet General Montgomery's rapidly advancing 8th Army. Three days later, the division between occupied and unoccupied zones was abolished, and German troops occupied the south of France as far east as Toulon, whose population they evacuated. Notable events of that winter were the assassination, in North Africa, of Admiral Darlan, the Casablanca conference between Churchill, Roosevelt and Stalin and a bad military defeat for the Germans at Stalingrad. The day before von Paulus's surrender there, the Germans in southern France embarked on the systematic destruction of that whole insalubrious district of Marseilles which lay to the north of the Old Port. This was a curious operation, without strategic value, long considered by the municipality as a measure of social hygiene, for that district had been the centre of vice and criminality. To the Germans, it had perhaps also seemed to be a centre of resistance to their authority, for there had been bombs, and an important part of the Marseilles *milieu* was indeed to play its part in the Resistance, a fact which led to the eventual supremacy of the Guerinis, their rivals Carbone and Spirito, with the political boss Sabiani, having chosen to collaborate with the Germans.

At any rate, the war itself bore a different complexion, and France as an entity was much changed, between the first long series of disappearances connected with Dr Marcel Petiot and those which were yet to come. The next recorded group, in March 1943, was again of ponces and their women, and it seems quite uncertain just where they wanted to go or by what route. There were two men and two women, and both men had been working for the Germans. One of them was Adrian the Basque, the Estébétéguy mentioned earlier. The other, Joseph (or Giuseppe) Piereschi was a Marseilles Corsican who had been running a brothel for German soldiers in the Pas de Calais. The woman with him, Chinese Paulette, was a prostitute from Marseilles. The nature of the trouble they were in seems as obscure as just what their plans were for a happy future. However, interested in the 'escape route' of the man his *rabatteurs* or touts called 'Dr Eugène', they made their way two by two to the house in the Rue Le Sueur.

The last to go, at any rate that year, was Yvan Dreyfus. This was a sad and complicated affair, and Mr Seth is closely circumstantial about it. It appears that Dreyfus and three of his cousins were in the concentration camp at Compiègne, that French agents of the Gestapo managed to soak Mme Dreyfus, who was rich, of a great deal of money to get him out and that he was then put on to one of the mysterious doctor's touts to spy out the escape route for the Germans installed at the Rue des Saussaies headquarters of the Sûreté Nationale. Yvan Dreyfus may have hoped to double-cross the Gestapo and in fact get away. He didn't. But, of course, when he disappeared, the Gestapo couldn't be sure that he hadn't got away. It seems that the *police judiciaire* at the Quai des Orfèvres were also hot on Petiot's trail at this time, but the Gestapo got there first. He was arrested in May and tortured, but did not reveal much, for the address in the Rue Le Sueur did not come to light, though it was discovered that he also owned a house in the south-eastern district of Reuilly, towards Vincennes. During this unpleasant interlude, Dr Petiot had somewhat to do with those eminent policemen, Bony and Lafont. Then he was sent to prison at Fresnes, where he would remain for eight months. He must at once have got a message out to his brother Maurice, for, barely a week after his arrest, a lorry appeared in the Rue Le Sueur and drove away with forty-five suitcases, which it took to the Gare de Lyon, whence they continued by train to Auxerre, the Petiots' home town, and were later transported, again by lorry, thirty miles or so, to a house at Courson-les-Carrières, the property of a M. Neuhausen.

DURING THE course of 1942, the younger of the Papin sisters, Léa, had been released from prison after nine years and Henri-Antoine ('Papillon') Charrière had escaped from one of the Guiana settlements, possibly Devil's Island and possibly on a sack of coconuts. The actual getting away cannot have been very difficult, for at that time neither the Vichy government nor the Free French occupied themselves much with the administration of penal settlements overseas, and by the end of the war the place would be found to have died a natural death, though many convicts and *relégués* and some warders remained, among them men of whom we have heard, Guillaume Seznec, for instance, and the Boyer brothers, of whom the elder, Alexandre, died the following year. The Salvation Army occupied itself with the welfare of these men. As we all know, Papillon went to Venezuela, remarried and started a night-club in Caracas, which was much the old *milieu* life all over again. With

Christine no longer there to guide her, Léa Papin continued in menial employment, as a chambermaid in rather good hotels.

Arrested in Orleans by Superintendent Charles Chenevier, Jean Belin's former colleague and worthy successor at the Sûreté, Émile Buisson was returned to the prison at Troyes from which he had escaped during the fall of France. He and four of his five accomplices in the Troyes bank raid, but not Émile Courgibet, appeared before assizes on May 13th, 1943. Awarded a life sentence, Buisson was then taken to Paris and the Santé prison to await trial on a capital charge for the later raid with Mammoth Abel Danos.

DR PETIOT was released on January 13th, 1944, his two 'leg' men, whose names were Fourrier and Pintard, having been set free two days earlier. There is an element of mystery about the release itself. The suggestion would later be made that Petiot must have undertaken to work for the Gestapo. It is possible also, as Mr Seth points out, that by following him the Gestapo still hoped to discover the escape route. A Frenchwoman who worked for them was to state that she heard arrangements being made whereby the doctor's brother, Maurice Petiot, paid a large sum for his release, which of course does not contradict either suggestion about the reasons for it, though itself may have provided sufficient reason. At any rate, it appears that the Germans had still not discovered that Marcel Petiot had a house in the Rue Le Sueur, nor do French police enquiries seem to have established the connection.

During the weeks which followed, these latter were puzzled by a number of dismembered bodies fished out of the Seine. They bore signs of having been expertly dissected, as though by a doctor, but the fact may have no connection with Dr Petiot. A fact very certainly connected with him was the appearance, in early February, of a lorry in the Rue Le Sueur. This lorry bore a load of quicklime. It had come all the way from Auxerre and was the same, with the same driver, as, eight months before, had taken forty-five suitcases from Auxerre station to M. Neuhausen's house at Courson-les-Carrières.

No. 21's twelve windows on the street had remained shuttered. On March 6th, black smoke began to rise from its chimneys, and by the afternoon of Saturday, the 11th, it had become a public nuisance. The smell was dreadful, and the whole neighbourhood was complaining. Two policemen came, and the caretaker at No.

23 had the Rue de Caumartin telephone number. Mme Petiot answered and fetched her husband. He asked whether the police had broken into the house and, being assured that they hadn't, said he'd be round in a quarter of an hour. It took him longer than that, and the fire brigade also was called. The corporal in charge of it was later to give evidence in court.

WITNESS, CPL BOUDRINGLIN : After I had broken a window-pane, I entered the house and, guided by the smell, went down to the basement. Near the boiler, I saw human remains. The boiler was drawing rather noisily. It was burning human flesh. I saw a hand, at the end of a skeleton arm. It looked like a woman's hand. I made haste upstairs. I opened the street door for the police and said to them : 'You'd better come and look, there's a job here for you.'

At this juncture, a dark-complexioned man in his forties rode up on a bicycle. It was Dr Petiot, but he announced himself to the police as the owner's brother. He asked the police whether they were true Frenchmen, because, he said, the corpses were those either of Germans or of traitors. If the authorities had been notified, that was bad. It wasn't only *his* head, there were others involved. He was a leader in the Resistance, and this house was the headquarters of a secret network. Dr Petiot took a paper from his pocket and showed it to the policemen, though not so that they could read it. He'd better be off, he said. He'd got files at home he must destroy at once, three hundred or more.

They let him go. A *Paris-Soir* reporter who turned up was not at first given much to go on.

Two men have been found burnt to death beside a central-heating boiler at a house in the Rue Le Sueur. Police inquiries have established that they were two tramps who had broken into the empty house and set fire to their garments as they tried to warm themselves.

The papers of the time are not easily come by, and this, with much of the immediately foregoing, I owe not to Seth but to Montarron.

The detective put in charge of the case at the Quai des Orfèvres was Superintendent Massu. He did not, as Mr Seth says, go round to the Rue Caumartin till next morning, but the fact does not call for an exclamation mark. Although, by comparison with our own, the French police often seem to be allowed too free a hand, French law has always been very strict about arresting, let alone breaking in, during the hours of darkness. It is true that a watch, if available, could have been posted outside the house or, with the caretaker's agreement, in his lodge or even on a landing, and it seems possible that the *police judiciaire*, themselves pro-Resistance and anti-German and perhaps half-ready to believe the story of documents which had to be destroyed if lives and operation secrets were to be saved, gave Petiot as much chance as they dared. We may, at any rate, be fairly certain that not calling till morning did not show mere negligence.

By then, there were no files, no Dr or Mme Petiot either. The caretaker had last seen them at some time after eleven the previous evening. The newspapers got their story on Monday, and there were photographs. Petiot was referred to as Dr Satan.

> This block and tackle stands over a pit twelve feet deep. The pit contains quicklime, in which are human bones. It is covered by an iron hatch. . . . As may be seen, the small triangular cell is windowless. Note the peep-hole in the narrow door. This, it is believed, was the death chamber. . . . The number of dismembered bodies is calculated to have been twenty or more. They had been dissected by a skilful hand.

By March 20th:

> Maurice Petiot, brother of the wanted man, a radio engineer in Auxerre, has been arrested and brought to Paris. Mme Petiot, wife of the doctor, is also in custody. She was traced to Courson-les-Carrières. At the house in which she was staying were found between forty and fifty suitcases, evidently taken there last year from Paris. They contained a wide variety of men's and women's clothes.

A few days later, the *rabatteurs*, Fourrier and Pintard, were also in custody.

Then Dr Satan slipped out of the news. A man who slipped in, very briefly and not for the first time, was Alain de Bernardy de Sigoyer, self-styled *marquis*, occultist and purveyor of brandy to the Germans. On March 29th, a Mme Kergot went to the police-station in the Boulevard de Bercy and reported that on the previous day her daughter had gone to a house along the street and had not returned home. The house was that of her husband, M. Bernardy de Sigoyer, from whom she lived legally separated and whom she had called on because she had not received the alimony due to her under a court order. The police went along to see. Two servants said that Mme Bernardy had indeed called the previous day but that they had seen her leave. The *marquis* made helpful suggestions and ostentatiously fingered a card which showed that he enjoyed German protection. The police went back to their station and reported the matter to the Quai des Orfèvres, where the case was handed to Superintendent Massu. He found no trace of the vanished wife, and her mother boldly went to the Gestapo. Bernardy de Sigoyer was sent for and, according to Alistair Kershaw, whose account I largely follow, subjected to the customary tortures, but revealed nothing. He was released.

On June 6th, the Allies landed in Normandy. Among the premature Resistance operations which followed was the descent upon Tulle next day of the local *maquis* (a word which had come into use since the liberation of Corsica, *maquis* being the traditionally bandit-infested scrub of the island's interior). Moving north at that moment, to join in the defence of Normandy, was the *Reich* S.S. Division, which did a little hanging in Tulle before proceeding to the atrocity for which it is principally famous, the burning of a church full of people at Oradour. An atrocity of a more personal nature was committed on the outskirts of Paris on June 26th. This was the taking 'for a ride' of an inspector of the Quai des Orfèvres vice squad, Henri Ricordeau, a man active in the Resistance, who was pushed out of the car, had five bullets put into him and the car's wheels driven over him in the Clamart woods (he recovered). The abductors were French gestapists, and their trigger-happy leader was Pierre Loutrel, who, as 'Pierrot le Fou', was to become known as the deadliest individual killer in France during the next two and a half years, abducting among others, though not with similar intention or results, the film actress Martine Carol.

On the morning of the last day of July, the airman-writer Antoine de St Exupéry, took off on his last flight from Corsica and, so far as we know, was blown out of the sky over the Mediterranean or the Alps. On August 24th, Paris was liberated from within, by none with more gallantry than the police, of whom more than two hundred were killed. Two days later, troops under General Leclerc entered the city, and (if I may dispute Mr Kershaw's date) it must therefore have been on the 26th that Alain de Bernardy de Sigoyer was spotted by two policemen in the Place de l'Hôtel de Ville and arrested, not for causing the disappearance of his estranged wife

but for over-enthusiastic collaboration. He wore an armband pro-
claiming him a leader of 12th District resistance. He was taken to
Fresnes, to await, with a daily increasing number of others, trial
before one of the new Courts of Justice, with some likelihood of
thereafter being shot as a traitor.

Dr Satan was back in the news on September 19th, when *Résist-
ance* published an article claiming to show that he had been a Nazi
agent. It was headed PETIOT, SOLDIER OF THE REICH, and
assumed that he would now be beyond the Rhine with the retreating
German armies. Foolishly, the doctor reacted. His lawyer (at that
moment engaged with the interests of his brother and of Mme
Petiot) received a letter with a Paris postmark, enclosing a reply to
the article. This appeared on October 18th.

Dr Petiot rebuts the suggestion that he was ever a collaborator.
The source of your columnist's information can never have
existed, except perhaps in the imagination of the police. Throughout the Occupation, Dr Petiot was an active resistant, and, as
the police know, he was imprisoned by the Gestapo. The moment
he was released from Fresnes, he resumed his former place in the
Resistance under a new code-name. He demanded to be given
the most active part to play, so that he might avenge the hundreds of thousands of Frenchmen tortured and killed by the
Nazis. Despite the threat of prosecution which hangs over his
head, he remains in touch with his friends and is still playing an
active part in the Liberation. A friend showed him your newspaper. Deprived of all but life and honour, he lives and serves
under a false name, awaiting the day when tongues and pens
unfettered shall declare the truth which might be so easily discovered.

                                        Marcel Petiot

The document was handwritten. It was passed to F.F.I. (that is
to say, French Forces of the Interior) headquarters in the Paris
region, who found that the handwriting resembled that of the reports of a Captain Valéry in the Reuilly neighbourhood, where it
may be remembered that Petiot owned a house (and where, as it
happened, Bernardy de Sigoyer had both lived and had his wine-
and-spirits warehouse). On the 31st, Petiot was arrested by an F.F.I.
captain who was in fact as phoney as himself. On November 2nd,
however, he was turned over to Superintendent Massu at the Quai
des Orfèvres. He had grown a black beard, was thin and liverish
and looked indeed truly satanic, mad. He was told that he was

suspected of no fewer than sixty-two murders. That was wrong, he said. The number of his victims was sixty-three, every one of them either a German or a traitor. Among the documents found on him was a Communist Party card, though we cannot be certain of the significance of that fact.

The Germans were making their last stand in Alsace. That month, their rearguard left Strasbourg and crossed the Rhine by the pin-nacled Kehl bridge. To this day, a little way upstream on the French side, stands a rough-hewn slab of pink stone, polished on one side and bearing the names of nine men murdered at that point, their bodies thrown into the great river, by the departing Gestapo, who then crossed over to Kehl, leaving engineers to blow the bridge up. All crimes committed in France thereafter would lie within the jurisdiction of French courts, even if for the moment too many of these were the hurriedly improvised and vengeful *cours de justice* and even if too many of the murders which proclaimed themselves executions never came into court.

The *épuration* or purge was under way, and very nasty reading much of it made. Two of its earlier and, certainly, unregretted victims were those two eminent policemen, Chamberlain known as Lafont and the Pierre Bony of whom perhaps we have already heard enough. They were at least brought to a form of trial before they were shot on December 27th, 1944, and that is more than could be said, abroad, for Mussolini and the unfortunate Clara Petacci, shot and strung up ten days before the lights came on in the better parts of Europe. Not that a public trial always guarantees justice, as we were to see at Nuremberg.

THE FIRST new, post-liberation French murderer I have any note of was Roland Gosselin, a former pork-butcher in Paris, and even he had a long record of conviction for minor offences. It was on New Year's Day, 1945, that he committed the first of his two murders, cutting a second-hand dealer's throat, rifling the apartment and disappearing until, on April 11th, he savagely killed an old manservant, again rifled the apartment, took some time to catch and, when arrested, soon confessed. This simple and uninteresting brute was still at large when a marked change occurred in the judicial position of Alain de Bernardy de Sigoyer, still at Fresnes.

Before he and his wife separated, a peasant girl, Irène Lebeau, a servant in the house, had born a child to the *marquis*. From prison, he wrote to her in February 1945, telling her to collect a small box, containing private papers, from the house in the Boulevard de Bercy and put it away in a safe place. Mlle Lebeau had meanwhile married a soldier and was no longer interested in black magic. She gave the letter to her brother-in-law, who opened the box. Finding that it contained not papers but a number of readily identifiable objects, including a handbag, a lady's watch and a fur tippet, he took these to the police. They had, said Mme Kergot, when shown them, belonged to her daughter. In April, Irène Lebeau was summoned to the Quai des Orfèvres.

Bernardy de Sigoyer had been arrested in the first place by Chief Inspector Hillard, at that time fully convinced that he had murdered his wife but in no position to make the charge stick. It may be that in April 1945 Bernardy's former mistress was questioned by Hillard. It may, on the other hand, be that she was questioned by *officier de police* Émile Casanova, who had a special gift for mild but effective questioning. In his office stood a threadbare plush armchair with which, in later years, we are assured by André Larue in *Les Flics*, he would unnerve suspects by telling them that Petiot had once sat there. Though true, this would hardly be said that April

day, since the Petiot case was then still *sub judice*, but Irène Lebeau
was shown the fur tippet, lady's watch, handbag and so on.

In her original statement, taken at her local *commissariat*, she had
said merely that Mme de Bernardy de Sigoyer had indeed called at
the house in Reuilly on March 28th of the previous year but, after
a short visit, had left. The new statement was longer and more
circumstantial. Bernardy had garrotted his wife from behind, as she
sat in a red armchair smiling. She, Irène Lebeau, had watched help-
lessly as he did it, pulling on the cord, his knee against the back of
the red armchair. Afterwards, she had helped her former master
and lover bury the body in a pit dug the previous day in the floor
of his wine-and-spirits warehouse. A magistrate signed a warrant for
the arrest of Irène Lebeau, and she was taken to the Petite Roquette
prison.

Fetched from Fresnes, Bernardy admitted helping to dispose of
the body, but said that his wife had been shot by Irène Lebeau.
After an exhumation on April 20th, he said that it was always nice
to know where the dead were resting. Autopsy showed no bullet
wound, but there was some evidence of death by strangulation. The
case was passed to M. Goletty, the examining magistrate who also
had Petiot to deal with. For his defence, Bernardy enlisted the services of Maître Jacques Isorni, also at that time engaged as junior
counsel in the forthcoming trial of Marshal Pétain. Before this
came up, what was not yet known as an identikit picture or *portrait-
robot* led to the arrest of an eccentric person, Théodore Pluvinage,
who, eight years before, in a fit of neighbourly rage, had shot the
caretaker and two other women on the landing outside his premises.
While the Marshal's trial proceeded, a uniformed policeman was
shot by a former gestapist, Ferdinand François, and the Japanese
sued for peace.

The trial of Pierre Laval followed that of Marshal Pétain, and
on the day of the verdict, October 10th, another policeman was shot
by a black-market dealer in spare parts, Lucien Rouy, caught re-
moving a wheel from a parked car. On the 21st, elections accompanied by a referendum produced a Constituent Assembly and
decreed the end of the Third Republic, promptly replaced by a
Fourth. On the night of January 22nd, 1946, the two policeman-
shooters escaped from the Santé. On the 26th, a policeman-shooter
of longer standing, Pierre Gilblaise with a gendarme and two plain-
clothes inspectors notched up, was tracked down and besieged by
men from the Quai des Orfèvres, including Chief Superintendent

Pinault himself and Émile Casanova (in the end, Gilblaise, leaving eight hot, empty pistols on the bed, shot his mistress and himself). On February 1st, other members of the crime squad shot Ferdinand François. They got Lucien Rouy on March 23rd, five days after the opening of the trial of Dr Marcel Petiot.

PETIOT WAS charged with the murder of twenty-seven people. He admitted nineteen of these, the ponces and their women and some of the Jews, who also, he said, had been working for the Gestapo. He further claimed to have killed many Germans and collaborators not named in the indictment. The trial began on the March 18th, 1946, a Monday, and was to continue for almost three weeks.

To the right of the dock, past the clerk of the court, were stacked forty-seven suitcases and hold-alls, so that the courtroom looked a bit like the left-luggage office of a railway station. Among the contents of the suitcases (it is among the merits of Mr Seth's account that he gives us an inventory of these) were indeed several German uniforms. Below the dock sat Maître René Floriot and his four juniors, for the defence. Opposite sat no fewer than eleven black-gowned advocates for the civil complainants. In the public ministry horse-box sat the prosecuting magistrate, M. Dupin, red-gowned. An usher called the gentlemen to their feet, and there entered the president of the court, Councillor Leser, and his two assessors, also red-gowned. Through a little door at the back of the dock appeared the accused with two policemen, one of whom unclicked the hand-cuffs. All those with seats sat down.

Dr Satan no longer had a beard. He wore a double-breasted jacket and a bow-tie, a dapper man, though with a touch of the artist (a pianist, say) in the length of his dark hair, which waves lightly. His complexion is sallow, his eyes rather hollow. There is a contemptuous twist to his mouth. He seems quite at his ease. He is not an attractive figure, but hardly the monster that people expected. A jury of seven is empanelled and sworn. The witnesses are sworn and withdraw. The clerk to the court reads the long indictment or *acte d'accusation*, which in effect is an opening speech for the prosecution.

The defendant is called to his feet, and the *interrogatoire* begins.

PRESIDENT OF THE COURT, M. LESER: Your name is Marcel-André-Henri-Félix Petiot, married and the father of one child.

a son. By profession you are a doctor of medicine. You were born at Auxerre, Yonne, on January 17th, 1897. Your father, a post-office employee, died when you were eight, your mother five years later, whereupon you and a younger brother, Maurice, were confided to the care of an aunt. As a child, you were noted for your fits of violent temper.

PETIOT : Oh, come now, if we start like this, we shan't get on very well.

PRESIDENT : At the age of sixteen, you came before the juvenile court in Auxerre on a charge of robbing letter-boxes, but were discharged.

PETIOT : That's better.

PRESIDENT : Your scholastic record was excellent, and on leaving school at eighteen you began to study medicine, but in January 1916 were called up into the Army. You served in the 89th Infantry. Wounded in the foot by a hand-grenade in 1917. . . . Is that right?

PETIOT : It wasn't serious. I can walk.

PRESIDENT : You were nevertheless awarded a disability pension. You were finally discharged in 1920 on psychiatric grounds, first pleaded in your defence at a court martial in 1918, when you were accused of stealing drugs from a casualty clearing-station and selling these to your own private profit. Shall I stop there?

PETIOT : No, go on.

PRESIDENT : Having completed your medical studies, you set up in private practice in 1924 in Villeneuve-sur-Yonne. Three years later, you were elected mayor of that town as a candidate of the Left. That year, you married Georgette Lablais, and your son, Gérard, was born the following year. At various times, you were charged with the diversion of electric power to the detriment of the municipality and with theft of petrol from the railway sidings.

PETIOT : The charges were dropped.

PRESIDENT : You were also questioned in connection with two mysterious disappearances. A charge was brought in connection with one of these, that of Mme Debauve.

PETIOT : She'd been claiming to have had sexual intercourse with me. I declined the honour.

PRESIDENT : The gentleman who brought the charge died suddenly. He was a patient of yours.

PETIOT : It happens on occasion.

PRESIDENT : The local gossip became such that you judged it desirable to leave Villeneuve. That was thirteen years ago. You settled in Paris, at No. 66, Rue de Caumartin. You put up your plate, and you issued a prospectus, which I propose to read to the court. (*He does so.*)

PETIOT : Thanks for the publicity.

PRESIDENT : It was the prospectus of a quack. You boasted of earning astronomical sums, but your tax-returns did not show these.

PETIOT : That is traditional. When a surgeon makes millions, he declares a quarter. It proves how French I am.

PRESIDENT : Three years later, on being charged with the theft of a book in the Boulevard St Michel, you pleaded madness, as on previous occasions.

PETIOT : You never know how mad you are. It's all a matter of comparison.

PRESIDENT : At any rate, by 1941, a year after the German occupation of Paris, you had made enough to buy a house in the Rue Le Sueur.

PETIOT : Houses were cheap then.

PRESIDENT : And you caused certain alterations to be made.

PETIOT : I see that we are coming to the famous 'ante-room of death'. It was intended for radiotherapy. The apparatus was at that time unobtainable.

PRESIDENT : It contained a bell which did not ring.

PETIOT : Electric wire also was unobtainable.

PRESIDENT : It further contained a false door which did not lead anywhere.

PETIOT : It made the room look more comfortable.

PRESIDENT : And in the real door was a spy-hole.

PETIOT : It was papered over.

PRESIDENT : There was also a lime-pit. Those whose bodies were found in this pit had met their deaths by one means or another.

PETIOT : The bodies were there when I came out of Fresnes. My comrades in the Resistance had to have somewhere to dispose of the traitors they had executed.

PRESIDENT : Who were these comrades?

PETIOT : I shall not give their names. There were members of my group who wanted to come here and testify. I would not let them. On men who deserve the Liberation cross you would put handcuffs. And there's no need for you to throw your arms up in the air.

PRESIDENT : I shall raise my arms if I want to.

PETIOT : Well, you'll be raising them higher presently. I was in the Resistance from the time the Germans arrived.

PRESIDENT : In your earlier statements, you gave the name of your supposed organisation as 'Fly-tox'. That is the name of a common insecticide, isn't it?

PETIOT : That's what the organisation was, a common insecticide.

PRESIDENT : No mention of such an organisation has been found in F.F.I. records or elsewhere. Tomorrow, I shall ask just what you did. . . .

PETIOT : You'd do better to ask me what I didn't do. I blew up trains full of Germans. I. . . .

PRESIDENT : . . . But now we shall adjourn.

PETIOT : Why? I'm not tired.

TUESDAY, MARCH 19th

PETIOT : . . . When we discovered an informer, we'd arrest him, pretending to be German police. The fellow'd say : 'That's all right. I'm one of you.' That put an end to all doubt. We questioned him and then took him in a truck to the forest of Marly.

PRESIDENT : Not to the Rue Le Sueur?

PETIOT : We only went there if there was some need to hurry.

FOR THE PROSECUTION, M. DUPIN : And, in the forest of Marly, what exactly did you do to your prisoner?

PETIOT : Got sadistic tastes, have you? These traitors were executed and buried, that's all you need to know. When I'm acquitted. . . .

DUPIN : Acquitted? You?

PETIOT : I'm counting on it. It won't be you who judge me, it'll be the gentlemen of the jury. In them I have confidence. I got my hands dirty all right, but I didn't soil them by holding them up to swear oaths of allegiance to Pétain.

PRESIDENT : Everybody knows under what conditions. Don't be insolent.

PETIOT : To whom? To Pétain?

In 1940, a formal declaration of allegiance to the new constitution under the government formed at Vichy had indeed been required of all State employees. With whatever mental reservations, most State employees had made it and thus remained at their posts. In distant retrospect, it must be clear to all but juveniles and a lunatic fringe on the Left that they had been right to do so, but in 1946 it was less clear to many who yet were neither utter fools nor interested parties. It would be nice to have a stereophonic recording of court reaction at this juncture in the Petiot trial. It is specifically enjoined upon French jurymen that they must not allow what they feel to appear even from their facial expressions.

ON WEDNESDAY, March 20th, the disappearances, in the summer of 1942, of Dr Braunberger and the Knellers were considered. Petiot claimed to have heard from both after their escapes, from Braunberger in South America, from the Knellers in Bordeaux and thereafter. The Knellers had had a son, René, with them.

> PETIOT : Yes, he was a nice little boy.
> PRESIDENT : In one of those suitcases, the boy's pyjamas were found.
> PETIOT : They were dirty, and they had his initials on them. His mother said he should leave them.

Next day, it was the turn of the ponces and their women. Petiot admitted killing Adrian the Basque, Boxer Joe and two Corsicans, with four of their women, including Chinese Paulette, but not that any of these had been among the bodies found in the Rue Le Sueur.

> PETIOT : . . . We didn't need to question Adrian. We knew his rotten mug. We stuck a revolver into his back to make him climb into the truck. He pulled a knife. It was like a butcher's shop.
> DUPIN : Was it necessary to execute the women?
> PETIOT : They'd have given us away. What do you think we ought to have done with them?
> PRESIDENT : The Wolffs, the Ansbachs, the Stevenses, they were not criminals. They were Jews who were hiding from the Nazis.
> PETIOT : They were Germans. They'd been told to hide. When I was first married, I used to hide under the sheets and say to my wife : 'Come and find me !' That's the way they were hiding.
> PRESIDENT : And Yvan Dreyfus?
> PETIOT : A traitor to his race, his religion and his country.

But Petiot denied that any of these were among the bodies found at the Rue Le Sueur. The following morning, Friday the 22nd, those premises were visited by the whole court, the lawyers, the jury, twelve car-loads altogether. The road had been blocked, but people leaned out of upstairs windows, and a crowd had gathered outside the barriers. There being no electricity in the house, those who descended to the basement had to make do with a police inspector's taper, quite enough, as Petiot said, to enlighten the law. The walls of the triangular room were exceptionally thick. They'd deaden any cries, said Dupin. They had to be thick, said Petiot, for protection against X-rays. Lead had been quite impossible to obtain. As the court might easily see, there was no room to kill anyone in that room. Nor, suggested Dupin, was there room to practise radiotherapy. Once the apparatus had been installed, where would the patient lie? Councillor Leser thought it curious that, with so many rooms in the house, the doctor should have set up his consulting-room in an outbuilding at the rear of the basement.

The crowd had already brought in its verdict, and the twelve cars drove away to a chorus of hostile shouts. In court, during the afternoon, the chief expert witness was called, the French Sir Bernard Spilsbury, Dr Paul, white-moustached, fat, old, as often made a fool of by clever defending counsel as his English counterpart, the one real-life legal character to whom, in his novels, M. Simenon gives no fictitious name.

PRESIDENT : Dr Paul, you examined all the remains that were found two years ago in the Rue Le Sueur. In your view, how did those people die?

DR PAUL : It cannot be established. It was not by a bullet or a blow on the head, that is certain. Asphyxiation, strangling, poison, a knife-wound – all those are possible.

PRESIDENT : Injections?

DR PAUL : It is possible, but I must not theorise.

PRESIDENT : Might gas have been used?

DR PAUL : Again, it is possible. Not coal gas, however. The discolouration produced by carbon-monoxide poisoning would have been apparent in the fragments of skin which remained.

PRESIDENT : The bodies had been skilfully dissected?

DR PAUL : The man had a knowledge of anatomy. I said to M. Goletty : 'A doctor has done this. Pray God it was not one of my pupils.'

FOR THE DEFENCE, MAITRE FLORIOT : Mr President. . . . I don't know whether Dr Paul is aware of the fact that, in the course of his medical training, my client never followed any course in dissection.

DR PAUL : That surprises me. It's a pity, too. He dissects very well.

FLORIOT : Excuse me, Dr Paul, what we must say is that the dissector, whoever he may have been, dissects very well.

AT SATURDAY's hearing and all the second week and again on the following Monday, April 1st, some eighty witnesses were heard. They included relatives and friends of those who had disappeared, as well as the touts who had sent people to 'Dr Eugène'. There were also psychiatrists and handwriting-experts. Among witnesses for the defence was a Richard Lhéritier, who'd been trained in England and parachuted into France by the R.A.F. He'd been captured and had spent five months in Fresnes with Petiot.

PRESIDENT : You were sharing a cell?

LHÉRITIER : Yes.

PRESIDENT : And what impression did you form of your enforced companion?

LHÉRITIER : I found Dr Petiot an intelligent man. He gave me very good advice on how to behave under torture. He raised everybody's morale. He passed messages out of prison, and he gave me safe addresses I could go to if I escaped.

PRESIDENT : Did he speak to you about his alleged work in the Resistance?

LHÉRITIER : Constantly.

PRESIDENT : What did you think about it?

LHÉRITIER : He wasn't working alone, he worked for a party, which gave him orders.

PRESIDENT : A party of the Left?

LHÉRITIER : Yes.

PRESIDENT : Did you learn the code-name of his organisation?

LHÉRITIER : Yes.

PRESIDENT : What was it?

LHÉRITIER : 'Fly-tox'.

ME FLORIOT : It has been suggested that no such group existed, that Petiot invented it after the discoveries in the Rue Le Sueur.

LHÉRITIER : No.

FLORIOT : He talked to you about a group under that name?

LHÉRITIER : Yes, about that and about his escape route.

FLORIOT : You spent five months together. Do you think that a man can hide his true feelings as long as that?

LHÉRITIER : You can't share a cell for long and not know your companion.

PETIOT : Lhéritier, do you think that any sane man could accuse me of working for the Gestapo?

LHÉRITIER : No. . . . Mr President, whatever the result of this trial may be, I shall always recall with gratitude that I shared a cell with Dr. Petiot.

And there were others who testified that he'd made out false medical certificates to keep them from being deported and that he'd got warnings out to Jewish families when they were in danger.

During the first week of the trial, the courtroom had been crowded. The crowd dropped off during the second week. There were very few there when on Tuesday of the third week, April 2nd, the lawyers in the civil action began (a thing which of course doesn't happen in British criminal proceedings). They were very tedious, especially the barrister representing the family of Chinese Paulette, who no doubt hoped for handsome damages and who were not in the least Chinese. Petiot sketched these lawyers and wrote a poem about them, understandably savage and not unamusing. He'd been doing a good deal of writing in prison – in prose, a treatise on the laws of chance and how to overcome them (it was later published). One of these lawyers, the most effective of them, Maître Véron, ventured a notable image.

VÉRON : You knew the legend of the wreckers, those cruel men who lit fires on the cliffs designed to lure mariners in distress into the belief that they'd found a haven of refuge. Unable to imagine that any such blackness of heart existed, the steersman landed his vessel on the rocks, with the loss of all souls aboard and all that they owned. Those very men who gave the illusion of safety enriched themselves with the spoils. Well! that's what Petiot was : the false saviour, the false refuge. He attracted people to him as though to save them. He murdered and despoiled them!

On the afternoon of the 3rd, the crowd began to drift back. Shortly before half past five, red-robed M. Dupin began his concluding speech for the prosecution. He continued next morning. With brilliant timing, the defendant spoiled his peroration.

DUPIN : . . . But we shall no longer let Petiot foul the sacred name of the Resistance. . . .

PETIOT : Signed : State Prosecutor of France.

DUPIN : Petiot, the role of administrator of justice hardly becomes you.

PETIOT : What about yourself?

DUPIN : . . . Gentlemen, let Petiot go from here to join his victims !

Me Floriot followed for the defence. He spoke for almost seven hours, and by all accounts it was magnificent. At half past nine, court and jury retired. The court, that is to say, the presiding judge and the two assessors by whom, throughout the proceedings, he had sat dumbly flanked, retired with the jury. This practice had been established under the government of Vichy, which had also reduced the number of jurors from twelve to seven. Together with the three red-robed *magistrats*, who were not supposed to attempt to lead the argument but merely to answer questions of law, they deliberated for well over two hours, with three questions to answer in respect of each of the twenty-seven murders alleged. Floriot also retired, to replenish his forces in the barristers' refreshment-room. Returning to the cells below the dock, he expected to find his client agitated and in need of calming words. Petiot was sleeping peacefully. When the court again took its place and the jury came in with the verdict a little before midnight, he had to be awakened to be taken up to the dock again.

He was found guilty, without mitigating circumstances, of wilful murder upon all but one of the twenty-seven persons with whose deaths he was charged. He listened to the verdict and to the sentence of death contemptuously, but, as he was led away once more, called out : 'You must avenge me !' It is not known to whom he called, whether to his wife and son (she, certainly, had been sitting in court and now rose) or to the public at large or to a group of friends among the public. It is also unknown on whom revenge was to be wreaked.

On Wednesday, May 15th, Petiot's appeal was rejected by the Court of Cassation. By Friday, May 24th, the Fourth Republic had not yet elected a President, and so the appeal to presidential clemency was void. At a quarter to five on the morning of Saturday, May 25th, Marcel-André-Henri-Félix Petiot, then in his fiftieth year, was awakened and enjoined, in the customary formula, to have courage, which he had.

IN HIS book on miscarriages of justice, Maître Floriot does not instance the trial of Dr Petiot, and so I suppose that he thinks his most famous client was guilty as charged and found. He is on record as saying that, among all the murderers he has known, Petiot alone was a man of intelligence.

Not long after his trial and execution, the house in the Rue Le Sueur was pulled down. There was still no trace of any of the valuables and money which had presumably passed through the doctor's hands, estimated to be worth something like a quarter of a million pounds sterling. If I have understood him properly, Mr Seth's theory is that they went to swell Communist Party funds. During the first year of the Occupation, the French communists collaborated, as far as the occupying forces would allow them to do so. Only when the Germans invaded Russia did communists first play any part in the Resistance, which all too soon they came to dominate. According to Mr Seth, it was members of the communist Resistance, possibly including another doctor, who dumped bodies at the Rue Le Sueur while Petiot was in prison. On his release in early 1944, finding them in his lime-pit, he said, 'Ah, well!' and, being told to get on with it, started to burn them. The reason why he didn't talk, at or before his trial, was that threats had been made against his wife and son if he did. *He* was 'for it' anyway and had only one head to lose

ON JUNE 5th, 1946, Interpol picked up what the Russians had left of its files and moved from Vienna to Paris. On November 6th, after a raid in which a jeweller was killed, the atrocious young gunman, Pierre Loutrel, known as 'Pierrot le Fou', tucked his pistol carelessly into his belt. It went off and wounded him fatally, a fact which was to remain unknown to the police for a year and a half. Bernardy de Sigoyer came up for trial in mid-December. Sentenced to death on the 23rd, he remained unexecuted until the late spring of 1947. That was a fearsome year for murder in France. Indeed, it is estimated that, in the three years after the Liberation, more Frenchmen were killed by other Frenchmen than had been killed by Germans all through the war. In the south-west, a communist reign of terror was still raging.

On a capital charge for the murder of a bank cashier, Émile Buisson ('Mimile') had, it may be remembered, been transferred from Troyes to the Santé in May 1943. By early 1947, he had convinced the authorities that he was mad and had been taken to the asylum at Villejuif. From there, on September 3rd, he was 'sprung' by his elder brother, Jean-Baptiste, *Fatalitas* or 'le Nus'. Within a week, they and three other men held up a restaurant in the street of which we have already heard so much, the Rue Le Sueur. At the share-out, Mimile suspected one of the other men of keeping a piece of jewellery back and, two days later, on a job outside Paris, shot this other man in the nape of the neck while he was lighting a cigarette. During his five years' confinement, Émile Buisson had become, at the age of forty-five, a hardened killer and, for the next four years, was to replace Pierrot le Fou as Public Enemy No. 1. There remained something appealing about this terrible little man, who, for instance, was always nice to children, but, after his arrest in 1950, he talked. This got him a nasty reputation as a *casserole*, too loudly insisted on, in the outer *milieu* of Montmartre, by one Michel Cardeur, known as 'Michel l'Avocat'. Jean-Baptiste Buisson shot

184

him down in the Sirène bar on Christmas Eve, 1952. In consequence of this over-emphatic loyalty to his kid brother, *Fatalitas* was to spend the rest of his life in prison at Clairvaux.

By then, Abel Danos, the Mammoth, Mimile's associate in his first fatal bank-raid, first sentenced to death by a court of assize in 1949, had been further court-martialled for war crimes and, in 1951, faced a firing squad. An earlier, non-lethal accomplice and momentary victim of Émile Buisson's indiscretion was Émile Cour-gibet, who, in the course of his first seven years in New York, had become an expert in the restoration and imitation of antique French furniture and in 1945 set up on his own, under the name of Fernand Châtelain, at 227 East 50th Street, four years later marrying an American wife. In 1952, M. Châtelain was picked up by the New York police or the F.B.I., and Montarron's story is that they asked him to swear on the Bible that he was not Émile Courgibet, that he did so swear and was extradited, whereas he would not have been extradited had he told the truth. It sounds improbable. In fact M. Châtelain was not to suffer too badly from his old friend's treachery. Never a killer except once in his youth, he was discharged by the French prison authorities in 1954, returned to New York and, for all I know, may still be consulted about Louis XV chairs at 227 East 50th Street. Mimile himself was tried the following year and executed early the year after that.

In the more picturesque gangsterland of Marseilles, the Guérini brothers now reigned. Whereas Carbone and Spirito had collabor-ated, *they* had resisted heroically, and Mémé Guérini, the second brother, displayed a Resistance medal. It was a smarter world over which they reigned. Marseilles had performed prodigies in the way of rebuilding on that area north of the Old Port, so oddly razed by the Germans, as though to render the municipality a service. But the development and ultimate downfall of the empire of the Guérinis form an epic which is not for this book.

THE GUIANA convict stations were being closed down, the remaining convicts repatriated in batches, to Bordeaux or Le Havre. Return-ing, by way of the latter, to Brittany in 1948, Guillaume Seznec found that his daughter Jeannette, a child when he last saw her, had married Le Her, the man who, then a bus conductor in Paris, had given eloquent but unconvincing evidence on his behalf, at the trial in 1924. Le Her had turned out to be a dreadful brute, and,

shortly after her father's return, the former Jeannette Seznec shot
her husband dead as he was about to start beating her again.
Twenty-five years after her father's appearance in the dock at
Quimper, she in turn stood there. She was acquitted. With her
father, a white-haired, broken old man, she moved to Paris. The
body of Pierre Quémeneur had never been found, nor had anyone
heard of him alive. On November 14th, 1953, crossing the Avenue
des Gobelins, Guillaume Seznec was knocked down by a lorry and
taken to hospital. Delirious, he said that the place where, thirty
years before he had buried his friend was at Plourivo, by the foun-
tain. A search was made, but no remains were found. Seznec died
on February 13th, 1954, murmuring that the world had done him
too much harm.

In prison at Fontevrault at the time was a man who once, in St
Laurent du Maroni, had put Seznec in hospital before. This was
Eugène Boyer, who had only just returned to France when the
stations were finally shut down and who still had four years of his
sentence to serve. His escape attempts had always failed. Among
the many whose attempts had succeeded, Henri ('Papillon') Charrière was installed in the *milieu* of Caracas, where it seems that he
met Dr Bougrat, who had opened a clinic in the Venezuelan capital,
while still mainly living on the island of Margarita, with five
daughters of his second marriage and a daughter adopted to replace
the one taken away from him, first by his deportation and then by
divorce. Pierre Bougrat died in 1962, honoured locally as a saint.
Two years later, Eugène Boyer, wrapping an arm-sling tightly round
his neck to make doubly sure, succeeded in drinking himself to
death at a workhouse in Touraine.

Those who closely followed the controversy about Papillon may
remember that, in the account of one of his first-person hero's
escapes, Charrière was said to have taken his detail from Bougrat's
earlier real-life escape. When he was in London, in May 1970, for
the publication of the English translation of his fine novel, Papillon
told me that, in the original manuscript, there was a great deal
about Bougrat which the publishers had persuaded him to cut. As
I said that I was writing about Bougrat, he promised to send me
the suppressed material, which of course I still eagerly await. Three
months later, *France-Soir* reported that, on Sunday, August 2nd,
at Juan Griego on Margarita, there had been a kind of Bougrat
festival, marked by the apposition to his tombstone of an official
plaque on which was engraved : 'Doctor and exemplary citizen, he

rendered himself worthy of the affection, the admiration and the respect of all.' There is also a Bougrat museum, whose principal exhibit is the native canoe in which, in 1928, the miracle-worker and his six companions first touched shore and were brought into the fishing village of Pedernales.

It is inherent in the nature of the subject that few of our *dramatis personae* can be expected to put in later appearances. The number of those who do will exclude not only victims but all the murderers who were men held to have acted in full responsibility for their actions and without extenuating circumstances, unless they escaped between sentence and execution (but none of ours did) or were sentenced in their absence and never caught (but, again, this happened to none of ours) or benefited by unexpected presidential clemency or such an odd stroke of fate as befell Eugène Boyer. It will be different for criminal historians of the future, but ours was a period which in France (even in France) carried out almost all the many sentences of death it passed, except those on women. Besides, the last crime we noted was committed a quarter of a century ago, so that the youngest even of our commuted killers would be young no longer now.

Even so, it does to keep a pair of scissors handy. The last *dramatis nostri persona* whose name I noticed in a newspaper was Gabriel Socley, not prominently featured but our only child-murderer, a transvestite, it may be remembered, found guilty of abducting and killing a little girl in Chaumont, on Good Friday 1935, and sent to the special prison at Château Thierry. We may read already in Montarron's *Histoire des Crimes Sexuels* that, in early 1960, Socley was released and returned to his family in Dijon, but that in less than a month he was seen holding by the shoulders a little girl who was struggling to get away. 'This time,' says Montarron, 'he was shut up for ever.' As recently as March 27th, 1971, *France-Soir* printed what I translate as follows :

DIJON, Friday
'I escaped to prove my innocence. It wasn't I who killed Nicole Marescot. . . . My whole life has been ruined by a miscarriage of justice.'
Those words were uttered by Gabriel Socley, sixty-five, during the short visit he paid the other morning to a woman neighbour of his sister's, Mme Grillot, Impasse Berthioux, Dijon, after

escaping from the psychiatric hospital at Sarreguemines (Moselle), where he was confined for life.

In 1960, after his release from prison in Château Thierry, he had had his own room in her apartment there for several weeks. He left four suitcases of linen behind when he took flight after his attack on a little girl in the Rue Jules Ferry, Dijon, on July 27th.

A year or so previously, I had seen, also in *France-Soir*, a photograph of a man on a bicycle who had escaped with Émile Buisson from Villejuif, a daring criminal but not a murderer and therefore not one of mine. From an earlier Montarron book one had gathered that in 1967 the younger of the Papin sisters, Léa, was still working as a chambermaid in a luxury hotel, which M. Montarron rightly did not name or situate. To me, the most evocative of my clippings is one which comes from *Le Monde* for January 30th, 1968.

LANDRU'S LAST MISTRESS. Mme Fernande Segret, aged 72, living in an old people's home at Flers in Normandy, has taken her own life by drowning in the lake of the château nearby.

After living for many years in Lebanon, Mme Segret had returned to France and, at the time of the Claude Chabrol film on the famous murderer, was much sought after by journalists. She brought a libel action and was awarded 10,000 new francs' damages.

It is thought that her suicide may have been due to the renewed publicity.

The age is wrong. Fernande Segret must have been four years older than that when she drowned herself in Flers Hall pond.

BIBLIOGRAPHY

Belin, Jean, *My Work at the Sûreté*, translated by Eric Whelpton, London : Harrap, 1950. (The *cagoulards*, Philippe Daudet, Davin, Dervaux, Landru, Red Max, Stavisky, Weidmann)

Bolitho, William, *Murder for Profit*, London : Dennis Dobson, 1926. (Landru)

Browne, Douglas G., and Tullett, E.V., *Bernard Spilsbury: His Life and Cases*, London : Harrap, 1951. (Red Max, Vaquier, Voisin)

Faralicq, René, *The French Police from Within*, translated anonymously, London : Cassell, 1933. (Mme Bessarabo, Burger, Girard, René Jean, Mlle du Bot de Talhouët, Train 5)

Gide, André, *Journals*, Vol. III, translated by Justin O'Brien, London : Secker & Warburg, 1949. (Dufrenne)

Greenwall, H.J., *They Were Murdered in France*, London : Jarrolds, 1957. (Olive Branson, Nurse Daniels, Drinan, Annie Gordon, Gourlay, Dora Hunt, Lee, Pamela Raper, Ross, Mrs Wilson)

Gribble, Leonard, *Famous Manhunts*, London : John Long, 1953. (Landru, Train 5)

Hale, Leslie, *Hanging in the Balance*, London : Jonathan Cape, 1962. (Seznec)

Hastings, Patrick, *Cases in Court*, London : Heinemann, 1949. (Vaquier)

Kershaw, Alister, *Murder in France*, London : Constable, 1955. (Henriot, Petiot, Sigoyer)

Mackenzie, F.A. (ed.), *Landru*, London : Geoffrey Bles, 1928.

Masson, René, *Number One: A Story of Landru*, translated by Gillian Tindall, London : Hutchinson, 1964.

Miller, Webb, *I Found No Peace*, London : Penguin, 1940. (Landru)

Morain, Alfred, *The Underworld of Paris: Secrets of the Sûreté*, translated anonymously, London : Jarrolds, 1929. (Germaine Berton, Mme Bessarabo, Bonomini, Burger, Nurse Daniels, Girard, Mata Hari, René Jean, Landru, Merabashvili, Nourric, Schwartzbard, Mlle du Bot de Talhouët, Train 5, Mrs Wilson)

Parrish, J.M., and Crossland, John R. (eds), *The Fifty Most Amazing Crimes of the Last 100 Years*, London : Odhams, 1936. (Mme Fahmy, Landru, Vaquier)

Rickards, Colin, *The Man from Devil's Island*, London : Dawnay, 1968. (Bougrat, Davin, Red Max)

Seth, Ronald, *Petiot, Victim of Chance*, London : Hutchinson, 1963.

Smith, F.E. (Lord Birkenhead), *Famous Trials*, London : Hutchinson, undated. (Landru)

Tenyson Jesse, F., *Comments on Cain*, London : Heinemann, 1948. (Weidmann)

Waagenaar, Sam, *The Murder of Mata Hari*, London : Arthur Barker, 1964.

Wakefield, H. Russell, *Landru, the French Bluebeard*, London : Duckworth, 1936.

Wilson, C., and Pitman, Patricia, *Encyclopaedia of Murder*, London : Arthur Barker, 1961. (Mme Bessarabo, Olive Branson, Émile Buisson, Girard, Henriot, Landru, Nourric, Seznec, Sigoyer, Train 5, Voisin)

Wolfe, H. Ashton, *The Thrill of Evil*, London : Hurst & Blackett, undated. (Mme Bessarabo, Bougrat)

——, *The Underworld*, London : Hurst & Blackett, undated. (Mme Fahmy, Vaquier)

Bourdrel, Philippe, *La Cagoule*, Paris : Albin Michel, 1970.

Chavardès, Maurice, *La Droite Française et le 6 Février 1934*, Paris : Flammarion, 1970.

Delarue, Jacques, *Trafics et Crimes sous l'Occupation*, Paris : Fayard, 1968.

Devèze, Michel (ed.), *Cayenne, Déportés et Bagnards*, Paris : Julliard, 1968. (Bougrat, Davin, Dervaux, Seznec)

Garçon, Maurice (ed.), *L'Affaire Bernardy de Sigoyer*, Paris : Albin Michel, 1948.

Gide, André, *Ne Jugez Pas*, Paris : Gallimard, 1930. (Reiser, Robitaillie)

Jardin Birnie, Renée, *Le Cahier Rouge d'Eugène Weidmann*, Paris : Gallimard, 1968.

Larue, André, *Les Flics*, Paris : Fayard, 1969. (Buisson, Courgibet, Danos, Loutrel, Pluvinage)

Le Clère, Marcel, *L'Assassinat de Jean Jaurès*, Paris : Mame, 1969.

——, *Histoire de la Police*, Paris : Presses Universitaires de France, 1947.

Ménager, Georges, *Les Quatre Vérités de Papillon*, Paris : La Table Ronde, 1970.

Montarron, Marcel, *Les Grande Procès d'Assises*, Paris : Planète, 1967. (Bougrat, Gorguloff, Landru, Papin sisters, Petiot, Sarret, Seznec, Weidmann)

——, *Histoire des Crimes Sexuels*, Paris : Plon, 1970. (Dufrenne, Henriot, Socley)

——, *Histoire du Milieu*, Paris : Plon, 1969. (Buisson, Courgibet, Loutrel, Marseilles and Montmartre gangsters generally, Red Max, Train 5)

——, *Tout Ce Joli Monde*, Paris : La Table Ronde, 1965. (Boyer, Gauchet, Gorguloff, Socley, Stavisky, Train 5)

Ragon, Michel, *L'Avant-Guerre*, Paris : Planète, 1968. (Assassination of Alexander I, Violette Nozières, Ernst von Rath, Stavisky)

Sicot, Marcel, *Servitude et Grandeur Policières*, Paris : Les Productions de Paris, 1959. (*Cagoulards*, Weidmann)

Villiers, Gérard de, *Papillon Épinglé*, Paris : Presses de la Cité, 1970.

Zimmer, Lucien, *Un Septennat Policier*, Paris : Fayard, 1967. (Alexander I, Dufrenne, Gorguloff, Mestorino, Stavisky)

INDEX

Apart from a small number of people in earlier French criminal history, only the names of persons active or significant within the period are listed.